Team Chemistry

SPORT AND SOCIETY

Series Editors
Randy Roberts
Aram Goudsouzian

Founding Editors
Benjamin G. Rader
Randy Roberts

A list of books in the series appears at the end of this book.

Team Chemistry

The History of Drugs and Alcohol in Major League Baseball

NATHAN MICHAEL CORZINE

UNIVERSITY OF ILLINOIS PRESS
Urbana, Chicago, and Springfield

Library of Congress Control Number: 2015954827
ISBN 978-0-252-03979-9 (hardcover)
ISBN 978-0-252-08133-0 (paperback)
ISBN 978-0-252-09789-8 (e-book)

For Gwendolyn and Eleanor

You don't play this game on ginger-snaps.

—Leo Durocher, 1966

Integrity has no need of rules.

—Albert Camus

Contents

Acknowledgments

On many days history is a lonely endeavor, a solitary trek along a twisting paper trail through archives, memoirs, and other printed materials. But not always. This has been, as they say, a team effort. Its failings are mine and mine alone. Its strengths are the product of contributions for which even the smallest I am eternally grateful. Thanks, firstly, to the staff at the University of Illinois Press, my copyeditor Jane Curran, Jennifer Comeau, and especially Willis G. Regier, for their patience and faith in this project. Among others to whom I would like to extend my gratitude are the archivists and staff of the various libraries I visited during my extended baseball tour: the A. Bartlett Giamatti Research Center at the National Baseball Hall of Fame in Cooperstown, New York, the Robert F. Wagner Labor Archives at New York University's Tamiment Library, and the Joyce Sports Research Collection at the University of Notre Dame. Also indispensable was the contribution of the staff of the Purdue University Library System who aided me in tracking down hard-to-find memoirs and various government document collections.

The faculty in the Department of History at Purdue University is an amazing group of scholars and teachers. I was blessed to learn the craft of history under their guidance. This book owes a great deal to their teaching, and I am especially grateful to Michael Morrison, Darren Dochuk, and James Farr, three whose enthusiasm and insight were so appreciated and whose criticisms and suggestions were tempered with kindness and humanity. I also had the benefit of my graduate student colleagues—Eric Hall, Andrew Smith, and Jamal Ratchford—whose input, even in informal conversation, was so valuable. In this arena I want to extend special thanks to Johnny Smith, a model scholar and dispenser of extremely useful advice. I wish to extend my deepest gratitude to Randy Roberts. His guidance throughout the research and writing process as well as his unflagging support were in many ways the foundation of this project. He is the heaviest hitter in my lineup and I am doubly fortunate to call him both mentor and friend.

Members of my extended family—my parents, Jim and Carole Corzine, siblings, in-laws, and a host of other relatives—eased the burdens of this project with their love and support. My late grandmother, Reva Elliott, inspired me as child with her love of learning and of the written word.

The greatest measure of my gratitude, however, belongs to the day-to-day heart of my order. Gwendolyn Lane, watching you grow up gives me far more pride and a far greater sense of accomplishment than any other achievement ever could. Your weekend soccer matches remind me what is purest and most enjoyable about sport. Eleanor Rose, my own *Le Grande Orange*, your irrepressible enthusiasm has sustained me throughout. And to Tammi, my dearest friend, thank you. Your patience during this journey has been exemplary. On every step of this journey, from library to written page, you've been there—even if you didn't know it. In that sense this is as much your book as mine.

Team Chemistry

Introduction

The Last Pure Place

This is the last pure place where Americans can dream.
. . . This is the last great arena, the last green arena,
where everybody can learn the lessons of life.

—A. Bartlett Giamatti

It turns out that integrity may have need of rules after all. In fact, a history of baseball in the new century might largely be about the debate over rules, the quest for a reliable and universally agreeable drug-testing system designed to restore gloss to the besmirched integrity of the professional circuit. The testing movement, for two decades the persona non grata of Major League Baseball, surged to the forefront of Major League thought following the embarrassing congressional hearings of 2005, culminating in the 2006 establishment of the Joint Drug Prevention and Treatment Program between the league and the Major League Baseball Players' Association (MLBPA). The new testing protocols were buoyed by the findings of the Mitchell Commission in December 2007. The Mitchell Report was, in essence, a $20 million display of self-regulation meant to add transparency and needed context to the problems confronting Major League Baseball and the measures deemed necessary to combat those problems. The report explicitly warned against retroactive punishment—the league could not slash and burn its way to integrity by torching past transgressions—and instead focused rather blandly on the need for diligence in the future. If the new Joint Policy's sole purpose was to expose cheaters and facilitate punishment, a superficial appraisal would suggest that it worked. Commissioner Allan H. "Bud" Selig could proclaim, with some justification, the end of the disastrous Steroid Era and the advent of a new, more just, Testing Era. Rules now in place, the integrity of the great game was assured. Or was it?[1]

In January 2013, building on the initial triumphs of the Joint Agreement protocols and inspired by the international shaming of former Tour de France champion Lance Armstrong, the league and the union agreed to add random, in-season, tests—so-called biological passport testing—for synthetic testosterone and human growth hormone (HGH), two of the most difficult performance-enhancing drugs to detect. Despite this proactive stance, and despite a handful of apparent successes in rooting out cheaters, reality was that the new testing regime was still a house of cards. Now it came crashing down. The *Miami New Times* cracked open a story about an anti-aging clinic, Biogenesis of America, located in Coral Gables, Florida, with alleged ties to the Major League Baseball community. A disgruntled former employee of the clinic provided the *Times* with documents linking a handful of current Major Leaguers to the clinic and its owner, Anthony Bosch. Other major media outlets rushed to pick up the story. Several of the players on the list had failed drug tests in the previous year, but it was the inclusion of troubled superstars Alex Rodriguez and Ryan Braun, both with serious doping allegations in their past, that really set alarm bells ringing.[2]

Now, at what was supposed to be the *end* of the Steroid Era, it was time for a new round of heated discussions about the actual efficacy of performance enhancers, about the true extent of drug-induced damage to Major League Baseball's reputation, and about the irreparable harm being done to youth and amateur athletes. The sports-talk media machine cranked into high gear to debate whether baseball could sustain yet another hit to its tarnished reputation, whether any system of tests could ever secure the game's once unimpeachable integrity, and whether baseball's belated efforts to add teeth to its testing regimen may have actually led the league to break privacy laws. Overlooked in the maelstrom of expert analysis and punditry was a stunning moment of clarity courtesy of a *60 Minutes* interview with Anthony Bosch, the man behind Biogenesis. Hewing to the usual narrative about the damage being done to baseball's wholesome reputation, journalist Scott Pelley asked Bosch about the difficulty in preserving baseball's integrity in this current climate. In this instance, and given Bosch's history, it would be easy to shoot the messenger. The message is nonetheless edifying. Bosch was blunt: "Unfortunately, this is part of baseball," he said. "This is part of baseball. This has always been part of the game."[3]

* * *

One could say that Major League Baseball has a paradise problem. Major League Baseball was never the Garden of Eden. Of course, you would probably never reach this conclusion from reading generations of writers waxing eloquent about the unique rhythms of the game, celebrating baseball's cultural significance in plum-colored prose. For baseball's knights of the pen, and for more than one generation of their readers, the game of baseball was a reliable pinch-hitter for Eden, a perfect proxy for the purest of places. Baseball, in the hands of the most adroit scribes, became an almost sacred metaphor for nation, the daily reenactment of American exceptionalism. The game's mostly urban theaters were imbued with agrarian religious sanctity. Ballparks became steel-and-brick chapels wherein the masses convened, amid clipped grass and sunlight, to receive an education in good, clean, Americanism.

The inimitable essayist Stephen Jay Gould once speared the pretense of ascribing such metaphysical significance to baseball—baseball's true beauty was extant in the simple action of the game itself. Nevertheless, the dominant tradition is to polish the metaphor. Baseball is America. Dining at Delmonico's in 1889, no less a literary light than Mark Twain feted the game by proclaiming it the "very symbol, the outward and visible expression of the drive, and push, and rush and struggle of the raging, tearing, booming nineteenth century!" In Ron Shelton's *Bull Durham* the character of Annie Savoy, the quintessential "Baseball Annie," proclaims the gospel of the Church of Baseball and offers an abridged recital of Walt Whitman: "I see great things in baseball. It's our game—the American game." Like Twain, Whitman's particular focus was on the game's celebrated reflection of what sportsman Albert Spalding called "American Vim, Vigor, [and] Virility." Baseball was exuberant. Baseball was manly. Whitman prophesied that baseball would take Americans outside, spur them to greater health, and improve their "physical stoicism." The game itself was the ultimate form of performance enhancement. Baseball was an extension not just of America, but of a manly, healthy, rushing America. We might all be exiled from Eden, but there was salvation in the game.[4]

To Americans who grew up with what Bart Giamatti called the "Last Pure Place," baseball was often cast as the very soul of their democracy. It was a mirror of the best American qualities and a barometer of important social transitions. Imagine Jackie Robinson, a black man, walking onto a Major League baseball diamond for the first time, a harbinger not only of integration within his own sport, but also of the remarkable social change destined for all of American society. Americans looked to the diamond in times of crisis and of tranquility in order to confirm that the promise of the American dream was still within reach. If a man—even a black man—could make it on the field, he (and all the rest of us with him) could make it anywhere.[5]

Baseball was always more than just a mirror, though. Baseball—and sport in general—is also an arena geared toward self-invention. Writers used the playing field to craft narratives explaining who Americans were and who they wanted to be. Part of the resonance of Jackie Robinson's story is that it reminds us of a time when, to all appearances, we got things right, maybe even despite ourselves—as is very often the case with Major League Baseball. Even the shadows that on occasion fell over the sunlit diamond—think of the Black Sox scandal of 1919—added something to the mythology of the "Last Pure Place." There was something resonant and inspiring about baseball, phoenix-like, rising from the ashes of rampant skullduggery behind the prolific bat of Babe Ruth on the diamond and the unassailable, shock-haired, justice-wielding Judge Kenesaw Mountain Landis in the offices beyond it.

Sure, it is common for aging writers, their hair thinning, their midriffs expanding, to condemn the modern iteration of the sport, recalling from the press box a better time, and a purer game. This hand-wringing actually illuminates baseball's remarkable resilience. The dark times stand out because they run against the grain of the game's celebrated lightness. Baseball imagined as a bonding game of catch between fathers and sons, hot dogs, and endless summertime emerges a more vivid image because the somber memory of harder times lingers. Cranks might bemoan the state of the game, but they still recognize that baseball survived and even thrived despite the troubling persistence of chicanery, racial injustice, and economic inequality.

Drugs, however, seem to present a crisis of entirely another sort. Writers, fully aware of the game's imperfect past, nevertheless write hysterically about drugs, as though they have just uncovered some dread truth that will prove the undoing of the entire sporting enterprise. Nothing threatens the sacred covenant between baseball past and present in the way that drugs, especially performance-enhancing drugs, do. We can always reinvent (and maybe even forgive) gamblers like Shoeless Joe Jackson or Pete Rose, but there is less room to rehabilitate Mark McGwire or Barry Bonds because their sins were greater. Their transgressions struck at the very soul of the "Last Pure Place"; they waged war on the numbers, the holy scriptures of the church of baseball, the sacred links tying each passing baseball generation to the next.

Start to talk about drugs and baseball, and the narrative quickly threatens to become tiresome. There is no doubt that Americans are suffering from a case of steroids fatigue. The search for scapegoats, the disingenuous hand-wringing, the congressional grandstanding—it has all been played out. It is so much sound and fury, often to no useful end. Why should we care anymore? Let the old writers polish their myths. Baseball's long-burnished reputation as the preeminent sporting institution in the United States has grown dusty. Major League Baseball has long since taken up lagging behind the National Football League in the race for America's sporting hearts and minds. Although baseball's once sterling reputation is still something of a byword, if nowhere else than in the somewhat anachronistic title of "National Pastime," there is a definite sense that the heyday of Major League Baseball's cultural resonance is passed. Maybe we have come to know that baseball was not all that it was cracked up to be. It was never Eden. It was not exceptional. So what?

We may still love the old baseball myths, but we have learned to take them with a grain of salt. We know the game was never perfect when it came to matters of race, economic equality, or social justice. But look a little deeper. Author Don DeLillo wrote of the "deep eros of memory that separates baseball from other sports." It remains true that baseball's reputation, perhaps even the game's future, is tied to the game's past in a way that one finds in no other major American sport. The problem is that our understanding of baseball's past, its influence on American society and culture, and perhaps even on its future course, remains obscured by the persistence of that exceptionalist mythology. The mythmakers retain a maddening hold over the narrative. They ask us to save baseball (by which they almost certainly mean the sacred past upon which the game is built) from drugs (which break crucial links between present and past) by denying the very memory of the existence of drugs in the game even from the very beginning. They are defending a myth—a myth that insists that Paradise was lost when performance-enhancing drugs found a way in. We know there is more to it than that.[6]

The story of baseball and drugs needs to be recovered from the tyranny of baseball mythology. As we can see in many other circumstances, baseball does provide a valuable reflection of society, but only when we separate idyll from authenticity. We can begin with some big questions. Forget Eden. What if the baseball Elysium that a century of writers did so much to canonize never really existed? What if Barry Bonds, and Mark McGwire, and Roger Clemens, and Jose Canseco, and Alex Rodriguez are not so different from the icons of those earlier, supposedly purer, eras? Maybe there is not such a wide gulf between Bonds and Mickey Mantle, between Clemens and Sandy Koufax. Forget exceptionalism, comforting as that idea may be. What if baseball actually was America, and what if drugs, legal and illicit, were always part of the story?

*　*　*

Team Chemistry is an attempt to answer those questions by exploring that story. This book operates on the premise that Major League Baseball provides a distinct, and meaningful, reflection of America. *Field of Dreams*' fictional "boat-rocker" Terrance Mann was not wrong when he proclaimed that as Americans progressed through the twentieth century, baseball marched alongside them. It did. And drugs were always there. Baseball was connected to the brewing and tobacco interests almost from its professional inception, not only using their products, which some even then suggested was decidedly unhealthy, but providing a useful vehicle for selling those same products to the public (especially to the impressionable young). In the years after World War II, as Americans celebrated the fruits of modern science's pharmacological cornucopia, it was only natural that baseball reflect the newfound appreciation of ameliorative drugs, painkillers, and even performance enhancers. There was a Cold War to be won (and stresses of the Cold War to escape from). However much the purists loved to celebrate the sacred sameness of the national game, baseball at the Major League level was rapidly evolving, reacting, and adapting, like Americans themselves, to the dislocations of the American Century.

This book, then, is about baseball, about drugs, and about America. A good deal of what is addressed here is done so not in the interest of providing any policy prescriptions, but rather in an effort to provide much-needed context to one of the prominent questions in sports today. The combination of drugs and baseball is not new. The real trick is pinpointing when drugs actually became a "problem," why at that point, and, most importantly, what might that say about America?

A story as broad as this has to start on a solid foundation. The first part of *Team Chemistry* introduces the long tradition of drugs in baseball by tracing, in brief, the history of alcohol, tobacco, and new postwar pharmaceuticals in the Major Leagues. These mostly legal drugs were not only ubiquitous within the game, essential partners in the economics of the baseball business, but they were also key elements in baseball mythology. Look back, and you will find that many of the stories that in one context might be read as tragedies of drug abuse are actually some of the most beloved and oft-told stories in the pastime's mythic canon.

The latter half of the book focuses more closely on the perceived problem of drug use, transitioning into the world of illegal recreational and performance-enhancing drugs. The story on those pages is how the "problem" was handled (or not handled, as the case may be) by the regimes of commissioners Bowie Kuhn, Peter Ueberroth, and Bud Selig. There the story of drugs becomes entwined with the internecine labor struggles of the late twentieth century as well as, by comparison, the increasingly relevant substance abuse issues of the mythologized past. In the end there is one fundamental theme at the heart of this book's narrative: baseball is America. We cannot truly assess the sacred covenant between baseball past and baseball present without making drugs a central part of the story. It is time to separate myth from reality and to consider that, in the end, our reaction to troubling revelations about drug use in baseball says less about baseball, the "Last Pure Place" of the imagination, than it does about our society in general.

With this in mind, some brief definitions are in order. What exactly do I mean by "drugs"? My concern is with drugs both licit and illicit, performance enhancing, recreational, and ameliorative. The House of Baseball is home to all kinds of drugs—from alcohol to nicotine, to various legal painkillers, to street drugs like cocaine or marijuana, and, finally, to performance enhancers like amphetamine, human growth hormone, and steroids. Definitions in this arena are often difficult and quite variable, but for my purposes I am including anything that when taken into the body may modify one or more of its physical or mental functions. Obviously this covers most of what can traditionally be called a drug, but keep in mind that while water or basic nutrients also fit this broad definition, they are not what this history is about.[7]

Within the world of baseball, and sports in general, there are basically three broad groupings of drugs. The first and most expansive group includes recreational drugs. Here we are talking about legal substances like alcohol or tobacco as well as illegal substances such as marijuana, cocaine, or LSD. In one form or another, these have been a part of baseball since the game's inception in the nineteenth century.

The second group includes the restorative or ameliorative drugs. These are usually taken to manage an injury or some other existing condition, enabling an athlete to return, as nearly as possible, to his normal state of performance. In this group we find painkillers, muscle relaxants, various sedatives, and topical sprays. Most of these came into baseball along with the evolution of the field of sports medicine and the dramatic growth of the pharmaceutical industry in the years after World War II.

Finally there are the ergogenic drugs, what are today known as performance-enhancing drugs. The primary purpose of these substances is to increase the performance of the athlete beyond the boundaries to which he is usually constrained. Here we find amphetamines, anabolic steroids, and a host of other designer chemical agents.

Obviously, all of these drugs are not the same, and it is not my intention to suggest that a ballplayer who was fond of the bottle and who drank his career away should be wholly equated with a player who snorted and sold cocaine or who injected Winstrol into his buttocks. What *Team Chemistry* argues instead is that those acts, broadly conceived, all derive from similar origins and are part of a connected narrative. The alcoholic of the early 1900s or the amphetamine user of the 1960s is inextricably linked to the steroid user of the 1990s not by the moral equity of their behavior but by a unified cultural and social framework far more complex than what most baseball writers have previously conceived. In other words, *Team Chemistry* suggests that we can better understand baseball's Steroid Era if we first try to understand the century (not just the decade) of drug use that led into it.

Delving into this past means assessing, above all, the way in which the relationship between drugs and baseball distorts the traditional baseball narrative. On one level this is about restoring baseball to a more human dimension. *Team Chemistry* says something about how we define heroism and what, in the end, we want from our sports heroes—why do we lament the tragedy of Mantle but turn away in shame at the story of Bonds, commend Koufax but condemn Clemens? There are no obvious answers to the questions at the heart of this book, but to ask them is to enter an ongoing debate, one that exists well beyond the sports world, about ethics. It means navigating the rise of a culture of instant gratification and narcissism, and contemplating the timeless human quest for eternal youth and permanent virility.

Team Chemistry is about drugs and baseball. About America as it wants to be and America as it is. About heroes in one time becoming the villains of another. It is about the concept of purity and perfection and the hard reality that the game is anything but. Major League Baseball is not Eden, and it is not perfect. This is what makes it so interesting, so important, and so utterly American. It is time to examine the undisguised reflection of America in the game of baseball by looking beneath the carefully polished metaphor.

Where to start? The writer Thomas Boswell once suggested that the game of baseball was diffracted by the town and ballpark where it is played. Baseball at any given time, both in how it is played and what it means to those who view it, is defined by where it is played and who plays it. "Does baseball," Boswell asked, "like a liquid, take the shape of its container?" The container is America, and for the first few generations of players, it looked an awful lot like a bottle.[8]

PART 1

This Is Your Game

1

Time in a Bottle

As long as I could pitch a little, no one cared that I was
getting drunk.

—Don Newcombe

Alcohol is tied in with masculinity—the more you drink,
the better man you are.

—Ryne Duren

Mickey Mantle was dying. It was clear to everyone who saw him in
those last few weeks, a gaunt figure in an ill-fitting All-Star Game cap, his
face ravaged by hard living, pain, and no small measure of regret. Five weeks
after the most controversial liver transplant in American history, this Mantle
seemed a hollow shell of the legendary Mick. At a moment when baseball
needed good memories, Mantle was taking his leave, offering only a solemn
elegy for the golden days of his sport and the men who played it. Baseball,
which Mantle had dominated with his violent swing, once peerless speed—
peerless, at least, before repetitive leg injuries slowed him—and humble "aw
shucks" smile, was struggling through the aftermath of a devastating labor
stoppage, a strike that had led to the first cancellation of the World Series
since 1904. Like Mantle, it seemed as if baseball itself were slowly passing.
Fans from Main Street to Pennsylvania Avenue lamented the creeping cor-
poratism, greed, and stupidity that had overtaken Major League Baseball in
the summer of 1994. Now, scarcely a year later, seeing Mickey Mantle ravaged
by the liver cancer that had first been diagnosed just that May was almost
too much to endure.

In the age of the skeptic, nostalgia is no shield. That didn't stop some
from using Mantle as a diversion from baseball's mounting troubles. Misty-
eyed baseball writers mourned the passing of an era (not yet the passing

of the game) and found an endless array of ways to work the word "hero" into print or televised commentary. Considerably less time was given by the cognoscenti to a discussion of the uncomfortable elephant in the room: Mantle's lifelong battle with alcoholism. Mickey's disease was acknowledged, of course, but almost always in a manner that suggested the man's fatal attraction to the bottle actually made his baseball accomplishments even more laudable. The hangovers made the homers seem longer and more majestic. After all, a man in such physical pain surely needed to take the edge off. Who could or would blame him? It was not what the bottle kept Mickey from accomplishing, but what he accomplished despite the bottle. Few writers at the time proffered the starkly honest assessment of John Anders in the *Dallas Morning News*: "The first great disappointment in joining the sports staff here in 1967," he wrote, "was learning that my boyhood idol, Mickey Mantle, was a big drunk."[1]

Oddly enough, nobody did more to counter the hero talk and bring the saddest aspect of Mantle's life to the fore than Mantle himself. After checking into the Betty Ford Clinic in early 1994, he gave numerous interviews highlighting the high cost of decades of excessive drinking. Having come so late to sobriety, he endured the highly contentious debate over the legality and morality of his liver transplant with admirable stoicism. He emerged from that struggle determined to redefine his legacy and, in doing so, to begin redefining an entire baseball era.

Weakened and sick as he was, Mantle started revising his legacy almost immediately, beginning at the posttransplant press conference. "I owe so much to God and to the American people," he told the assembled reporters that day. "I'm going to spend the rest of my life trying to make it up. It seems to me all I've done is take. Have fun and take. I'm going to start giving something back. I'd like to say to the kids out there, if you're looking for a role model, this is a role model." Mickey thumbed his own chest. "Don't be like me. God gave me a body and an ability to play baseball. God gave me everything and I just . . ." His final words were overwhelmed by raw emotion. It seemed clear that Mantle meant to say that he had squandered his many physical gifts for love of drink.[2]

Later that summer, Mantle was unable to be on hand for the annual Old Timers' Game at Yankee Stadium in the Bronx. He appeared instead in a taped segment on the stadium scoreboard. There he once again sought to recast his image while targeting baseball's young audience. "To all my little teammates out there," he pleaded, "please don't do drugs and alcohol. God only gave us one body, and keep it healthy. We really need it."[3]

Throughout his final weeks, Mickey Mantle lamented to all who would listen the high cost of the lifestyle he had chosen. His was too many mornings greeted with the "Breakfast of Champions" (a cloying concoction of Kahlua, brandy, and cream). His was a wrecked marriage, the loss of a son (Billy Mantle in March 1994) and of his dearest friend (Billy Martin on Christmas Day, 1989) to demons too much like his own. In the end, and though he might not have known it, Mantle's were the shared regrets of a century of baseball men very much like him. "I know it should have been so much better," he said of his life and career, as those other players surely would have said of theirs, "and the big reason it wasn't is the lifestyle I chose, the late nights and too many empty glasses."[4]

In eulogizing Mantle in August 1995 it was time to remember those long nights. Understanding them is a more difficult proposition. Baseball was born wet. Alcohol, the drug that, if it did not lead to an early grave, had wrecked many a baseball man's career, retirement, or marriage, was, with nicotine (by way of tobacco), an ubiquitous presence throughout the formative years and during the Golden Age of professional baseball. Despite a few weak reform efforts, alcohol remained an accepted, even essential, element in the game's masculine subculture. Eventually, alcohol became an integral part of baseball's economic system as well as a component of the game's rich mythology. The myths were perpetuated by writers who relied on friendly teams for support, who sometimes lived vicariously through the athletes they covered, and who celebrated displays of athletic prowess despite inebriation as evidence of masculine excellence. If baseball's endless binge was hidden from the public, or given a glossy veneer, it was because writers simply could not afford to expose the worst excesses of the game. The ethos of the time was simple: "Drink Hard, Play Hard."

From time to time in recent years players and writers have questioned Major League Baseball's relentless assault on ergogenic drugs while the league seemingly ignores the long history of alcohol abuse and excess of beer money in the game. The response to these concerns is typically something along the lines of "but alcohol is legal—steroids are not." That misses the point. The influence of alcohol on baseball cannot be measured by resorting to the concept of legality alone. Peer through the fog of nostalgia, and you will find that alcohol both shaped and misshaped baseball, in myth and in reality. For the better part of a century many players were victims of an ill-informed tradition that actually celebrated drunkenness. For decades, the purity of the game was a surrogate, in the ad copy of Madison Avenue, for the purity of barley, hops, and water. The history of baseball and alcohol runs deep into the past and well beyond the neon-illuminated New York skyline of midcentury. Nevertheless, this hard-drinking world reached its apotheosis in New York, center of the baseball world, during the 1950s when Mickey Mantle, young and vibrant, was the brightest star in the brightest constellation in the baseball firmament.

* * *

It was a little after 1:00 in the morning, and a man was sprawled on the floor at Mickey Mantle's feet. Chaos ruled the cloakroom of Manhattan's Copacabana night club as several men, most of them blurry-eyed and uncoordinated after a long evening of drinking, awkwardly swung their fists at opponents they could barely see. Or maybe it was that everyone was trying to restrain everyone else, giving the impression that fists were flying, or were about to fly—Yogi Berra later summed up the episode in his own inimitable style, insisting that "nobody did nuthin' to nobody." Somewhere in the confusion was Mickey's teammate, Billy Martin. It was Billy's birthday. Outside the cloakroom, in the dining room of the Copa, guests mingled under electric blue and pink palm trees, sipped cocktails, and listened to music. Opening in 1940, the Copa, on East 60th Street in New York City, had become a regular watering hole for mobsters and celebrities, a place to see and to be seen, where "every night was New Year's Eve." In the early morning hours of May 16, 1957, however, the scene was closer to something out of Gillette's Friday night fights.[5]

Concerned that the man at his feet might be Martin, Mantle leaned down to check. It was not Billy, so Mantle dropped him back to the floor and waited. Months later the man on the floor, a Bronx delicatessen owner, sought damages before a grand jury. Mantle would tell the New York City courtroom that "it looked like Roy Rogers had ridden by, and Trigger had kicked the man in the face." Mickey had not thrown a single punch. In fact, the only thing he had laid a hand on was scotch and soda. He would have been surprised to know that Billy Martin had not thrown any punches either. Nevertheless, the man on the floor was no Yankee. And *someone* had decked him.[6]

The evening had started innocently enough. Mantle, Whitey Ford, Hank Bauer, Yogi Berra, Johnny Kucks, and Martin, along with the wives of the first five, had arrived at the Copa to celebrate Martin's twenty-ninth birthday. Sammy Davis Jr. was headlining that night, and the Yankees were eager to see him perform. While Davis worked, a raucous group of bowlers, apparently intoxicated, started hurling increasingly nasty racial slurs toward the stage. Mantle recalled that they called the singer "Little Black Sambo and stuff like that." Others insisted that the bowlers had referred to Davis as a "jungle bunny." This behavior incensed the Yankees, who recalled the daily struggles of their teàmmate, Elston Howard, the first black Yankee. Yet another account suggests that the drunken revelers had approached the Yankee table for autographs, thrown insults at Davis, and then been invited outside by Billy Martin for a "talk." No matter what version of *L'Affaire Copa* one finds, the end result was a cloakroom full of people eager to confront each other, if not yet trading blows. For his part, Mickey Mantle was so drunk he could barely remember what had happened. Whitey Ford stayed at the table and, as he later lamented, was stuck with the check for the evening's festivities.[7]

The confrontation was broken up quickly, but as the Yankees were attempting a quiet escape out the Copa's back entrance, they were spotted by a reporter for one of New York's major newspapers. Joe Trimble of the *Daily News*, possibly the reporter in question, rang Yankees manager Casey Stengel, pulling the aged skipper out of bed for his reaction. The next day headlines across the city blazed with some version of "YANKEES IN COPA BRAWL." Hank Bauer, when confronted with reports that he had allegedly hit a drunken Yankees' fan, pointed to his less-than-robust .255 batting average. "Hit him? Why I haven't hit anybody all year."[8]

If the players seemed barely fazed by the party-gone-wrong, the fracas was an embarrassment for the Yankees brass, who felt the players should be concentrating more on clinching the pennant. Their team had a well-earned reputation for excessive nightlife, and although manager Stengel was generally accepting of his player's off-the-diamond behavior, he had to make a stand. "We have twenty-five birthdays on this club, not to mention wedding anniversarys [sic]," explained Stengel. No club, he was suggesting, could survive too many Copa-like celebrations. To further drive the point home, Ford, Bauer, Berra, Mantle, and Martin were each fined $1,000. The struggling Bauer was dropped to eighth in the batting order for the next day's game against the Detroit Tigers, but Mantle remained ensconced in the third spot. "I'm mad at him, too, for being out late," said Stengel, "but I'm not mad enough to take a chance on losing a ball game and possibly the pennant." As Mantle went, so went the Yankees. Besides, the punishment was paternalistic farce. The Yankees would get the money back after playing in (and losing) the World Series that fall. There was, however, one significant result stemming from the Copa escapade.[9]

If Mantle was the Yankees' offensive engine, Billy Martin, the team's plucky second baseman with a reputation for expressing his competitive fire with his fists as often as his sharp tongue, was the team's soul. George Weiss, the

Yankees' general manager, tended to believe that the light-hitting Martin was a chronic troublemaker and, more distressingly, a bad influence on Mantle. The Copa incident was a perfect excuse to excise a potential cancer, and Martin knew it. "I'm gone," he told Mantle and Ford the day after the fight, "George Weiss is just looking for an excuse to get rid of me."[10]

Martin had not even thrown a punch at the Copa. Still, the blame would be his since everyone knew that "Billy the Kid" was eager to resort to punches at even the slightest provocation. More than any other Yankees player, Martin got aggressive when deep in the bottle. And he was often in the bottle. In that, he was seldom alone. He was fast friends with the young, impressionable Mantle and the urbane Whitey Ford. Together, these nocturnal "Dead End Kids" ruled New York City's nights, and although Ford would later insist that they didn't actually drink all *that* much, almost everyone else acknowledged that their diet was often more liquid than solid. Even Ford himself admitted that those who roomed with Mantle "said [Mickey] took five years off their career."[11]

Billy Martin, who would eventually become the sacrificial lamb in George Weiss's hopeless crusade to impress prudence on his troublesome ballplayers, was shipped to the baseball Siberia of Kansas City on June 15. When news of Martin's trade was announced, the "Dead End Kids" hit the bars once again, drowning their tears in an endless round of drinks, one more night on the town like so many nights before. Mantle and Martin remained close friends even after the trade. Recalled Mantle, "We used to tease each other about whose liver was going to go first."

Sundered partnerships aside, it was a great time to be a baseball player. In New York, the "National Pastime" ruled the daytime, and a vibrant nightlife turned the evening to neon. In those days there was no pastime more beloved within the National Pastime than drinking. Before the game or after the game, it was just what you did. Bob Lemon, who pitched with the Cleveland Indians in those heady days, once summed up the attitude of the era. "After my team wins, I drink to celebrate," he said. "After my team loses, I drink to cheer up."[12]

* * *

A troubling fondness for the bottle was not unique to the "Dead End Kids" of the 1950s. In fact, alcohol abuse had been the doom of a long line of ballplayers stretching back to the professional game's nineteenth-century inception. The casualty list is a "Who's Who" of star-caliber players, not to mention a host of lesser-known athletes whose on-field accomplishments were never significant enough to have their tragic off-field escapades elevate them into baseball's curious pantheon of bacchanalian icons.

Concerned that well-to-do fans might be put off by baseball's association with alcohol, the game's owners had once tried desperately to cut booze out of the game. If the players, usually of a different class or ethnic background than their employers, wanted to imbibe, management's appeal to middle-class Victorian moral codes and the temperance crowd did little to deter them. In fact, although progressive reformers bemoaned demon rum, an obtuse argument could be made that alcohol was actually the first, and most revered, of performance-enhancing drugs to take root in the game of baseball. The sport's history is littered with stories of players who claimed that they performed better after a few drinks. Leo Durocher once incurred the wrath of the teetotaler Branch Rickey when he administered brandy to minor league castoff Tom Seats, who suddenly turned into a serviceable pitcher. When Rickey forbade the special tonic, Seats's career quickly petered out. Numerous other players swore by the remarkable effects of a few nips (or more) just before game time. Smiling Mickey Welch, an ace screwballer who won over three hundred games playing in New York in the 1880s, ascribed his pitching success to beer and offered a paean to malt beverages, singing: "pure elixir of malt and hops / beats all the drugs and all the drops."[13]

Foremost among the idols of baseball's hard-drinking early days was Ed Delahanty, the very best of a five-brother baseball fraternity, and one of the greatest power hitters of the nineteenth century. Big Ed was also a prodigious drinker who used alcohol to escape his unhappy personal life. Delahanty died in 1903 at the age of thirty-five when, after one particularly wild bender, he wandered away from his train's Niagara station platform, strolled onto a railroad bridge, and fell into the Niagara River, where he drowned or was swept over the falls. He was hitting .333 at the time.[14]

Fortunately, not every player was cut in the mold of Pete Browning, who, in addition to lending his nickname ("The Louisville Slugger") to his custom-made Hillerich & Bradsby bats, relied on alcohol to ease the pain of chronic mastoiditis. Browning famously averred that he could not hit the ball until he had hit the bottle. Nevertheless, more than a few players used alcohol to ease their tensions before a game, to escape personal problems as Delahanty, and, of course, to unwind in postgame celebrations of the sort that remain a tradition within the sports world of today.[15]

The veteran sportswriter Roger Kahn, himself no stranger to the bottle, once suggested that a complete history of baseball's hard drinkers would make a "very long book indeed." Thanks to writers like Kahn, however, hard drinkers do hold a special place in the history and mythology of the game. Some of the most-oft told and beloved baseball stories—tales of Ruth's epic bellyache, Hack Wilson playing a batting practice carom as though it were a crucial in-game play, almost all the tales of the Bronx Zoo–era Yankees— involve a distinctly boozy element. These stories tend to take one of several standard forms, and drinking tales about players of one generation tend to get repeated about players of the next, so that one never really knows what tale is true and what one may be apocryphal. A few examples of the traditional forms will suffice.[16]

Take, as a fairly typical model, the tale of the absent alcoholic. Flint Rhem, who led the National League in wins in 1926 while pitching for the world champion St. Louis Cardinals, disappeared from the team for a brief spell in 1930 just as the Cardinals and Brooklyn Dodgers were locked in a tight pennant race. When he eventually turned up, bedraggled and a little worse for wear, Rhem swore to manager Gabby Street that he had been kidnapped by gangsters (of the Dodger partisan variety) and forced, at gunpoint, to drink copious amounts of alcohol. Phil Douglas of the New York Giants once insisted, or so writer Hugh Fullerton claimed, that members of the Cincinnati Reds drugged his lemonade, forcing him astray on an ill-fated bender during a crucial part of the season. Similar stories were often told of man-boy Rube Waddell, the eccentric, but undeniably talented, flamethrower for Connie Mack's Athletics who was famously fond of booze, women, and fires—not necessarily in that order.[17]

Baseball history is a constellation of stars and lesser lights whose careers were snuffed out by their love affair with the bottle. From Grover Cleveland Alexander to Hack Wilson, the list is illustrious and lengthy. Numerous players of less stature died young, alone, made mendicant by alcoholism, casualties of a disease that was, for much of the twentieth century, misunderstood by the medical community. Yet, as one can see from just a sampling of popular stories, there has always been a peculiar spin on the history of the baseball drunk, a nostalgic gloss that suggests not only were these players part of the game's charm, but their obsession with the bottle ultimately became part of the definition of what a real baseball player ought to be: rough around the edges, fun loving, and as hard-living off the diamond as he was hard-playing on it. The best players were not necessarily copies of the tragic Pete Browning, but they were men who could hold their liquor, tie on a few drinks the night before a game, and then perform at their best the next day. This bizarre mythos of macho performance ethic and paternalistic "don't ask, don't tell" response spelled a century of alcohol-induced heartache for the game of baseball.[18]

The "Drink Hard, Play Hard" ethic imbues many of the stock tales in baseball's rich mythology—stories of ballplayers who are physically capable of heroic game-time feats even while playing drunk or hung over. The heroic, superhuman, and often comedic aspects of these stories have tended to obscure any concern about the human cost and adverse health effects of excessive drinking.

Though alcohol abuse was undoubtedly the single greatest scourge of the baseball community in the first half of the twentieth century, there was no institutional response to the problem. In fact, no problem was ever recognized so long as excessive drinking did not interfere with on-field performance. Jacob Ruppert, the Yankees aristocratic brewer-owner, was typical of his peers, adopting a paternalistic stance when dealing with Babe Ruth's excesses. Ruppert treated the Babe as one might treat an unruly, but undeniably beloved child. Along with manager Miller Huggins, Ruppert would firmly push Ruth back into line whenever the star slugger's excesses threatened the team's larger goals. Ruth might bluff a bit, but was ultimately always malleable. Sam Breadon, the Cardinals owner, treated Grover Clevelend Alexander more like a charity case, providing money, disguised as a pension, to keep Pete on his feet well after his baseball career ended. Nothing was ever done to combat his raging alcoholism. Alexander survived until 1950, two years before he was immortalized in film, when he died, at age sixty-three, drunk and alone in a Nebraska boarding house.[19]

In large part the attitude of baseball men toward the bottle was informed by simple ignorance of alcoholism—what caused it, how it manifested itself, how to fight it. Few experts could agree on the answers to those questions. More to blame than medical ignorance, however, was the common belief that there was a cosmic connection between booze, especially beer, and baseball. Echoing Mickey Welch, Senators manager Bucky Harris remarked in 1933 at the end of the Prohibition experiment that there was an inexplicable connection between beer and baseball success. This unusual relationship between booze and baseball, however, had less to do with cosmic serendipity than it did with the masculine culture of the game.[20]

The baseball world features a distinctly male subculture built around complicated notions of hierarchy and rites of passage, emphasizing action and physical prowess. In this manly world highly educated players were rare, and those who possessed college educations were often made the butt of jokes. A college kid was, contemporary thought suggested, "a rarity, a near-freak on a major league diamond." Nobody with serious ambitions would waste time in college when he could be working his way through the minor leagues. Bill

Rigney summed up the era's thinking: "we used to think the dumbest guys we had in the game were the college men." The rambunctious Billy Martin felt that college graduates were too refined to be good ballplayers. Martin was typical of an era that saw ballplayers as part of a hypermasculine universe built around hard drinking, sex, and a privacy-performance rule that said so long as a player performed on the field, his private activities were no business of the public or management.[21]

Heavy drinking and obsession with manly virtues tended to go hand in hand. Thorstein Veblen wrote in 1899 that "infirmities induced by overindulgence are, among some peoples, freely recognized as manly attributes." In baseball, drinking was a critical component of the bonding process that created clubhouse cohesion and team chemistry. Young boys, many of them lonely, far away from home for the first time in their lives, found acceptance by joining old hands in postgame drinking binges. Outfielder Rick Reichardt would later acknowledge what he saw as baseball's "built-in insecurity." It was, he said, "a very lonely life. Our working day may be only three hours long. Our worst enemy may be spare time." By the 1950s, when Mark Harris's fictional Henry Wiggins parted the veil on baseball's clubhouse culture, drinking remained a primarily male activity, and along with the first sexual experience, a symbolic rite of passage into manhood. The more one man could drink, the more manly he was.[22]

The ubiquitous culture of drinking in baseball helped to keep the players united. It livened the hours on long train rides between cities, easing the boredom of a mostly transient life. It also helped to keep ballplayers separated from women. In one profound example of the misogyny and sexism inherent in baseball, journalist Al Stump wrote a blistering article about how women—"baseball Sadies" (groupies), girlfriends, and wives—all threatened the carefully crafted cohesion of the locker room. Women, viewed primarily as little more than sex objects in the sophomoric and alcohol-tinged culture of the game, did not really have a place in baseball's masculine universe. Particularly in the 1950s, when national concerns about emasculation, homosexuality, and softness in the face of dire Cold War threats were paramount, it was imperative that baseball men uphold the old standards. Beer and liquor were the glue that held that manly world together, the heart of a "holy trinity of alcohol, sports, and hegemonic masculinity."[23]

Heavy drinking, then, was a key part of baseball's macho tradition, not only tolerated but often applauded. Ralph Houk, manager of the Yankees in the early 1960s, echoed several generations of forebears when he proclaimed, "I'll take nine whiskey drinkers over nine milk-shake drinkers any day." If a player happened to be a booze hound, so what? It was taken for granted that he was young and strong, and that he could sweat the alcohol out of his system. Heavy drinkers were sometimes celebrated, described as "Fun Worshipers," as lively throwbacks to some mythical rough-and-tumble baseball frontier. Most of the time the activities of the most outsized carousers simply were not reported. When Milwaukee's Earl Torgeson wrecked his car after an acknowledged six-drink evening at the bar, the *Sporting News* went out of its way to emphasize that Torgeson had not been ticketed for driving under the influence.[24]

Few ever took notice of the game's struggling retirees, the old men with puffy faces and pot bellies, wasting away in some postbaseball alcoholic Purgatory. Pitcher Ryne Duren once showed a reporter for *Sports Illustrated* group shots of former teammates. "This guy drank himself to death," Duren said, pointing to one player. "This fellow died of an alcohol-related sickness," he said of another. "This one died an alcoholic, though the papers said it was heart trouble."[25]

In many ways, it was the sports pages that protected and celebrated the 'Drink Hard, Play Hard' culture of alcohol abuse in Major League Baseball. They did this in large part because it was good business. In the era before television, the sports press had a highly symbiotic relationship with the teams they covered. Teams often paid for writers to travel with the team, providing lodging and food. Few would dare bite the hand that fed them. But the writers also relished being included in the players' lives—especially their nightlife. If the media had reported everything that happened at popular watering holes, they would soon find themselves barred from admission. In short, the difference between the old "heroes" of the sporting Golden Age, who seem to shine so brightly when compared to the tarnished idols of today, is, in large part, simply a matter of how little of the bad was actually ever reported in the old days.[26]

Roger Kahn, who chronicled the Brooklyn Dodgers of the 1950s, noted that writing about drunkenness had been absolutely beyond the bounds of sports pages for as long as writers had covered the game. Kahn recalled how the famous Yankees manager Joe McCarthy once went on a bender during spring training in 1938 and failed to show up at the ballpark for five days. The few reporters who bothered to mention the missing manager wrote that McCarthy's absence could be attributed to a nasty bout of "Florida flu."[27]

Similarly, Babe Ruth's drinking and training habits were no secret to anyone who came near him, but they were largely glossed over by the newspapers. In addition to baseball players Hack Wilson and Grover Cleveland Alexander, papers seldom exposed the boozing of athletes such as Jim Thorpe, Notre Dame golden boy George Gipp, or the Chicago Bears' Red Grange. One former sportswriter explained the relationship most clearly. "Baseball players," he said, "were like pool hustlers back in the early 1900s. They were animals. The railroads would cordon off whole cars to isolate them from other passengers. Old-time sportswriters—Ring Lardner and Grantland Rice—rode on trains and played cards and drank with those guys. None of that stuff ever got in the papers."[28]

Instead, writers helped to craft a rich baseball mythology, illustrating for posterity the pervasive macho performance ethic. They perfected the ubiquitous story of the star player who, after a night on the town, played with a seismic hangover and still hit the decisive home run. The ending of that story is almost always the same, no matter who the smashed player happens to be: "I see three baseballs," the hero says, "but I only swing at the middle one." This heroic archetype survived well into the 1960s, when Jim Bouton recalled Mickey Mantle, after hitting just such a home run, squinting out into the stands and proclaiming, "those people don't know how tough that really was."[29]

*   *   *

Mickey Mantle's death in August 1995 became a touchstone for the National Pastime and the nation, a moment for fans to forget the desperate months of critical wrangling over the appropriateness of Mickey's last-minute liver transplant, to forget the cynical outrage that spilled out of his posttransplant press conference, to dismiss baseball's many recent transgressions, the strike, the scabs, the lost World Series. It was, instead, an opportunity for many to wax nostalgic about a time when the game, and the men who played it, stood above commercialism and displayed loyalty to club and country. Those men, true role models, real heroes, played the game the "right way," and Mantle towered over all of them. The story of Mantle—brawny, blond, the son of a poor but hard-working Oklahoma zinc miner—was the American dream. He was, suggested one writer, "more than a baseball star. He was fast and strong and handsome. He was who we wanted to be."[30]

In the atmosphere of partisan culture war that clouded the 1990s, there was undoubtedly something deeply appropriate and even therapeutic about the sudden urge to celebrate the era that Mantle so vividly symbolized. After all, for baseball as well the United States, the 1950s had seemed a Golden Age marked by confidence in the progress of the American way at home and abroad, soaring economic abundance, and a comfortable ideological consensus. Mantle himself was the most cherished symbol of American masculinity before the era of Vietnam and runaway celebrity; a snapshot of the time when sports dreams and pure American manhood were one, when fathers and sons played together, our relationships virtuous, the dream always accessible.[31]

Baseball's ruling class has always responded to contemporary crisis by looking into the sport's hallowed past, trading baseball's storied and carefully crafted mythology for the good will of fans and public officials. Mantle's passing afforded a rare opportunity to firmly put aside the bitterness of the strike and troubling rumors of potential performance-enhancing drug abuse in order to celebrate that past. The memories spilling out onto the sports pages after August 13, 1995, were often gilded. Mantle, one writer opined, had forged his legacy "in a time before free agency, investigative sports reporting, stratospheric salaries and the accompanying fan cynicism." He was, wrote another, baseball's flag bearer "at a time when money wasn't the issue and loyalty was." Bob Costas, eulogizing the hero of his childhood, said that Mantle "was the most compelling hero of our lifetime. And he was our symbol of baseball at a time when the game meant something to us that perhaps it no longer does."[32]

Historians, of course, have long delighted in showing how the age of Eisenhower was far more complex and nuanced than recalled through the rosy haze of nostalgia, exposing inequality, unrest, and the roots of social rebellion amidst the plenty. For those writing about baseball, the 1950s were equally complicated. This was, after all, a decade marked by precipitously declining attendance, congressional wrangling over juvenile delinquency, and antitrust exemption, as well as a number of opportunistic franchise relocations that left loyal fans in several cities feeling abandoned. On the other hand there was the rousing image of New York's Boys of Summer—Mantle, Willie Mays, and Duke Snider running down fly balls and hitting majestic home runs. The urge to quote Jacques Barzun's famous line from 1954's *God's Country and Mine* was impossible to resist: "Whoever wants to know the heart and mind of America had better learn baseball." It was gospel, especially as that golden era faded from memory, that baseball in those days really stood for something, was a vibrant allegory of the American experience—the living embodiment of the values of democracy, individualism, and fair play.[33]

No doubt the same problems that existed in cosmopolitan New York were extant in the hinterlands of the Major Leagues, but New York's teams and players were indisputably the center of the baseball world at this time. In the 1950s, Mickey Mantle's Yankees symbolized and upheld the American obsession with victory, perfection, and manly arête. They were damned, in fiction and in truth, as often as they were celebrated for their dominance. They were also more than a symbol of excellence. The Yankees were the quintessential representatives of the paternalistic attitudes and performance ethic that defined baseball drinking culture for more than half a century. In the heyday of the postwar Yankees, hard drinking still possessed a sort of high-life cachet: it was the height of manliness so long as you could perform the next day. And it was glamorous. Yankees stars of the era—DiMaggio, Mantle, Ford, Berra—were the brightest in baseball's firmament. The Yankees were high class, the purest sporting distillation of America's Cold War devotion to victory. Not just the Bronx, the Yankees were also the Stork Club, the Copacabana, and Toots Shor's.[34]

Toots Shor's eponymous place on West 51st Street in Manhattan was the epicenter of postwar New York nightlife, a remarkable feat considering that Shor was an inept businessman with a gambling problem. Most patrons even acknowledged that the food at his restaurant—stereotypically some version of steak and potatoes—wasn't very good. Nevertheless, celebrities flocked to Shor's. On any given night vice presidential candidate and future Supreme Court justice Earl Warren might be found rubbing elbows with mobster Frank Costello, while Shor himself stood drinks at the bar with Frank Sinatra, Jackie Gleason, football star Frank Gifford, Yankees DiMaggio, Mantle, Ford, and Berra, and a host of local reporters among others.[35]

So prominent was the barkeep in the world of sports celebrity that Shor's face eventually graced a 1959 *Sports Illustrated* cover. In his 1977 obituary the *New York Times* opined that Shor "was a magnet around which flowed many of the special streams of New York's greatness." *New York Post* writer Maury Allen recalled how Shor made it his mission to connect sportswriters and athletes in a way that they might come to understand one another. In an age before the sports tabloid press made every athlete's foible front-page fodder, Shor's was a haven for a "boys will be boys" club wherein the biggest stars could tie a few drinks on and never worry about the repercussions. For many of the New York Yankees it was *their* pub. And they frequented it often.[36]

A fondness for the New York nightlife, for the bottle, and for women was a distinctive hallmark of the late Golden Age Yankees. But in some ways it seemed the Yankees barely held together for all their drinking. Most of the focus was on the "Dead End Kids," Mantle, Martin, and Ford. But long nights and empty glasses was a Yankee tradition stretching back at least as far as Joe McCarthy's clubs of the early 1940s. Those Yankees, however, seemed to know how to control themselves, and like their peerless star, Joe DiMaggio, they had a knack, with considerable help from the press, for crafting an impenetrable facade of high-class professionalism. The problems for the Yankees really began in 1947 when Bucky Harris assumed the managerial position in the Bronx.[37]

Harris, onetime boy-wonder manager for Clark Griffith's Washington Senators, was a lifelong baseball man, but like so many managers of his time, he lived by the creed that so long as a baseball player did his job on the diamond, his personal behavior was not the manager's business. In particular, Harris struggled to control relief ace Joe Page. Page, a bulky fireballer affectionately dubbed "The Gay Reliever," was widely regarded as the key player in the team's 1947 pennant run. In 1948, however, Page started hitting the bottle harder than ever, and the Yankees slid in the standings. In 1947 Harris had toasted Page after every successful conclusion to a game, but he never offered the reliever a drink. In 1948, Page, it seemed, simply went out and got his own.[38]

Yankees brass, concerned that Harris was losing control of the club, disappointed by losing, and eager to remind their charges who was boss, started the practice of hiring private investigators to keep tabs on the player's nighttime activities. Harris was unmoved by the detective's reports. Alcoholism, he believed, was simply something that you put up with in baseball. In fact, for the man who once suggested beer and success went hand in hand, it was not necessarily a bad thing. "They told me a certain pitcher was drinking too much," said Harris. "He was. I didn't say anything to him. I felt like Lincoln when his cabinet fussed about Grant drinking, and Lincoln said he wished some of his other generals would try Grant's brand of whiskey."[39]

Page wasn't alone in sowing some wild oats. Other Yankees were having a fine time under Harris's watch, outfielders Johnny Lindell and pitcher Frank Shea foremost among them. When the Yankees faltered down the stretch in 1948, finishing 2.5 games out of first, the front office saw too many empty glasses as the culprit. A change had to be made.[40]

The man Weiss chose to replace Harris and reassert control over the club, and who would ultimately preside over the Yankees' emerging dynasty, was Charles Dillon "Casey" Stengel. A disciple of the legendary John McGraw, Stengel was known for his clownishness and occasionally indecipherable language ("Stengelese"), and was soon to be known for advancing the underappreciated art of the platoon (starting different players in a certain position based on their particular strengths as well as the opponents' particular weaknesses).

Expected to rein in a club given to excess, Stengel himself was a hard-drinking man. He, too, lived by the "Drink Hard, Play Hard" ethic. Like his mentor McGraw, Stengel wanted his players to embody masculine virtues: play smart, play tough, play dirty if you had to, in order to win. Despite receiving a slew of detectives' reports about his player's nighttime shenanigans, Stengel just winked, saying "those are my boys." Although he would occasionally admonish players about staying up late, drinking, and chasing women, saying, "it ain't the getting it that hurts them, it's staying up all night looking for it. They gotta learn that if you don't get it by midnight, you ain't gonna get it, and if you do, it ain't worth it," he always favored drinkers over teetotalers—men he derided as milkshake drinkers. When Bob Turley, a notoriously clean-living player, was in a prolonged slump, Casey lamented, "Look at him. He don't smoke, he don't drink, he don't chase women, and he don't win."[41]

No episode from the Stengel era, or any other, better illustrates baseball's romance with the bottle and its expectations about stepping up and delivering a macho performance than the perfect game pitched by Don Larsen (one of Stengel's "boys") against the Brooklyn Dodgers on October 8, 1956, the fifth game of the World Series. Larsen had a well-earned reputation as an incorrigible "fun lover." Headlines made much of Larsen's famous exploit, celebrating how an "imperfect man pitches the perfect game."

Larsen long argued that he had not actually been drinking the night before the perfect game, although some others insisted he had. In the end, it did not really matter whether Larsen had been out drinking all night or not. His reputation was such that the rumors seemed plausible. Besides, and more importantly, the idea that he'd been out drinking all night made his accomplishment seem all the more remarkable. It was the finest example of the "Play Hard, Drink Hard" performance ethic in action in the entire history of the game. If Larsen had been a good boy the night before, the story would have been shorn of its charm, and the macho element of the tale lost. Once again, baseball writers' penchant for mythmaking underscored and affirmed a culture that, for all of its literary allure, was profoundly destructive.

*   *   *

The New York Yankees were the model of hard-drinking excellence in baseball's Golden Age, but they were not the sport's only hard-drinking team. Almost every franchise possessed some night-crawling element in those days; it was just that some groups were more notorious than others. The Dalton Gang, described as "a group of wild-living, fun-loving, hell-raising players" and led by hard-throwing reliever Dick "Turk" Farrell, made life difficult for Philadelphia Phillies management while upholding the "tradition" of the raucous old days. What repeated fines and suspensions could not accomplish—curbing the gang's nocturnal rides—trades eventually would.

Passing through Philadelphia during the last days of the Dalton Gang was another hard-drinking reliever who had played, and had drunk, with the finest exemplars of the "Play Hard, Drink Hard" era. Ryne Duren was six feet two, a muscular and imposing presence on the mound, who stared out at the world through glasses that were cut milk-bottle thick. It was a psychological advantage for Duren that batters wondered about his eyesight. For emphasis, he often squinted at the plate as if he couldn't see it. His first pitch would purposely sail over the head of batters, rattling against the backstop. A flame-throwing right-hander with control problems was a nightmare for any batter, and Duren knew it. Of course, the wildness was not entirely an act, and Duren always struggled to harness his considerable talent. His addictive love of the bottle, however, ultimately got in the way of every effort to achieve his Major League dreams.[42]

It was perhaps ironic that Duren was one of the key players traded by the Kansas City Athletics in return for Billy Martin. In the universe of baseball's drinking lodestars, Mickey Mantle was cut in the mold of Ruth, a celebrity drunk whose heroics excused his excesses. Billy Martin was an old-school drinker, a baseball man's baseball man à la Stengel or John McGraw. Ryne Duren, on the other hand, was simply an incorrigible, sometimes mean, utterly hopeless alcoholic.[43]

Mickey Mantle recalled chumming around with Duren when the reliever came up to the Yankees. "I used to run around with Ryne a lot. But, thank God, I was lucky enough to have had a greater tolerance or stronger stomach. I don't know." Duren soon had a dim reputation as a man who could not handle his liquor, notorious for keeping roommates awake as he drunkenly berated total strangers on the telephone, or for loudly haranguing mysterious adversaries once he finally fell into bed. "Drinking got me out of the big leagues," Duren would later say. "I was an alcoholic . . . the guys (Yankees) knew I had a problem. But I really had a problem. It got bad toward the end."[44]

Duren had a number of notable alcohol-related incidents in his time with the Yankees. In fact, almost as soon as he arrived at their minor league affiliate in Denver, he was involved in a barroom brawl that earned him the nickname "The Little Copa." The most highly publicized incident during Duren's Yankee tenure occurred when he got drunk on a road trip flight, had an argument with backup catcher Ralph Houk, and shoved Houk's cigar into his face. It was one of several episodes that exposed Duren's drinking problem, but in the world of the macho performance ethic, it also saw him celebrated by writers as one of baseball's throwbacks to the "good old days."[45]

After wearing out his welcome in the Bronx, Duren would enjoy a brief renaissance pitching out of the bullpen for the surprising Los Angeles Angels, an expansion team in 1961, mounting a shocking chase for the pennant in the summer of 1962. That Angels team, including Duren, fellow reliever Art Fowler, and Pacific Coast League icon Steve Bilko, was celebrated as "perhaps the last generation of a hell-raising baseball breed that dated to a time when the salaries were low and the living high." The 1962 Angels were one of the last, pure, team embodiments of the "Drink Hard, Play Hard" era.[46]

The early 1960s, recalled author Ron Fimrite, may have also been the last days of the vintage newspaperman, soon to be displaced by the more sober and less garrulous journalists of the new era. Everyone on that Angels team played together, he noted—even off the field, including the sportswriters. "We were like a family then," said one Angels player. "The writers protected the players, and the players protected the writers."[47]

Drinking was something that baseball insiders winked at so long as you lived up to your contract on the field. Sam McDowell, another pitcher in the Duren mold, provided a succinct overview of the era's macho atmosphere. "The persons who drank the most on a team," he recalled, "were the ones held in the highest esteem. Back in the days of the "Play-hard, Drink-hard Syndrome," it showed you were someone, showed how much you could drink and still stand on your feet." Some players never achieved what they should have in the game of baseball because of the unwritten rule of the bottle. Such was the case with McDowell, and before him, the Brooklyn Dodgers' imposing right-hander, Don Newcombe.[48]

Newcombe's experience with alcohol, as was shown to be the case with many alcoholics, began when he was a kid. Both of Newcombe's parents drank. "I was raised on home-brewed beer," he recalled in a groundbreaking interview with *Ebony* magazine. "My father used to make it in the cellar when we were kids and give it to us innocently, you know."[49]

Newcombe grew quickly. At the age of fifteen he stood six feet tall and weighed close to two hundred pounds. Looking so much like an adult, he could enter a bar, sit down, and order a drink. Nobody ever asked him his age. "When Pearl Harbor got bombed," he recalled, "I was sitting in a bar in Staten Island, drinking beer. I didn't know where Pearl Harbor was, but I sure as hell was getting bombed that morning!"[50]

Newk, as he came to be called, dropped out of school his junior year and began to pitch professionally with the Newark Eagles of the Negro National League. He was the third black player signed by a Major League franchise in the wake of Jackie Robinson, also by the Dodgers. The strapping hurler soared through the minor leagues at Nashua and Montreal before landing with the big league club in Brooklyn. From 1949 to 1956 (excluding military service in 1952–53), Newk was one of baseball's best pitchers, the ace of a Brooklyn team that was always in World Series contention, earning a Cy Young Award and MVP plaudits along the way.

But Newcombe always struggled to control his drinking. He would pitch and win a night game, then, he recalled, "have six cans of beer in the clubhouse before I went into the shower. Then I'd drink another can or two after the shower. I'd get dressed, meet my father and my wife. We'd drive four blocks to a delicatessen, buy more beer and I'd drink a six-pack on the way home—40 miles into New Jersey." Newcombe blamed not only the glamorization of drinking, but also racial tension for contributing to the alcoholic culture.[51]

Pressure was enormous for the black ballplayers in that era. "We had to have a way to release those tensions," he said. "A lot of guys would go out and get drunk to relax and ease the tensions associated with the game. But we had a completely different thing altogether. We were not only baseball players, we were black baseball players on a pedestal." "I think," said Newcombe in later years, "very few people know that Jackie Robinson came very close to having a nervous breakdown because of the pressures heaped upon him in his first year in Montreal and in his early years in the Major Leagues. Jackie neither drank nor smoked in his life. He had other ways of relieving tensions." Newcombe was different. "I got involved with the drinking of beer."[52]

Drinking destroyed Newcombe's personal life. His first marriage collapsed beneath the weight of chronic loneliness—the burden of all baseball wives—and heavy drinking. Newcombe's considerable talents faded prematurely. Unable to win with the Dodgers after the team moved to Los Angeles in 1958, he struggled in Cincinnati and in Cleveland before retiring. Although he would later find a way to turn his experience into a positive for the baseball community, he always lamented that his career ended at the age of thirty-four. Newcombe insisted that if not for the carousing and drinking he could have pitched until he was thirty-nine.[53]

"Sudden" Sam McDowell, like Don Newcombe, possessed one of the best fastballs in the game. As it did for Newk, raging alcoholism also spoiled his career. A poster child for the what-might-have-been crowd, McDowell was one of just a handful of pitchers to twice fan over three hundred men in a season. He averaged almost a strikeout an inning, quite an accomplishment for a man about whom teammate Dick Radatz once said: "We thought he was stupid. Turned out he was never sober."[54]

Throughout his early career McDowell exhibited scintillating promise and head-scratching inconsistency (the hard-throwing McDowell always seemed to get torched by baseball's lightest hitting players). The man routinely hailed by writers as "the next Koufax" finally broke through and won twenty games in 1970 with the Cleveland Indians. That year he struck out 304 hitters. Few pitchers in baseball history had ever been as feared. But drinking and success went hand in hand, and McDowell, who would later admit that he was "the biggest, most hopeless, most violent drunk in baseball," never could maintain that level of excellence. He eventually wore out his welcome in Cleveland, bounced around to the Giants, to the Yankees, and then to the Pirates, where he ended his career in 1975, washed out at only thirty-two years of age.[55]

The Yankees, knowing about McDowell's drinking habits, assigned a full-time guardian to keep him out of bars. "I used to get HIM drunk," says McDowell. "Back when I played, you weren't respected if you didn't drink the night before, then go out and have a good game the next day." Like so many others before him, Sam McDowell was badly served by a baseball culture that prized a macho performance ethic, winked at excessive alcohol abuse, and had no institutional answer for players whose careers, and lives, were endangered by that culture.[56]

* * *

Baseball's last Golden Age passed long before Ryne Duren and Sam McDowell were washed out of the game, but the "Drink Hard, Play Hard" ethic did not necessarily pass with it. It was just not celebrated anymore, or it was celebrated differently. The Yankees of the Mantle era imploded after 1964. The Columbia Broadcasting System inherited an aging team rife with internal tensions; the old cadre of drinking men set against a young gang of clean-living teetotalers exemplified by the devoutly religious Bobby Richardson, who with young shortstop Tony Kubek formed one-half of the so-called Milkshake Twins. As the Shor's crowd left, or retired, the Yankees became less interesting and eventually less successful.

With the drinking man's model franchise on the skids, hard drinking lost much of its glitter. Frustrated managers tried desperately to curb the after-hours activities of the Dalton Gangs of the baseball world, but for every Turk Farrell who was rehabilitated by paternalistic sanctions, there was a Ryne Duren who was unperturbed. As the league moved into the expansion era there remained no organized internal outreach program for dealing with baseball's problem drinkers. Besides, old mystique faded reluctantly. Decades later, as baseball struggles for attention in the age of hype and media saturation, there is still the occasional article expressing longing for the colorful old players of a bygone era. Forgetting, if one ever truly knew, the high cost of that wet age, a sad lament is heard echoing through the baseball world. In this age of increasing homogenization and corporatization one could only wonder "where are the drunks of yesteryear?"[57]

2

Tobacco Road

This is old stuff . . . We've got alcohol that's the No. 1 killer in America and we legalize that to buy in the store. You've got tobacco number two or three killer in America; we legalize that. There are other issues.

—Barry Bonds

In my day, and I'm talking about 1952 to 1960, to be a big-leaguer you had to chew.

—Joe Nuxhall

Bill Tuttle did not always look like a monster. Pick up any Bill Tuttle baseball card from the 1950s or 1960s, and you will find him, whether in the uniform of the Detroit Tigers, Kansas City Athletics, or Minnesota Twins, faithfully depicted with a wad of tobacco stuffed into his left cheek. Introduced to the practice of chewing by teammate Harvey Kuenn, Tuttle chewed tobacco anywhere from ten to twelve hours a day for more than forty years. In 1993 he was diagnosed with oral cancer, cancer he logically saw as stemming from all those years of chewing. A seemingly endless series of operations cost him a large section of his jawbone, parts of his cheeks, his taste buds, and numerous teeth. The operations left Tuttle so badly disfigured that several of his grandchildren refused to visit his hospital room, all of them too afraid to look at him.[1]

In the spring of 1996, joined by his wife Gloria and Joe Garagiola, the former player, broadcaster, and now head of the National Spit Tobacco Education Program (NSTEP), Tuttle was on a mission to warn Major Leaguers about the dangers of smokeless tobacco. Driven by his passion to educate others on the topic, and with his horribly disfigured face as a harsh object lesson, Tuttle was the most effective speaker in a program that included retired superstars Hank Aaron, Tom Seaver, and Rod Carew. Tuttle's crusade attracted attention. A year earlier he received the U.S. Surgeon General's highest award, the Exemplary Service Medallion, for his tireless campaigning. When Tuttle spoke in baseball clubhouses across the country, players sat silently and listened, as eager schoolchildren gathered on the floor around a beloved teacher. Canisters of snuff were quietly stuffed into lockers. Later, when Tuttle was finished speaking, those same canisters would be dumped into in a nearby trashcan.[2]

When Tuttle visited Toronto one afternoon, his speech had a dramatic effect on pitcher Bill Risley. Risley was one of the heaviest users of smokeless tobacco on the Blue Jays. He had a dip of Copenhagen in his mouth when Tuttle began to speak. "I took it out about halfway through," the pitcher recalled. "Luckily, I was in the back of the room. I didn't want anybody to see me." Risley, convinced by Tuttle to get help with his nicotine addiction, said he typically went through a can and a half of Copenhagen each day. "I'm up at 7:15 in the morning, take a shower, then put some dip in," he admitted. "I don't even eat breakfast. That is my breakfast. I quit drinking six years ago. This stuff is much tougher (to quit) than alcohol. I get very cranky if I go two hours without it. I've tried to stop. The longest I've gone is a week." Bill Tuttle understood. "It's a powerful addiction. I miss it right now. If they assured me I had a 100% chance of not getting cancer again, I'd have some chew in my mouth tomorrow."[3]

Not every Tuttle presentation led to immediate conversions like Bill Risley's, but Tuttle was persistent. This crusade was not just about the health of Major Leaguers; this was about the health of kids all across America. At every stop he explained to players that he wanted them to consider the example they were setting for youngsters. Don't chew, he told players, while they could be caught by television cameras. Garagiola, the former Game of the Week broadcaster and *Today* host who was spending his retirement lending his time and his celebrity to numerous causes, was as adamant as Tuttle about eliminating tobacco use from baseball. At the same time, Garagiola was realistic about the prospects for the crusade. Tobacco use could not be legislated or unilaterally ordered out of the game. It must be each player's personal choice to eliminate tobacco. This was the pragmatic position that Tuttle adopted with his audiences when he asked them to avoid chewing on camera. "It's going to be pretty hard to tell someone making $4 million a year not to chew," he said. "So what we're trying to do is get it off TV."[4]

Bill Tuttle's story should sound familiar. Much like his peer Mickey Mantle, Tuttle became a living lesson on the high price of ignorance, negligence, and economic hypocrisy in American sport and American society more generally. Mickey Mantle's ravaged body reflected the human cost of a culture that celebrated alcohol while simultaneously (sometimes willfully) remaining ignorant of alcohol's dangers. Bill Tuttle's deformed face told the story of a similarly deadly and double-edged relationship between baseball, Americans, and tobacco. Unable to speak in his last days, Tuttle left a written note for his family and peers expressing remorse for the choices he had made in life. His last lament echoed Mantle's: "I know what I did to myself was wrong and I'm so sorry I hurt everybody. But maybe I can show them how sorry I am by teaching other people."[5]

*   *   *

Even if he sincerely believed that players must make the choice to eliminate tobacco on their own, Joe Garagiola was confident that they would come around to NSTEP's way of seeing things. "I've yet to have a player give me a good reason why he chews or dips," said Garagiola, who chewed leaf tobacco when he caught for the Cardinals and Pirates in the 1950s. "It's either a macho thing or peer pressure. People have made tobacco a part of baseball, but tobacco isn't a baseball tradition. Cancer isn't a baseball tradition."[6]

Like so many other crusaders, Garagiola summoned the ideal of baseball purity as proof against baseball's vice-ridden tradition. In Garagiola's proffered vision, real, honest-to-goodness baseball was not about chewing, or spitting, or smoking. There was, insisted Garagiola, no real tradition of tobacco use in baseball. Joe Garagiola was wrong. If the Spirit of Baseball Past (which surely must look like Babe Ruth) could become manifest, it would undoubtedly have a big wad of tobacco stuffed into its cheek and a hip flask tucked in its back pocket. As with alcohol, and though it might seem trite to say so, baseball and tobacco just seemed to fit together. For more than a century, the tobacco companies used baseball to help market their products. In that same time baseball players earned much-needed income by lending their image to tobacco ad campaigns, and for decades, on a day-to-day basis, tobacco, like alcohol, served a wide range of more utilitarian purposes both on and off the diamond.

It is perhaps easiest to make sense of the relationship between the sport, its players, and tobacco if we first consider the similarities between tobacco and alcohol. Tobacco, alcohol, and baseball were together from the beginning. So, too, were the hard questions about their compatibility. NSTEP was hardly the first group to express concern over professional baseball's tight relationship with vice interests. In fact, as far back as the game's nineteenth-century adolescence, temperance organizations, socially conscious newspaper editorialists, and youth advocates had targeted baseball's growing economic ties with the tobacco and alcoholic beverage industries. They exposed and criticized, usually with limited effectiveness, the grim reality that the National Pastime, a game that the staunchest defenders of exceptionalism believed inculcated the values of teamwork, integrity, and physical vigor in American youth, was simultaneously being used as a vehicle for inspiring addiction and misbehavior in the American population. Those early critics pointed out the hypocrisy in tying the supposedly pure national sport to vices like smoking and drinking. Much like the majority of the populace, the lords of baseball, then as later, were hardly ever swayed by such criticisms. The heady mixture of ballplayers, beer, and tobacco was not, to their mind, evidence of any hypocrisy. It was the basic nature of professional baseball. It was the simplest social equation: Drinkers and smokers played the game. Drinkers and smokers consumed the game. It was never really about the breweries or the tobacco companies. It was never about vice or the health of the players. It was always about money. The relationship, such as it was, was all down to plain, sensible economics.

From the start and throughout the twentieth century there was a symbiotic relationship between the brewing and tobacco industries and the sports world, especially professional baseball. That relationship took on various forms through the years. Sometimes the tie-up, especially when it came to alcohol, occurred naturally via the team's ownership. Beer baron owners were not uncommon in the world of professional baseball. Look into the past, and there you will find men like Chris von der Ahe, who turned his St. Louis Browns ball club of the late nineteenth century into one giant sudsy circus. Jacob Ruppert, the Colonel, the man behind Knickerbocker beer, signed the paychecks of Babe Ruth and other members of New York's legendary Murderer's Row in the golden glow of the Jazz Age. By midcentury there was the irascible Gussie Busch, patriarch of the Anheuser-Busch juggernaut, then owner of the St. Louis Cardinals, spreading the gospel of Budweiser over radio with the help of fifty-thousand-watt KMOX. By that point, thanks in large part to the influence of radio, you did not need a brewer in the owner's box to associate a given team with specific brands of beer and cigarettes. It was easy for a baseball fan in those days to bastardize Savarin's famous dictum: show me what you drink and what you smoke, and I will tell you what team you root for. The celebrated tradition of purity aside, for more than a century it was the most natural thing in the world to connect beer, tobacco, and baseball.

In fact, the values that were celebrated in the game of baseball were the same virtues that sponsors wanted to co-opt for *their* products. For the whiz kids on Madison Avenue dreaming up ways to tie cigarettes and beer to the

National Pastime, it was a simple case of acquiring virtue by proxy. To garner just a bit of baseball's vim, vigor, and vitality would make their product that much more marketable and would appeal to the consumers that marketers most wanted to reach—young men between the ages of eighteen and thirty-five. In order to adopt baseball's virtues, the tobacco and brewing industries soaked the game in money. With ballpark attendance waning in the 1950s, the accounting offices around the Major League circuit were significantly buoyed by the influx of money from the beer and tobacco companies. If we return to New York City in the age of Mantle, still the center of the baseball universe, a portrait of a baseball world inextricably linked to the vice industries becomes crystal clear.[7]

In the summer of 1957, as Bill Tuttle, chew firmly in cheek, was playing for Detroit, and as the Yankees, who very much wanted to acquire the Tigers outfielder, were raising hell in New York City nightclubs, the average fan of the New York Giants, tuning into the team's radio broadcast on WMCA 550, would be greeted with a heady mixture of baseball, beer advertisements, and cigarette spots. Announcers Russ Hodges, Jim Woods, and Bob Delaney, although nominally in the employ of the baseball team, were also under contract to sell products for the American Tobacco Company and the Jacob Ruppert Brewery, makers of Knickerbocker Beer. Provided with records of musical scores, prerecorded ads, and scripted commercials, the three Giants radio men would turn the baseball game into a lucrative platform for telling as many people as possible about their sponsor's products.[8]

A game usually began with the playing of the "Knickerbocker March"—supplied on record by the sponsor's advertising agency. Listeners were informed that Knickerbocker, the beer that would best satisfy their thirst, and Pall Mall Famous Cigarettes were to be thanked for bringing them today's game. One of the team's announcers—Russ Hodges, for example—was then expected to introduce himself, provide some kind of ad-lib color commentary to "build the game excitement," and then segue to *more* advertising. Before lineups could be announced, Hodges exhorted listeners to visit the fridge: "why not treat yourself to a tall glass of the beer that's bringing you the ballgames. KNICKERBOCKER, the beer that's brewed to satisfy your beer thirst better! Try it." Then it was on to another Pall Mall plug: "Pall Mall is the cigarette for you!" Finally, mercifully, the broadcaster provided the day's lineups.[9]

Well before the actual baseball *game* started, the listener had already been encouraged—several times—to grab a beer (Have a Knick!) and enjoy a smoke (smoking Pall Mall is *fun*). In between innings of that day's game the

Knickerbocker jingle (Have a Knick / You feel refreshed / Have a Knicker-bocker Beer) could be heard up and down the Atlantic seaboard courtesy of the New York Giants baseball broadcast.[10]

Some in the media were taking notice. In 1954, *Time* ran an article for opening day pointing out that fans by the millions were gathering around their television sets for the opening slate of games. Before the games, however, viewers had to listen to "hard plugs for Chesterfields and National Bohemian, Valley Forge and Hamm's beer. Beer and cigarettes are today as much a part of the league and the national game as bat and ball." With radio and television broadcasts saturated with advertisements, with the game's broadcasters known as much for the products they sold as for the action they described, it was becoming difficult to imagine a time when the game had not been closely associated with the beer and tobacco business.[11]

This is hardly different from baseball today, minus the tobacco ads, of course. Then, as now, we have solitary half-innings of baseball action struck between alternating plugs for this product or that service. What loyal Vin Scully listener is not familiar with Farmer John sausages (or with the infamous parody of Scully's product pitch on TV's *The Simpsons*)? It was not, and is not, enough to just listen to America's game—for the love of freedom and baseball, *go buy something*! Then as now it was not just routine between-innings advertisements, either. If something extraordinary happened during the game, the announcer had a mandate from his sponsors that granted him the right to award the sponsor's product to the public. For example, if a Giants player were to hit a home run at a key juncture of the game, or if a double play was turned in a critical inning, a thousand Pall Malls might be sent to the patients of a local hospital "with the compliments of the makers of Pall Mall Famous Cigarettes and Knickerbocker Beer." Each special event was worth a certain amount of free smokes. Shutouts and grand slams were worth ten thousand cigarettes, no-hitters and triple plays twenty thousand. Other special or extraordinary plays were left to the announcer's discretion. If a certain play merited it, up to five thousand cigarettes could be given away at any time.[12]

Giants' broadcasts were typical of broadcasts from around the Major Leagues. Any listener tuning into any game in any Major League city in the summer of 1957 would be subjected to a similar mixture of baseball and advertising, of plugs for regional breweries and one of two or three major brands of cigarettes. Some listeners might have even wondered what had happened to the baseball game. Was it drowning in a deluge of glib ad-speak? The question became even more relevant as the game moved into the 1960s and baseball's relationship with sponsors, and with the radio and television networks that tied the sport to its commercial financiers, began to draw more serious criticism. Major League Baseball had seemingly become the big sale, surpassed in the hearts of many fans by the more lively game of professional football. Baseball players not only played a square sport in a hip era, but they were overly conscious of their image—an image all too often buffered by advertising gurus to sell some product. The diamond's beloved "drunks of yesteryear" had been replaced by a bland band of aspiring businessmen in flannel suits. It was not always thus.[13]

*　*　*

One need not go all the way back in their history primers to John Rolfe and Pocahontas to recognize the prominent place of tobacco in the American story. Americans chewed and spit their way through the rough-and-tumble nineteenth century. By 1890, as the sport of baseball solidified its place as America's National Pastime, the average American gnawed through more than three pounds of cut tobacco per year. Cigarettes were less ubiquitous. There was a fairly commonly held notion at the time that while chewing tobacco was perfectly safe, cigarettes were actually rather dangerous—dangerous to your health and dangerous, if you played baseball, to your stat line. In the same era that saw Mickey Welch compose his ditty in praise of alcohol's performance-enhancing powers, some of his peers condemned cigarettes for their negative impact on performance. Cigarettes caused slumps. In 1892 Michael "King" Kelly, a career .308 hitter, saw his average dip catastrophically to .189. Kelly blamed the precipitous decline on a lifetime of smoking. It should be noted, however, that the infamous Kelly was also among the more notorious drunks of his era. However you look at it, the combination of hard living, booze, and smoking clearly had a deleterious effect on his play.[14]

As with other controversial vices of the time—drinking alcohol, for example—progressive temperance and prohibition forces also targeted the tobacco industry in the years around the turn of the century. Health was a major concern for the reformers, but they were also influenced by the growing national fear of immigrants. Just as with the crusade against alcohol there was a robust nativist component to the antitobacco movement. Like other lower-class groups, immigrants were more apt to take up smoking. That most baseball players, not to mention many fans of the game, themselves came from this sector of society further cemented the cozy relationship between the game of baseball and the tobacco industry, creating an island of stability amid the whirlwind of social reform. It was difficult for social reformers, in their assimilationist zeal, to criticize the national game when the game itself was seen as one of the finest tools for assimilation in the American cultural arsenal. In no small sense, due to both the demographic makeup of the players and fans, as well as baseball's reputation for exceptional Americanism, it became an ideal shelter for the vice industries.

That does not mean there were not robust efforts to root vice out of the game. Some reformers, troubled by an emerging fad in the early years of the twentieth century, sought especially to eradicate the nascent cigarette industry. Industrialist Henry Ford enlisted a host of well-known Americans, including baseball star Ty Cobb, to add weight to Ford's 1914 antitobacco tract, *The Case against the Little White Slaver*. Far and away the most strident antivice spokesperson was former diamond star Billy Sunday, who played for the Chicago White Stockings before jumping to the pulpit in 1890. From his perch, Sunday routinely railed against the evils of the world, especially saloons and smoking. In one sermon Sunday pointed out that "whiskey and beer are all right in their place, but their place is in Hell." Sunday's views were potent, especially where baseball was concerned, because he was a man with intimate knowledge of the game. His own sporting past surely informed his constant exhortations toward a more virtuous manhood, a manhood that hardly seemed to be shared by his former peers on the diamond. Sunday often used stories of baseball players to drive his point home. He spoke of onetime teammate John Clarkson, whose chain smoking (eight to ten packs of cigarettes a day) led to Clarkson's eventual death in a Massachusetts asylum. Clarkson's bath water, explained Sunday as he painted an evocative and horrifying portrait, was stained with nicotine whenever the player bathed. From his pulpit Sunday hardly portrayed professional baseball as Eden; rather, he painted baseball as a den of vice, a far cry from the purest of places. Baseball players, like the rest of American society, were a wandering flock. The lesson was clear: devote less money to booze and tobacco, said Sunday, and more money to God.[15]

World War I sounded the death knell for the sometimes quixotic crusade of the cigarette prohibition forces. The combination of new rolling machinery, widespread fear of tuberculosis (potentially spread by spitting tobacco), and the ubiquity of cigarettes in the trenches of the Western Front led millions of Americans to adopt cigarette smoking. The Red Cross and YMCA, once stridently opposed to cigarettes, now joined other patriots in providing box loads of cigarettes to the troops in Europe. As cigarettes boomed in popularity, there was still one place, the baseball diamond, where chewing and spitting remained just as vital as in the prewar past. As it turned out, in baseball the use of tobacco was always about more than just getting a nicotine buzz.

Just as we have seen with alcohol, and despite the extant story of King Kel-ley, tobacco was often suggested to have mild performance-enhancing effects. Oddly, this notion survived all the way to the end of the twentieth century. In "Chaws," a tongue-in-cheek exposé of the Major League tobacco-chewing tradition published in 1977 by *Sports Illustrated*, pitcher Gary Nolan concurred with the notion that it provided enhancement. "There's a little something in it. There's a little kick in there." Chicago Cubs pitcher Rick Reuschel added that "when the day is going bad, I'll stick a chaw in my mouth and everything seems to get a little brighter." Randy Jones began chewing in 1975 and won twenty games for the San Diego Padres. He thought the tobacco was part of his suc-cess: "I don't know why," he said, "but it seemed to help." Ignoring growing reams of scientific evidence, generations of players, from the late nineteenth century to the dawn of the twenty-first, passed along plugs of tobacco, swear-ing on the relaxation, relief, and concentration aid it afforded. This tradition thwarted reformers for a century. This was All-American, legal enhancement by way of Tobacco Road.[16]

As with alcohol, tobacco use was spurred in part because of the notion that it improved performance, largely because it served a fundamental utilitarian purpose and in the end became a celebrated part of the game's superstition and ritual. Aside from the rather silly belief in performance enhancement, in the baseball world chewing tobacco was also valued for its mainstream utility. Chewing produced saliva used to soften leather. Before the league banned the pitch in 1920, it was integral for the creation of spitballs. Leaf tobacco was valued because it could be inserted into the ragged holes that sometimes developed in baseball gloves, easing the sting from catching a hard throw. Inventing a unique hobby to pass the time, aspiring spit artists tried to paint their colleague's shoes with tobacco stains. In the 1970s, when chewing was revived as a Major League tradition, pitcher Steve Renko noted that "it's an unwritten law that you are permitted to spit on the shoes but not on the uniform." It was the law of baseball written as the law of the wild: burly pitchers, their jaws stuffed with tobacco, circled the mound like menacing animals, marking their territory with brown juice.[17]

Eventually even the much-maligned cigarette became an accepted part of the baseball universe. It did not matter whether tobacco was chewed or smoked, it was as fundamentally a baseball activity as drinking or batting or (if you were Rube Waddell) chasing fire trucks. As in the wider American society, there was a fundamental belief in the baseball world that tobacco and alcohol use was a gateway to manhood and a signifier of macho verve. College-educated baseball players who did not drink or smoke (the maligned "milkshake drinkers") were, unless they happened to be Christy Mathewson, not ideal types to emulate. Advertising played up the connection between baseball, tobacco, and virile manliness. Starting in the late nineteenth century, ad men routinely used baseball motifs to suggest that cigarettes, chew, and dip could help users attain some measure of their favorite hero's athletic prowess. This was not quite "performance enhancement" in the conventional sense, but it was definitely something like promising improved daily performance-by-proxy. Smoke this, chew that, the ads suggested, and find out what really separates the men from the boys.[18]

* * *

Marketing tobacco through baseball began in the nineteenth century with the use of color coupons and tobacco cards. The names of various brands of tobacco were sometimes inspired by sports themes. Early tobacco cards, designed to inspire brand loyalty, celebrated the Olympics, cycling, and auto racing. One of the most frequently invoked legends involving advertising tobacco and baseball involves Bull Durham, a brand of plug tobacco, so commonly advertised on the fences of southern baseball fields that it supposedly lent its name to the area where pitchers warmed up: the *bullpen*. For tobacco dealers, baseball provided a valuable image—it was a universally recognized symbol of American vigor and masculinity. Using baseball imagery, even in unconventional ways, helped to improve product sales. An Atlanta department store, Kimball House, displayed pictures of attractive women in baseball garb in their front window. So beautiful were the women in the pictures, they reportedly inspired suicidal heartbreak in the King of Bavaria. Crowds gathered daily to look at the stunning pictures, and though some citizens argued that the photos were indecent, they ultimately proved an excellent selling tool when local tobacco dealers began to use them.[19]

Although tobacco and baseball were certainly profitable partners, even in the earliest years of the relationship there was tension. Not everyone thought it was appropriate for baseball to prostitute its virtues in order to sell tobacco. From time to time the occasional sportswriter, haunted by a progressive social conscience, might launch a solitary assault on the evils of tobacco. Attacks from the inside carried even more weight. In 1870 Harry Wright, the famed Cincinnati manager, told a young player that he must abstain from both intoxicating drinks and tobacco. Those were the path to a ruined career. The detested cigarette was the subject of even more hyperbolic disdain. Player-manager Cap Anson remarked in the 1890s that "tobacco killed one of my players . . . two members of the team are slaves to cigarettes . . . you may as well cure a confirmed opium eater as wean them from cigarettes."[20]

The most famous clash between baseball and tobacco interests occurred early in the twentieth century when Pittsburgh Pirates star Honus Wagner demanded tobacco cards featuring his image be withdrawn from the market. To be fair, Wagner enjoyed chewing tobacco, and he did smoke cigars, but he did not want children to do the same. When the American Tobacco Company issued what collectors call the T-206 set in 1909 they were hoping the new cards would contribute to a spike in sales. Knowing that one of baseball's most important audiences happened to be American youngsters, Wagner demanded that cards bearing his image be pulled from the market. It was long thought that all but four of the cards were destroyed. Those that remain are today regarded as the most sought after and valuable baseball cards in existence.[21]

Wagner's stand was a rare exception to the usual rule. Ty Cobb had been one of the most recognizable celebrity spokesmen for automaker Henry Ford's ill-fated anticigarette campaign, asserting that "too much cannot be said against the evils of cigarette smoking . . . it lessens the moral fiber of a man." But Ty Cobb's image had earlier been used to endorse a loose cigarette tobacco bearing his name, and one of Cobb's peers suggested that Cobb "smokes more different kinds of tobacco than most men have ever heard of." Cobb, who also shunned sweet milk and chewing gum, ultimately explained that a cigar was all right after a meal, but cigarettes were to be avoided. Nevertheless, as a staunch symbol of the antitobacco movement, Cobb was a rather lackluster icon. In truth, as with so many of his fellow players, Cobb was simply padding his income by adopting whatever stance promised a paycheck. The genuine loyalty of the celebrity spokesperson is hardly ever to be relied upon.[22]

Although early superstars like Cobb and Christy Mathewson lent their names to product promotion, baseball's first truly towering celebrity endorser was Babe Ruth. The Bambino seemed to be everywhere, hawking everything. He even used a lot of the products to which his name was attached. Tobacco was a big part of the story. Babe's lifestyle included snuff, chewing tobacco, and many, many, cigars. The Bambino made his movie debut in a 1927 film entitled *Babe Comes Home*. That film is a first-rate illustration of the persistent notion that tobacco was a crucial performance aid in the world of baseball. The plot has Ruth giving up chewing tobacco at the request of a lady friend, only to fall into a terrible batting slump. Finally, when he comes to bat in the ninth inning of a big game, she relents and gives him a big plug of tobacco. Naturally, he hits a game-winning home run, and they live happily ever after. Given the numerous ads he lent his image to, and especially recalling the film, there is no small irony in Ruth's untimely death, from throat cancer, in 1948.[23]

As time passed, other players rarely turned down the opportunities to make endorsement money outside of the game. Endorsements provided a lucrative second source of income since the reserve clause served to keep player wages in check. Players appeared in various tobacco ads throughout the early decades of the century, but as advertising's methods matured in the 1920s, endorsements became an ever more profitable fact of life in the baseball universe. If a player was skilled enough on the field, if he looked the part—clean-cut, rugged, All-American—if he possessed the necessary charisma, the "color," he was a potential asset to marketers. The cigarette ads that were produced were colorful and usually intimated that one could achieve big league success by smoking a big league cigarette. An ad man for Viceroy once explained to journalist Robert Lipsyte: "We want to have our product associated with symbols of acceptance. Quality men use quality products. If [Gil] Hodges smokes Viceroys, it might do something for you, too." Cigarettes, the ads routinely implied, separated the men from the boys. "If you will smoke," they promised, "you will acquire the virtues and manners of manhood." The iconic image of the chewing baseball player, immortalized on baseball cards for a generation of midcentury card collectors, convinced historian Charles Alexander, then just a child, that serious baseball playing and tobacco chewing just naturally fit together.[24]

Ad men may have exploited the image, but it was also true that most baseball insiders revered the rugged ideal of the hard-drinking, ultra-masculine player. Many of baseball's most prominent tobacco chewers, especially in the 1920s and 1930s, hailed from America's agricultural heartland. There was something appealing about these homespun heroes, reminders of America's agrarian roots. Those selling the game played up these huckleberry heroes but more typically celebrated a very different, though no less macho, example of baseball excellence. Like the game he played, the ideal baseball player was "temperate, clean-cut, and religious." He was a visible extension of his game's highest virtues: a healthy, honest, plain-spoken individual who played the game correctly. And if you could paste a picture of him on a tobacco can or cigarette ad—which then imparted those virtues to the product—well, so much the better.

Using a baseball player's image in an advertisement was just one way of playing to a consumer's fantasies. Using a certain product might lend some of the player's skills to the consumer, smoking a certain brand of cigarette might make the smoker hit like Lou Gehrig or pitch like Walter Johnson.

And it was all—so the ads endlessly repeated—clean and healthy and manly. In an era during which the most popular celebrities smoked like chimneys, when sophistication could practically be purchased for a nickel at the five-and-dime, maybe one could, in fact, buy a slice of honest American vigor and swagger by smoking the same brand as their baseball heroes. It was taken for granted that players actually used the products that they endorsed.[25]

Despite a few pioneering scientific studies, and the colloquial usage of a popular nickname, "coffin nails," for cigarettes, it took a long time for health concerns concerning tobacco to really capture the attention of the wider populace. Although ads from this era highlighted the benefits (or at least, lack of ill effects) from smoking, there was already a growing body of research that indicated smoking was unhealthy. Dr. Raymond Pearl of Johns Hopkins University, for example, released a study in 1938 that summed it all up rather neatly: "smoking is associated with a definite impairment of longevity." It was also very much associated with Major League Baseball.[26]

The dearth of studies aside, there are obvious questions stemming from the relationship between tobacco and player performance. One particularly popular advertising motif in the late 1920s and 1930s was the assertion that smoking did not adversely affect an athlete's cardiovascular performance. A Lucky Strike ad featuring Pittsburgh Pirates star Lloyd Waner included the player's endorsement: "they never get my wind and my throat is always in perfect condition." The ad is underlined with the promise that Luckies are toasted—"no throat irritation, no cough." Could a product be any safer? Although the very idea that a good cigarette did not cause throat irritation suggested the lingering fear that some cigarettes did, in fact, do just that, the purported "health benefits" of cigarettes were regularly featured in advertisements at least into the early 1950s.[27]

Camel quickly jumped on the "they don't get my wind" bandwagon and routinely proclaimed that their product used "costlier tobacco," playing to audience notions of class and sophistication. Lou Gehrig and DiMaggio were both featured in Camel ads, usually in very colorful depictions of the athletes in action. In one famous example a Camel ad provided the first frame-by-frame photograph of Joe DiMaggio's legendary swing. Joltin' Joe would proclaim in another ad that he had smoked Camels for eight years and enjoyed their mildness. But, recalling the unreliability of the celebrity spokesperson, DiMaggio's image was also prominent in Chesterfield ads that proclaimed the cigarette "the choice of all baseball men." From ad to ad, the athletes were depicted either in action or posed with cigarettes in mouth or hand. Cigarettes made from costlier tobacco, cigarettes that were the choice of the best athletes, or smokes that did not cause throat irritation were re-peated refrains. Sometimes a fan could even discover the real worth of a team by knowing what kind of cigarettes its players smoked. An ad/article written by manager Frankie Frisch contended that twenty-one of twenty-three members of the 1934 World Champion Cardinals smoked Camels. The same had been true of twenty-one of twenty-three World Champion Giants in 1933. A certain brand of cigarettes, at least according to the glossy world of advertising, was a crucial part of on-field baseball success.[28]

Throughout the Golden Age of Major League Baseball it seemed that wher-ever there was baseball, there was tobacco. And more specifically, and most especially, now there were cigarettes. The game's greatest players all smoked (or, less frequently, chewed or dipped). Where market segmentation was practiced, tobacco advertisers happily employed aspiring black athletes who could most effectively reach the growing black consumer market. To that end, Giant stars Willie Mays and Monte Irvin endorsed Chesterfield cigarettes in issues of *Tan* while Dodgers stars Don Newcombe, Roy Campanella, and Joe Black endorsed Luckies in copies of *Ebony*.[29]

By no means was it all down to mere advertising shtick. Joe DiMaggio not only endorsed every cigarette brand under the sun, but he was indeed a chronic smoker. Biographer Richard Ben Cramer described reserve outfielder Hank Workman's game-time chore: "as each inning ended, he had to light a Chesterfield, take one puff and have it burning for the Dago [DiMaggio] when he came in from centerfield." DiMaggio would then duck into the runway behind the dugout to enjoy his cigarette and have a sip of coffee. The Yankee Clipper was hardly alone. An oft-told anecdote from former Brooklyn Dodgers pitcher Rex Barney illustrates the ubiquity of tobacco in baseball culture. As Barney remembered:

> When I First broke into the Dodgers' system, I was just a kid, 18 years old. And we had a coach, an old guy named Barney De Forge, or something like that. . . . I was sitting in the bullpen one night, and DeForge said to me: 'Kid, you want to get into the Major Leagues?' "I said, 'Sure, that's what it's all about.' He says, You don't chew tobacco, do you?' I said, 'No.' He said, 'Well, you'll never get there unless you chew tobacco.'

Barney also recalled that in those days "if you had 25 players, 24 chewed tobacco." Being young and easily influenced, Barney tried to chew. It made him sick. A terrifying thought crossed his mind—maybe he was not a Major Leaguer.[30]

Tobacco became part of the style and image of the game. Baseball was a regular subject of film in those years, both live action and animated. In 1946 a Warner Brothers cartoon featuring Bugs Bunny lampooned baseball's peculiar tobacco-oriented fixations. In "Baseball Bugs" the rabbit hero takes his act into a baseball game. On one side are the Gashouse Gorillas, a gang of hulking, muscle-bound brutes. On the other side is Bugs's team. They are a weak, effeminate band of no-talents known, not surprisingly, as the Tea Totallers. This inept team ultimately relies on Bugs and his bag of tricks to pull off a miraculous comeback. Throughout the cartoon, the game's relationship with tobacco is prominently set up. In one instance, Bugs drives a ball deep into the outfield where a Gorilla outfielder is lazily smoking a cigar. The ball smashes the cigar and drives the outfielder into the fence, where a sign above his head reads: "Does your tobacco taste differently lately?" (a takeoff on the Raleigh Cigarette wartime ad campaign—"Does your Cigarette taste differently lately?" "No! I smoke Raleighs!"). Elsewhere, an ad for Camuels (a thinly disguised spin on Camels) is displayed in the background. The mockery of the ads is in the best vein of Warner Brothers' social send-ups, but more telling still is the clear implication that vice was a crucial element in baseball success. Without Bugs and his unusual methods, the Tea Totallers were clearly sad-sack losers.[31]

From the animated satire of Termite Terrace to the flesh-and-blood of the ballpark, advertising was everywhere. The tobacco companies would do almost anything to generate good will, and baseball was a crucial element in reaching their desired targets. Chesterfield owed most of its considerable mid-century sales to the game. It was the self-styled "baseball man's cigarette" and the sponsor not only of the Giants but also the Chicago Cubs. Members of Chesterfield's "3-to-1 Club" would routinely visit the Polo Grounds to watch the Giants play. Chesterfield provided funds for building large scoreboards at the Polo Grounds, Wrigley Field, Braves Field, and Comiskey Park. As if this was not enough, Chesterfield, plucking the patriotic heartstrings of consumers, also provided copies of the *Sporting News* to men in the service or in Veteran's Administration hospitals, while simultaneously making sure the press knew, and wrote, all about it.[32]

Chesterfield even named its own annual all-star team composed of the players who had named Chesterfield their favorite cigarette. In 1950 that team included Eddie Stanky, George Kell, Ted Williams, Joe DiMaggio, Stan Musial, Yogi Berra, Phil Rizutto, and Robin Roberts. There were even enough Chesterfield "fans" in the league to provide a potent bench for the team, including Enos Slaughter, Andy Pafko, Roy Campanella, Don Newcombe, Ralph Kiner, and Larry Doby. Chesterfield, a tobacco company, crafted a "Dream Team" decades before the basketball Olympians became synonymous with the phrase.[33]

In the advertising world, rules were regularly broken or, at the very least, bent just a little. It had been an FDA policy since the 1930s that players had to use any product that they endorsed. This rule was not always obeyed. When George Kell was approached by Chesterfield, he told them he did not smoke. "We want to pay you anyway," they explained. They would use Kell's image and would state that Chesterfields were his favorite cigarette, nothing more. The endorsement—and Kell's time on the All-Chesterfield team—was short lived. Kell's father strongly disapproved of what he saw as an advertisement in awful taste. Kell refused to do any more tobacco endorsements. After becoming a Tigers broadcaster, he'd famously maintain his ethical stance when it came time to pitch the commercial segments.[34]

The companies could afford to lose the occasional George Kell. Cigarette endorsements were so pervasive at midcentury that it was almost second nature to associate a player's name with the brand of cigarette he smoked. In some circles, where people were only part-time baseball watchers, or ignored the game entirely, the player was actually better known for his choice of cigarette than for his prowess on the field. In a world of constant, repetitive advertising—on radio or on TV—this was not unusual. Longtime owner Bill Veeck once wisely pointed out that Joe DiMaggio was, to a later generation, probably better known for Mr. Coffee ads than for his great baseball career. Therefore, it might have been true that, in the minds of some Americans, Ted Williams and Stan Musial were as well known for smoking Chesterfields as they were for being two of the most prolific hitters of their era.[35]

Eventually baseball officials, buffeted by the early winds of public criticism about the glut of advertising, began to worry about the depiction of players in product endorsements and the effect of those ads on the game's image. Nellie Fox, the "tough-guy" second baseman for the 1959 AL Champion White Sox and the AL MVP that same year, had his face on an ad for ready-to-use plaster mix. The ad depicted Nellie with just a trace of his White Sox cap. This ad was interesting because the league had only recently issued a bulletin threatening fines for players wearing their uniform in beer, whiskey, or smoking ads. That went for everyone in the game—players, coaches, managers. The backlash from baseball's excessive advertising was widespread, but clearly some products drew more ire than others. Plaster mix was safe. Clearly there was a school of thought that saw beer and cigarettes as something else entirely.[36]

The ruling on the depiction of uniforms in certain ads exposed baseball's inherent hypocrisy. As Harold Rosenthal of the *New York Herald Tribune* editorialized, "this annual edict puts baseball in the strangest of positions—refusing to permit hired hands to pick up outside money endorsing beer, whiskey or cigarettes, yet welcoming radio and TV sponsorship by these products." It should be noted, however, that as long as the player was out of uniform, he was free to appear in any form of advertisement. If baseball was trying to take a moral stance, they erred in thinking that it was the big league uniform that made the player a marketable identity.[37]

* * *

In the late 1950s and early 1960s, athletic endorsements of tobacco products increasingly came under fire as medical research began to link smoking with carcinogenic effects. One fan wrote to the *Washington Post* to express his concerns that while President Kennedy was extolling the virtues of physical fitness, athletes—including Yankees Roger Maris, Mickey Mantle, Whitey Ford, and Yogi Berra—were sending a message through endorsements that smoking and sporting accomplishment were compatible. That the players smoked was not the problem, the concerned parent noted. What was a problem was that "they broadcast it to the world which includes many little leaguers who eagerly read the sports pages and are greatly affected by what they read in these formative years." Youngsters' esteem for these athletes was leading them "down tobacco road," impairing their health as well as their athletic proficiency. "Honest advertising is the lifeblood of American business," a critic pointed out, "players shouldn't exploit children." Nevertheless, as author Alan Blum points out, critics really could not fairly fault players or baseball officials for not taking a stand against tobacco when cigarette brands were being promoted at American Medical Association meetings through the 1940s and early 1950s.[38]

Not everyone saw a problem, although sometimes the defense of baseball's unusual position vis-à-vis the beer and tobacco industries undercut the game's self-proclaimed status as a major cultural institution. Commissioner Ford Frick, reiterating his 1954 statement before Congress, insisted that baseball would go wherever the television and advertising industries decided. The game did not make the rules—the media did. So much for the pastime as a major American mover and shaker! Sometimes players jumped to the defense of the "vices" now under attack. Legendary pitcher Satchel Paige, retired at long last, passionately insisted that smoking was a perfectly fine endeavor. "I guess it's sitting around and having nothing to do is what causes them to figure out these reports against smoking," opined the venerable Paige. Men used to smoke, pointed out Satch, and still lived to be "100, 115. It didn't kill 'em then, I don't see why it should now." "Some of the greatest athletes smoked," Paige said, "and I was one of them."[39]

While the big beer companies proved largely unassailable in a new tide of reformist zeal, the tobacco industry was in trouble by the 1960s. In 1955, some 68 percent of American adult men were smokers. Cigarette consumption by those Americans aged fifteen and older peaked in 1961. By the middle of the decade, however, those numbers began to decline. Why? One answer, the obvious one, would be the diffusion of scientific knowledge about the carcinogenic properties of smoking, which, although not unheard of in the years prior to World War II, had begun to appear more frequently in the 1950s. In 1964, the first Surgeon General's report appeared, which concluded that smoking was a causal factor in lung cancer. In 1965, their hands forced by the threat of government intervention, the tobacco industry began placing warnings on cigarette packs. In 1967, the FCC issued a Fairness Doctrine that compelled broadcasters who advertised cigarettes to provide free time for counter-advertisements. Antitobacco spokesman John Banzhaf was "concerned about the use of the public airwaves to seduce young people into taking up smoking without any attempt to tell the other side of the story on television and radio." The final blow against Big Tobacco, or so it seemed at the time, came in 1969 when the Public Health Cigarette Smoking Act banned all cigarette ads on radio and TV. Broadcasters, bitter about losing the massive sums of money from big tobacco, did win one concession: the ban didn't take effect until midnight on January 1, 1971, following the broadcast of commercial-heavy college football bowl games.[40]

Taking body blows throughout the decade of the 1960s, the tobacco industry did not go quietly and sought the support of Congress, pouring enormous sums of money into political lobbies. Self-regulation, said the tobacco industry, was the best answer. The industry had said this before, but its own proposed 1964 advertising code was never actually used. The 1965 labeling act, also born in the halls of big tobacco, was deemed weak by critics—the warning "Caution: Cigarette smoking may be hazardous to your health" was maddeningly uncertain and vague. Ultimately, the tobacco companies, denied the power of television, found salvation in sports. Money that once went to broadcast advertising now helped establish new sports events: Virginia Slims tennis and Winston Cup auto racing in 1971, Marlboro Cup horse racing in 1973—all emerging *after* the ban on TV ads went into effect.

For its part, baseball, where tobacco was as deeply rooted in the game's culture as alcohol, did not have an easy time extinguishing smoking even after its hazardous health effects became known. There were token efforts at control and reform, but they were minimal. Both the National and American Leagues forbid smoking in the dugout because of TV exposure, but as authors Jack Lang and Larry Merchant later pointed out, like Joe DiMaggio years before, the stars regularly went into the runway between the dugout and clubhouse to light up. Fans were hardly different—in the stands as in the dugout, ashtrays at New York's Shea Stadium were overflowing, and new spittoons were installed. Whether he was shown on TV or not, every baseball fan knew that Mets superstar pitcher Tom Seaver regularly smoked cigars and chewed tobacco.[41]

Even after 1969's advertising ban, cigarettes did not disappear from the game. Like drinking, smoking retained a potent measure of manly appeal, and there was always a subtly celebratory tone when writers described players like St. Louis Cardinals All-Star Ted Simmons, the consummate rebel, smoking in the dugout or keeping a lit cigarette between the webbing of his catcher's mitt during warm-ups. The Pittsburgh Pirates "Lumber Crew" of the late 1970s sat for photographs in a cloud of dugout smoke. The press made Keith Hernandez's pregame ritual of cigarette and crossword puzzle famous while he was with the New York Mets in the 1980s. Hernandez relaxed. The Mets won. Old traditions died hard.[42]

With cigarettes, driven by advertising clout, dominating the middle of the century, the older tradition of dipping was virtually unheard of at the time of the 1969 ban. Now the tobacco industry latched onto the notion, supported by dubious medical evidence, that smokeless tobacco was a safe alternative to cigarettes. Free samples of smokeless tobacco began appearing in Major League clubhouses in the early 1970s. Players combined tobacco and chewing gum to create a new baseball mania. Players now found themselves connected to competing brands of smokeless tobacco. Skoal used Bobby Murcer, the heir apparent to Mickey Mantle in New York, to plug their product. Skoal also produced advertising featuring Kansas City Royals star George Brett and Dallas Cowboy footballer Walt Garrison as spokesmen. Between 1978 and 1985, sales of smokeless products increased 55 percent even as cigarette sales declined nationally. Buoyed by the sports world, and especially Major League Baseball, smokeless tobacco was quickly restored to a position in the market it had not enjoyed since the days of the Great Depression.[43]

*　*　*

There is something noteworthy about the way in which the fight over tobacco products in baseball played out at the end of the twentieth century. The contours of the debate over tobacco use say a great deal about the fundamental approach taken by the league establishment in dealing with more general drug-related problems. Looking back, it would be easy to think that one of the most prominent spokesmen against tobacco would be a trained cardiologist with roots in the game. This is exactly what one found in the person of Dr. Bobby Brown, president of the American League from 1984 to 1994, a gentleman ex-player who once held down third base for the New York Yankees in the 1940s while simultaneously putting himself through medical school. After his playing career was over, Brown served with MASH units in Korea, and he knew, perhaps more clearly than any individual associated with Major League Baseball, that tobacco was not only bad for players, but that use of it by Major Leaguers sent the wrong message to young fans. Who in the ongoing debate was in a better position to make a difference than Dr. Brown? His voice was now amplified by his seat in the establishment leadership.

Brown, however, illustrates the limited capacity of the establishment to actually tackle such a widespread national phenomenon as tobacco use. There was too much money at stake. It was widely held that it was not Major League Baseball's job to make the difference, to lead the crusade. One sees the persistence of this position even in Joe Garagiola's argument that players could not be *forced* to change by any outside policy. When pressed by reformers to remove cigarette ads from stadium billboards, Dr. Brown took a libertarian position—he was obligated to recognize various individual rights, but the league would continue to look into the problem. It was, however, "unrealistic" for tobacco signage to be removed from baseball parks. There was already a rule on the books that forbid players from smoking in uniform, even if it was only loosely acknowledged. No need to rule players away from playing in front of tobacco signage. Although, in the interest of fairness, Dr. Brown's presence would be felt in the eventual push to implement a total ban on tobacco products in the Major Leagues, those bans were slow to emerge. When they did, they were instituted only at lower levels: in the rookie league by 1991, the minor leagues in 1993, and the NCAA in 1994. Major League Baseball, now confronted by greater problems, was as slow as ever to alter old traditions, however harmful they might actually be.

Part of tobacco's resilience in the Major Leagues resulted from the weakness of the league's leadership. It also resulted from economics—both inside and outside of the game. Tobacco money was not only funneled into subversive advertising in the Major Leagues, but it also underwrote many of the popular sports magazines in America. Knowing where their bread was buttered, magazines such as *Sports Illustrated* were seldom inclined to tackle the big social issues, preferring the lighthearted tone of the "Chaws" article, which hit the stands in 1977. For them, tobacco use was a fringe issue in sports. When cigarettes were acknowledged as a problem, they were typically lumped in with other health threats: sugary Kool-Aid, whole milk, too much butter! Alternative medical views were ignored. Greg Connolly, a Massachusetts dentist, was hired by Major League Baseball in an early effort to help athletes quit chewing tobacco. When he wrote a piece for *Sports Illustrated* about his program, it was never published. The magazine's baseball editor had warned Connolly that *Sports Illustrated* would be unwilling to alienate its tobacco advertisers. The same issue that emphasized the dangers of elevators and eggs featured ten pages of cigarette advertising.[44]

Oddly enough, *Sports Illustrated*, while unwilling to go against the tobacco powers, did run a compelling piece on the dangers of alcohol. Beer sponsorship and advertising in baseball led *Sports Illustrated* "to wonder just what kind of cultural hypocrisy is going on when Americans relentlessly insist on immersing sport—our most wholesome, most admired, even (sometimes) most heroic institution—in a sea of intoxicating drink." *Sports Illustrated* called the tie-up between baseball and the beer companies "cynical, ironic, immoral, [and] hypocritical." The numbers tell an even more troubling story. Brewers, so-called peddlers of hypocrisy and intoxication, spent more than $6.3 million on sponsorship and ads. Tobacco, apparently no worse than fat or sugar, spent as much as $35 million at the same time.[45]

Lost beneath the headlines about performance-enhancement scandals and other drug escapades, the ongoing debate about tobacco use in the Major Leagues has not really quieted in more recent decades. There is quite clearly something about the culture of tobacco use in Major League Baseball that makes it especially difficult to eliminate. Hall of Fame pitcher Nolan Ryan, an executive with the Texas Rangers and Houston Astros following his retirement, recalled his own difficult experience with tobacco. "When I first broke into the big leagues [with the New York Mets]," Ryan recalled, "30–40% of the Mets smoked, and only three of the remaining players on the 25 man roster chewed. No one dipped." Dipping returned with the advent of free samples later in the 1970s. What never left was the lingering connection, if only in the backs of some players' minds, between tobacco use and on-field performance. Ryan himself, now in upper management, struggled with the allure of the old link between tobacco and performance. When slugger Josh Hamilton, then with the Texas Rangers, quit tobacco and entered a midseason dry spell, Ryan blamed the slump on timing. Hamilton's ability to play had been negatively impacted by the *removal* of tobacco from his routine.[46]

Medical research conducted since the 1980s continues to underline the resiliency of tobacco use in the professional ranks. Studies by the *New England Journal of Medicine* and the American Medical Association exposed the regular use of tobacco in Major League spring training compounds, often concluding that many players used tobacco due to a mixture of addiction and the desire to maintain a baseball tradition. A later study of the 1999 Rookie League surveyed 30 teams and 616 players, focusing on American citizens only—since a look at the Latin population might have skewed the numbers significantly. According to the study's findings, 67 percent of the American players had tried tobacco, while 31 percent were current users. A total of 98 percent of the players had played Little League baseball at some point, and it was noted that almost half of the players who had a coach who used tobacco had taken up the practice themselves. Players, then as earlier, attributed tobacco use to boredom, ritual, and the difficulty of quitting.[47]

* * *

As with the bottle, baseball's historical connection to the tobacco industry is intricately knotted and runs deep. Much like alcohol, tobacco use—even after tobacco's carcinogenic effects were exposed—has been difficult to root out. Even as the numbers of users slowly decline, many Americans still smoke or chew. There is an insistent voice that suggests the choice to use a legal product, however unhealthy, is an inherently American right, and that no impinging on freedoms will be allowed—in baseball or elsewhere (although numerous antismoking codes springing up across the nation suggest otherwise). Research also suggests that players continue to use harmful products because of tradition; they grew into the game using them. They associate tobacco products with their idols, or with their own moments of greatest success. As the Josh Hamilton story illustrates, the ritualistic nature of baseball in which performance and product become conflated makes it not only unsurprising that tobacco culture persists, but suggests just how resilient it actually is and always has been.

Because they are legal vices, nobody paid much attention to the role tobacco and alcohol played in the untimely deaths of former superstars Curt Flood and Roger Maris. In 1985, when Maris died of cancer, tobacco products were still prominently advertised on athletic clothing, on stadium signage, and in sports magazines. It was not until 2010, when former Padres star Tony Gwynn announced that he had salivary gland cancer, blaming it on decades of using chew tobacco, that the movement against tobacco was well and truly rejuvenated. In the wake of the Gwynn announcement, Cleveland Indians manager Terry Francona and Washington Nationals pitching phenom Stephen Strasburg both publically struggled to kick their own addictions. Awareness was dawning slowly. Tony Gwynn's untimely death in the summer of 2014 raised the profile of tobacco's inherent dangers, and the fight to root its use out of baseball, even further.

Spurred by antitobacco backlash on the periphery of the steroid discussion, Congress, in 2010, held hearings with an eye toward implementing a complete ban of smokeless tobacco in the Major Leagues. The league itself moved, as always, to preempt government oversight. In 2012, as part of a five-year collective bargaining agreement between MLB and the players' association, players, coaches, managers, and other team personnel are no longer permitted to stash a can or package of smokeless tobacco in their back pockets or anywhere else in their uniforms when taking to the field or anytime fans are in the ballpark. Nor will they be permitted to have a wad of smokeless tobacco tucked under their lip when signing autographs or participating in on-camera interviews or fan meet-and-greets. The new direction appears to be progressive, but in other ways it sounds a lot like the anticigarette agenda of the 1960s. The rule of thumb is simple: If you want to use tobacco products, go ahead and do it. Just don't do it where fans can see you.

Back then, in the middle of the 1960s, Major League Baseball and its beer and tobacco sponsors could not have known what course the future would take. In those days, baseball still winked at alcoholism even if it no longer openly celebrated excessive drinking. It would handle tobacco advertising in the best way possible to meet federal standards without sacrificing valuable income. Increasingly shaped, dominated, and perhaps even diminished by television, and receding into the shadow of professional football, baseball could not afford to reject the rules of the sports-entertainment complex. In those days it often seemed to critics that the primary purpose of the game had become to provide a "narcotic dream with an inexcusable dose of dishonesty." True or not, it was all about to become even more complicated.[48]

3

Where's the Dexamyl, Doc?

The American League has no rules regarding
pep pills, painkillers, etc. Baseball players don't
use those types of things.

—American League executive assistant
Bob Holbrook, 1969

Who is to be the Tribune's new diamond expert now
that the diamond stars are chewin' tranquilizers instead
of tobaccy, and ministering themselves more with
amphetamines than with arnica? Dr. T. R. Van Dellen,
the health editor, of course . . .

—*Chicago Tribune,* 1957

In 1969, Major League Baseball celebrated its centennial spring. That year was also the twentieth anniversary of one of the more curious episodes in the history of baseball public relations. Here is the setup. In 1949, on a lonely college campus somewhere in America, a baseball crashes through the laboratory window of chemistry professor Vernon K. Simpson, spilling his latest concoction and dramatically altering his life when he discovers that the spilled chemical medley repels wood. In one serendipitous stroke, Simpson has accidentally discovered the answer to both his personal and financial problems, a surefire way to prove his academic chops while simultaneously earning enough money to wed the girl of his dreams (who also happened to be the daughter of his dean).[1]

Of course, Vernon K. Simpson, as portrayed by actor Ray Milland (something of a poor man's Cary Grant), was a fictional character. He was the protagonist of Twentieth-Century Fox's cinematic baseball fantasy *It Happens Every Spring,* the story of a nerdy chemistry professor, and diehard baseball fanatic, who relies on a secret chemical formula in order to moonlight as a phenom pitcher for the St. Louis Cardinals. Having borrowed Milland from Paramount to play the starring role, the film's producers had also expected to feature real professional baseball players and teams as well as popular Brooklyn radio announcer Red Barber in their film. About a month before shooting was scheduled to begin, however, the studio ran into serious complications during a series of meetings with representatives from Major League Baseball. Despite repeated efforts by Twentieth-Century Fox executives, Commissioner Albert B. "Happy" Chandler refused permission to use the names of real teams and players. The insurmountable problem with *It Happens Every Spring*, Chandler groused, was that it was "the story of a cheat, winning a pennant and a World's Championship series."[2]

In making their final plea, the studio offered to include a special foreword on the film:

> The adventures of Mr. Vernon K. Simpson, the central character of the story, are purely imaginary. Because they violate both the rules of the game and the law of nature, the things he does are impossible and quite fantastic—like so many other things that happen every spring.[3]

Chandler was unmoved. Nothing associated with Major League Baseball, he insisted, would ever be associated with cheating—the entire plot of the film, however fanciful it might be, was anathema to the spirit of the National Pastime.[4]

Now, most baseball fans know that cheating possesses its own lengthy thread in baseball's historical tapestry. Most recall the grim story of players in cahoots with gamblers, throwing games for financial gain, and of the permanent exile of eight players from the Chicago White [Black] Sox for their alleged skullduggery in the 1919 World Series. But, there was, and still is, a lighter side to cheating as well.

Just as insiders winked for decades at the game's most notorious drunks, they also smiled knowingly about pitchers who rubbed various greasing agents—Vaseline or KY Jelly—on the ball, or who used emery boards, files, and finger nails to cut the ball, enabling it to weave and dance as it would never have done under normal circumstances. This is to say nothing of the long history of corking, driving nails into, and doubling, or even tripling, the layers of lacquer on bats to improve their effectiveness. And what of the long tradition of stealing opposing teams' signs? Although gambling, or associating with gamblers, was strictly *verboten*, all of these other actions were moral or ethical failings only if you got caught. In some ways they were as intrinsic to winning baseball strategy as bunting or shifting fielders. Manifold, then, is the meaning behind one of baseball's most famous contributions to pro-verbial wisdom, "nice guys finish last." That famous Leo Durocher maxim is also the title of his autobiography, the first page of which contains this line: "I don't call that cheating. I call that heads up baseball. Win any way you can as long as you can get away with it."[5]

The literal, though admittedly fictional, case of Vernon K. Simpson aside, there is no more prominent or reliable cliché in the world of sports than the widely accepted aphorism that good chemistry is the key to victory. Next to the helping hand of God, in fact, fans are routinely told that good chemistry was the essential element in the forging of this team or that team's winning legacy. Despite the ironic and altogether troubling implications of that cliché in contemporary sports, for most of the twentieth century, when athletes and writers invoked chemistry, they were referring to the sense of fraternity, of clubhouse camaraderie, that united disparate bands of men in the solitary goal of winning a championship. The notion that *real* chemistry, even the utterly ridiculous notion that a baseball soaked in complicated liquid com-pounds, could alter the shape and course of the game was simply unthink-able. It was also naive.[6]

By the time baseball opened its centennial celebration in the spring of 1969, chemistry—*real* chemistry—had dramatically altered the American and global sports landscape; it had, in fact, transformed the entirety of American society. The previous summer, at the 1968 Mexico City Olympics, the Inter-national Olympic Committee (IOC) had for the first time enforced drug test-ing of its athletes. Olympic testing came on the heels of a number of minor doping scandals and several tragic, drug-related deaths in the cycling world, a place where doping was a century-old tradition. The steroid Dianabol had emerged as the chemical equivalent of ballistic missiles in the sporting Cold War between American and Soviet weightlifters. But that was global sport, the Olympics, not America's professional or amateur leagues. The percep-tion, especially in baseball, was that irresponsible, illicit drug use, not to mention "doping," was utterly alien, or at least European. Baseball players, league executives would insist, did not even use rudimentary painkillers.[7]

Yet chemistry was at the heart of baseball's 1960s transformation. In an era defined by pitching, and in turn by the subsequently large financial invest-ment in pitcher's arms, there was no more significant trend in baseball than the increasing reliance on preventive medicine. While old timers reviled modern players who seemed fragile and soft, a generation of pioneering trainers and team doctors introduced new methods to ease pain, spur heal-ing, and enable performance, slamming the door on a Dark Age wherein sports medicine had largely been a "black art consisting of a semi-educated trainer and a bottle of liniment."[8]

Not everything about this trend appeared undesirable. American society had, in the years after World War II, grown more and more enamored with the therapeutic possibilities of medical and pharmaceutical advances. While new wonder pills were making life more pleasant for many Americans, few could condemn Mickey Mantle, who needed antihistamines to fight through seasonal allergy attacks. Basketball players routinely took Vitamin B pills at halftime to restore energy. Sugar tablets were a mainstay of the hockey world. Juan Marichal, the great Dominican pitcher of the 1960s, was notoriously sickly and was often administered a mixture of vitamins, painkillers, and anti-allergens. True, it was different from the old days, but few took the use of a new medical ameliorative to be a sign of some imminent sporting apocalypse.[9]

But there were serious questions being raised. The questions went to the very heart of what sports were, what they represented, and how the public responded to them. What, some asked, was the social value of a game if it was not played in an atmosphere of righteous virtue? More than the paternalistic ignorance of widespread alcoholism, crass TV tobacco ads, or even gambling, the specter of drug use (legal or illegal) called into question the fundamental aspect of sport. In a sport, like baseball, where performance was the end-all and be-all, where did one draw the line on the medical and pharmaceutical relationship to performance? Could unrestrained drug use reduce sport to the status of mere entertainment, of shameless spectacle? Confronted with these questions, baseball simply denied the existence of any problem and stood its ground. Baseball players did not use drugs.

* * *

Everyone in Major League Baseball—in the entire world of sport—was at a loss at how to explain the sudden, unlooked for emergence of Detroit Tigers third baseman Reno Bertoia. Italian born but raised in a Windsor, Canada, neighborhood, Bertoia was a high school baseball phenom. In 1953 he signed a "bonus baby" contract with the Detroit Tigers. Pushed through the Minor League system, Bertoia arrived in the Major Leagues and struggled with culture shock and the unavoidable pressure to perform. He buckled in short stints with the Tigers in 1954 and 1955. Nevertheless, by the spring of 1956, Bertoia was the favorite to hold down the hot corner for the Tigers. Once again overwhelmed by pressure, he couldn't hit the ball, struggling to a dismal .182 average.[10]

That is when former New York Giants slugger turned Tiger broadcaster Mel Ott stepped in. Ott had noticed how tense Bertoia appeared at the plate. He sent Tigers trainer Jack Homel with a message and a suggestion for Reno. Bertoia promptly began taking the tranquilizers Equanil and, later, Sedayml. Buoyed by his new medicine, the handsome young infielder finally began living up to his contract. Weeks into the 1957 season Bertoia was leading the league in batting, his .380 clip placing him ahead of All-Stars Ted Williams and Detroit's own Al Kaline. His sometimes erratic fielding had improved as well; he was virtually errorless in the field. It was as if he had morphed into an entirely different player. When asked to explain his newfound success, Bertoia was honest. "I swallow one little white tranquilizer pill a half hour before each game. Occasionally, if things get a little tense, I'll take the top off my bottle and take another."[11]

Bertoia, however, was not the first Detroit-area athlete to try tranquilizers. Teammate Al Aber, a pitcher, routinely used tranquilizers to ease muscle tension in his legs. The pills were making the rounds in other sports, too. Osteopath Richard Thompson, the team physician for the Detroit Lions football team, recalled: "We used them on at least five Lions last year [1956], and we intend to continue to use them." Not everyone was thrilled with Bertoia's remarkable transformation. The Tigers' resident medical expert, Dr. Luther Leader, was concerned that Bertoia's success might convince others to seek the aid of "happiness pills" even if they didn't really need them. Leader suggested that Bertoia, now that his original worries had been eased, should dispense with the pills. Bertoia was understandably reluctant. "I wouldn't give them up for the world," he said. "Not with this batting average."[12]

The same year that Reno Bertoia finally discovered his batting stroke, the humorist S. J. Perelman published a book of essays entitled *The Road to Miltown; or, Under the Spreading Atrophy*. Perelman's acid wit seemed to provide a fitting summation for a decade that, in some ways, had become given to the wholesale swallowing of tranquilizers. These so-called wonder drugs, presaged by the synthesis of meprobamate in 1950, revealed the voracious public's "hunger for news of wonder drugs that promised to save lives, curb disease, and ease pain." When Miltown, the brand name for meprobamate, first went on the market in 1955, *Cosmopolitan* gave it a glowing report; it was, said the widely read magazine, safe and quick. Miltown "does not deaden or dull the senses and is not habit forming. It relaxes the muscles, calms the mind, and gives people a renewed ability to enjoy life." Sometimes it helped them hit a baseball.[13]

Throughout the 1950s, several euphemisms for tranquilizers entered the popular lexicon. People might take "happy pills," or perhaps they took "aspirin for the soul." Maybe they were downing "mental laxatives." And sometimes they were taking "don't give a damn pills" or "Turkish bath in a tablet." Whatever they happened to call tranquilizers, Americans were fascinated by them. By 1960, Americans were reportedly spending almost $280 million annually on Miltown, Equanil, Soma, Atarax, and Librium. Looking for any way to ease domestic Cold War tensions, Americans embraced the new wonders of pharmaceutical science, "rushing to buy up [a] panacea for tension and its handmaiden—anxiety." "It has become possible," suggested the *American Mercury* in 1957, "for people to annul . . . frustration artificially, enjoy a simulated happiness without paying the heretofore prevailing price."[14]

The fascination with tranquilizers coincided with the newfound, widespread, postwar belief in the absolute efficacy of drugs. New medicines were the triumph of postwar civilization, discovered to ameliorate the stresses of the Atomic Age. Newspaper, radio, and television advertising undergirded massive propaganda campaigns by pharmaceutical companies—whatever ailed you, a bad back, bad blood, or simple chills: drugs could help you. Drugs, Americans were informed each day, were *good* for you.

For some intellectuals, the sudden prevalence of tranquilizers in American life suggested that the country was branching away from its Protestant roots. If conventional wisdom was that psychotherapeutic drugs should only be used in situations where the ability to carry on important day-to-day activities was threatened, then the same pharmacological Calvinism (the notion that hard work cannot be replaced by drugs) suggested that pervasive tranquilizer use, the search for chemical happiness for happiness's sake, was the result of some creeping moral weakness in the American body.[15]

The case of Reno Bertoia was the first to raise important pharmacological questions for the defenders of sport, and particularly of baseball, as a field of virtue. He was not, however, the only player popping happiness pills. There were a number of high-profile cases of players making use of tranquilizers and other psychosomatic medicines in the 1950s. Billy Martin used tranquilizers, in addition to alcohol, in order to recover from the stress of marital problems that nearly led to a mental breakdown. Jackie Jensen of the Red Sox needed them in order to overcome his fear of flying. Gil Hodges of the Dodgers reportedly used them on occasion. And then there was Jimmy Piersall, the talented, but eccentric, outfielder from Boston who became the poster boy for psychological illness in athletes and the subject of the film *Fear Strikes Out*.[16]

Nobody was willing to go very far in suggesting that the clearly troubled Piersall shouldn't make use of whatever scientific advances were at his disposal, but what of the potential for tranquilizer abuse by other players? Was it fair, even if the effect was only psychological, for an athlete to be using such pills? How should one view the records that athlete might set? What about unscrupulous coaches who might endanger the health of their athletes by forcing them to take such pills without the necessary medical supervision? That various minor tranquilizers and barbiturates had their uses, easing the tension and drudgery of a person's daily grind was one thing. That they might actually be a useful tool for improving one's batting average was entirely another. The *Wall Street Journal* worried over the effect of the new drugs on the baseball record books. "Will the footnotes soon say something like this? Jones, Brooklyn, 1959: Played 30 games on Miltown, 20 on Equanil, 7 on Suavitil, and 40 on Thorazine?"[17]

Not everyone was convinced that the integrity of the game was in any kind of danger due to the infusion of tranquilizers and other pills. "What's the difference between Bertoia taking tranquilizers to quiet his nerves," asked White Sox manager Al Lopez, "and some clerk taking aspirin to ease a headache?" In the end any immediate controversy and long-term fallout within baseball from Bertoia's experience with the pills was made moot when, in midseason, he simply quit hitting the baseball again. "Now," moaned Bertoia, relegated to the bench, "everyone says that I'm over-tranquilized."[18]

The questions didn't necessarily go away with the rapid decline of Reno Bertoia. The biggest question of all loomed larger with each passing year. To what degree was it acceptable for athletes to use modern medical advancement in overcoming their own natural limitations? Certainly the inability of a .183 hitter to deal with Major League pressure was just that—a natural limitation. Was it any different from a runner or cyclist who was unable to reach top speeds without enhancement? Reno Bertoia took tranquilizers. Cyclists popped amphetamines. Both were looking to get from a pill what they did not naturally possess. In 1957, nobody was ready with answers to the big questions. Nobody in baseball thought answers were necessary because the question did not even need asking.

*   *   *

Doping, whatever people in the 1950s and 1960s may have believed, was as old as sports; it had been a part of athletic competitions for as long as civilized men held them. The ancient Greeks were known to eat animal parts, such as horns or testicles, which they believed would confer the strength of the animal. They and the ancient Romans also used toxic plants and mushrooms whose chemical derivatives enhanced physical performance. Mythology hands down the story of Pheidippides, the Athenian runner who collapsed, dead, in Athens after arriving with the joyous news that Athenian soldiers had proven victorious over King Darius's invading Persian army on the plain of Marathon. The only thing that likely distinguished Pheidippides from his modern counterparts was the specific absence of amphetamine in his blood.

From ancient myth to modern controversy, it was in the midst of the therapeutic 1950s that Roger Bannister of Great Britain succeeded in breaking through the seemingly impassible four-minute-mile barrier. The four-minute mile was a mark that nobody had thought possible in preceding decades, but in the wake of Bannister's run, suddenly a host of runners were coming in under four minutes: John Landy of Australia, the Hungarian Laszlo Tabori, Brian Hewson and Chris Chataway of Great Britain, and the American Don Bowden. Skeptics were certain that the runners had used pep pills, amphetamines, to achieve record times. The runners all angrily denied that *any* pill had helped them crash through the four-minute barrier.[19]

Dr. Herbert Berger, the American Medical Association's chairman of the committee on narcotics and alcoholics for the state of New York, launched his own investigation and concluded that "the recent rash of four-minute miles is no coincidence." Dr. Berger told of reports in the medical community on the shocking use of stimulating drugs by amateur and professional athletes, a "vicious practice" that he personally found deplorable. The culprit in the case of the four-minute mile, insisted Berger, was amphetamine, a stimulant commonly used in treating various minor aches and other complaints, commonly sold as Benzedrine, Phenedrene, or Dexedrine.[20]

More concrete than mythical Pheidippides, and stretching back a generation before Bannister, European cyclists had used elements as disparate as ether, caffeine, nitroglycerine, heroin, cocaine, and strychnine to delay fatigue and enhance performance. In 1886, twenty-four-year-old Welsh cyclist Arthur Linton, who had allegedly ingested the stimulant Trimethyl, died after a bicycle race between Paris and Bordeaux. Terry Todd, in his history of steroid abuse, described marathon runner Thomas Hicks's collapse at the 1904 St. Louis Olympics after downing a mixture of strychnine and brandy.[21]

"I dope myself," said cyclist Jacques Anquetil, five-time winner of the Tour de France. "Everyone [in competitive cycling] dopes himself. Those who claim they don't are liars." By Anquetil's time, amphetamine was ubiquitous in cycling. As early as 1939, sports medicine specialists were already noting widespread Benzedrine use among professional riders. In 1948 a British doctor attending several world championship competitions sounded the alarm that runners and cyclists were doping themselves like racehorses with concoctions of strychnine, caffeine, and Benzedrine. In the 1960 Tour de France, it was estimated that three-quarters of the competitors used speed, and it was that same year, during the Rome Olympics, that the Danish cyclist Knut Jensen died from the lethal combination of amphetamine and the heat.[22]

The primary catalyst for widespread amphetamine use was World War II. Amphetamine was among the drugs most regularly requisitioned by physicians with military units in the run-up to the German blitz of Poland. Throughout the war years phentermine and methamphetamine, which differs from amphetamine by a single carbon atom, were adopted by the military on all sides, embraced for their perceived ability to push the human body beyond normal capabilities, holding fatigue at bay. American servicemen, including not a few Major League baseball players, were introduced to amphetamine during their time in the service.[23]

In the postwar years, family doctors embraced amphetamine for the treatment of numerous psychiatric illnesses and hailed its marvelous utility as a weight-loss drug, transforming obesity into a preventable medical disease. Lester Grinspoon and Peter Hedblom in *Speed Culture: Amphetamine Use and Abuse in America* concluded: "Never before had so powerful a drug been introduced in such quantities and in so short a time, and never before had a drug with such a high addictive potential and capability of causing irreversible physical or psychological damage been so enthusiastically embraced by the medical profession as a panacea or so extravagantly promoted by the drug industry."[24]

In short, and far apart from its dubious place in the cycling world, amphetamine was the model miracle drug of the therapeutic decade. Despite knowledge that the drug had harmful addictive qualities and could even lead to psychotic rage, its popularity peaked in the late 1960s. By that time one in twenty American adults were active users of amphetamine by prescription. At least half as many were using speed without prescriptions. It was embraced by mods, beats, and the Hells Angels, among other period subcultures. Lou Reed of the Velvet Underground even celebrated amphetamine culture in the song "White Light / White Heat."[25]

In the 1950s, there had been serious worries about amphetamine abuse in university and high school sports. In 1957, the American Medical Association launched an inquiry into amphetamine use in college athletics, condemning what they saw as an alarmingly common practice. Although amphetamines were eventually banned in those arenas, professional sports officials were largely unimpressed by and disinterested in the study. Even as editorialists at the *Chicago Tribune* offered a sarcastic comment on the ubiquity of drug use in professional baseball, the heads of organized baseball still refused to see a problem.[26]

While most spokesmen for professional sports refused to acknowledge the increasingly obvious drug use of the 1960s, hindsight suggests that the National Football League quickly embraced the possibilities of amphetamine and other potentially performance-enhancing drugs. In the early 1970s players Houston Ridge of San Diego and Ken Gray of St. Louis actually sued their teams for having been forced to take amphetamines and other drugs. A doctoral dissertation observing the use of speed by thirteen NFL teams discovered that players were taking an average of 60 to 70 mg of amphetamine in every game just to get psyched up.[27]

A psychiatrist from the University of California, Arnold Mandell, investigated further. He discovered amphetamines were typically used once a week on game days entirely for psychiatric effects rather than for any technical improvement in performance. Quarterbacks, wide receivers, and defensive backs took a 5 to 10 mg dose, what was then the typical prescription for depression or fatigue. One quarterback reported that amphetamines made "everything slow down while I read the defense."[28]

Defensive ends and tackles were taking 50 to 200 mg of amphetamine, enough to induce a sort of semi-psychotic rage. Offensive linemen and running backs were taking approximately 15 to 45 mg, the desired psychiatric effects of such a dose being enthusiasm in the face of an attack. Similar doses, for similar reasons, were being taken by soldiers overseas. As Mandell, Stewart, and Russo pointed out, the thoughtful manner in which these drugs were being used indicated not only exceptional knowledge of their actual effects, but also a serious disregard for players' long-term health.[29]

Amphetamine was practically made for the baseball season, a long 154- (later 162-) game grind that left players tired and exhausted just as the game reached its midsummer plateau. For years, baseball men had been looking for some kind of edge, something to help carry them over that hill. During the early 1940s, as men were first heading off to fight in the war, the St. Louis Cardinals and New York Yankees experimented with a heavily enforced vitamin regimen at their training camps, certain that it would produce better results over the long haul. Convinced that beta-carotene would improve his batters' eyesight (it had supposedly worked for R.A.F. flyers dropping bombs on Hitler), the Washington National's owner Clark Griffith struck a deal with a California producer to deliver crate loads of carrots to his training camp.[30]

Baseball players called into military service began using amphetamine during games played on military bases. They called the amphetamine pills "greenies" because the most prevalent brand, Dexedrine, was produced as a green tablet. Benzedrine, the other common brand, was orange. Coming home from the war, the players discovered that the gospel of amphetamine had preceded them. "[Amphetamine use] spread like wildfire when all of those guys came home," said Dr. Charles Yesalis, one of the foremost experts on the history of doping in sport. Hall of Famer Ralph Kiner, the intimidating slugger of his era while playing with the Pittsburgh Pirates in the late 1940s, recalled that after coming home from his stint flying Navy seaplanes, he discovered amphetamines in baseball's training rooms. One time, before the second game of a doubleheader, a trainer offered an exhausted Kiner some Benzedrine. "All the trainers in all the ballparks had them," he remembered.[31]

Baseball, the old saying goes, is "five minutes of action packed into three hours," so one had to wonder what use a fatigue-fighting pill actually had in the Major Leagues. For starters, it is important to remember that the late 1950s and early 1960s was an era in which players seldom put a premium on off-season conditioning (they were often busy working to make ends meet). In fact, they were discouraged from any weight-lifting program for fear that it would make them muscle-bound, too bulky and inflexible to play the often subtle game of baseball effectively. Players would do anything to maintain hard-to-earn and valuable roster spots. The extra stamina supposedly afforded by amphetamine was just the ticket. "You needed to perform your best and you were going to use everything that's legal to help you do it," said Kiner. "You worked to get that job and you wanted to stay in the lineup. If you got out of the lineup, you might never get back in." Then, of course, there was the sense that amphetamine could ease the boredom of grueling road trips or help speed recovery from nights spent on the town. Greenies were great for hangovers, and ballplayers were no stranger to that particular affliction.[32]

Although World War II was the primary catalyst of widespread amphetamine use in Major League Baseball, it was the yearly tradition of playing winter ball in the Caribbean that truly made amphetamine a baseball mainstay. It was in the dugouts and clubhouses in Latin America that Major Leaguers were first introduced to the twin pots of coffee—one containing amphetamines, the other regular—that soon became permanent fixtures in clubhouses back home. Jim Willoughby, a relief pitcher who played in the early 1970s, remembered two giant coolers in the corner of the dugout. One, of course, was filled with water. When Willoughby tried to fill his cup from the other cooler, he was quickly stopped. "That one's red juice," he was told. Red juice was basically an amphetamine cocktail reserved for the veteran players.[33]

By and large, the use of amphetamine in baseball was a tightly kept secret—certainly more closely guarded than in any other sport. The press seldom wrote anything about "greenies," though they certainly knew of their existence. Players said even less, usually only admitting the existence of the drug in candid post-retirement interviews. Nevertheless, the picture that emerges is of a drug with numerous utility in the baseball world. Lenny Green of the Detroit Tigers remembered that amphetamines were suggested to him for recovering from an injured back—he thought nothing of it; players, Green suggested, didn't really know the difference between amphetamines and aspirin. Another player, Ray Herbert, recalled that in the 1950s and 1960s, team doctors had to write the prescriptions for drugs that were kept locked up, but trainers almost always supplied "greenies" for doubleheaders. Dick Drago, who came into the Major Leagues in 1969 with the expansion team Kansas City Royals, recalled that a common locker room saying of the era was "don't go out there alone." This meant, he explained, that you must remember to take your pep pills. Bernie Carbo, who played with the Cincinnati Reds, remembered how the training room always had large glass jars full of pills—painkillers, vitamins, and pep pills together. They were all called "vitamins," and the training staff in Cincinnati, and later in Boston, would sometimes ask Carbo or other players if they had taken their "vitamins" that day.[34]

Do amphetamines actually boost physical performance in any significant respect? That is a difficult question to answer. The military's considerable research into the effects of amphetamine during and since World War II failed to demonstrate any clear-cut gain. On the other hand, an influential 1959 study by Harvard Medical School, under the aegis of the American Medical Association, compared university swimmers and track and field athletes on placebo tablets to those on a moderate dose of amphetamines and barbiturates. Most of the weight throwers, runners, and swimmers, the Harvard study concluded, performed *better* while dosed with amphetamine than when taking the placebos. Still, there remained room for doubt. By the end of the 1960s, as amphetamine and methamphetamine were emerging as the nation's most significant illicit drug threat, the majority opinion was that judicious amphetamine use could produce a small gain in quickness and a helpful boost in courage and energy. Whether the small gain was worth the impaired judgment and potential psychosis, not to mention addiction, really depended on the personal belief of trainers and players in every sport.[35]

* * *

"If it wasn't for that stuff," said former Detroit Tigers manager Steve O'Neill in a 1951 interview, "we'd never have won the pennant because Hal never would have been able to pitch." He was speaking of the Tigers' 1945 championship campaign. The "stuff" he referred to was Novocain, a painkilling drug. That year, Hal Newhouser, the team's star pitcher and eventual winner of a second consecutive Most Valuable Player Award, won twenty-five games and posted a miniscule 1.81 ERA (throwing against many admittedly inferior wartime players). He was also troubled by relentless pain in his shoulder, pain that was relieved when Dr. Raymond Forsyth administered shots of procaine (another name for Novocain) to the shoulder. Although Newhouser was merely mortal in posting a 2–1 record against the Chicago Cubs in the 1945 World Series, there was some question in later years about the ethics of using Novocain to enable pitching. Future headlines blaring "DETROIT TIGERS WON FLAG BY DOPING NEWHOUSER" suggested such concern. Dr. Forsyth, who also worked with the Lions football team, maintained that there had been no "doping" involved; the administration of Novocain to baseball and football players naturally aided healing.[36]

Twenty-three years after Forsyth's administration of Novocain created a minor scandal, Denny McClain, another Detroit Tigers pitcher, won a remarkable thirty-one games, the last pitcher in either league to win thirty or more games. That autumn, McClain's Tigers matched up against the St. Louis Cardinals in the World Series. Despite some brash predictions on his part, McClain was largely ineffective in the series, winning only one game. He was able to pitch in game six's 13–1 drubbing of the Cards thanks only to pregame shots of cortisone and Xylocaine. However, in a series that seemed as much a competition between the two team's druggists as between the players, McClain's treatment was not exceptional. Willie Horton the slugging outfielder around whom the Tigers lineup was built had limped through much of the season on painkillers. Mickey Lolich, the other Tigers pitcher of note, who would emerge as the hero of that Fall Classic, was taking antibiotics. On the other side, the Cardinals' intimidating ace Bob Gibson gobbled up muscle-relaxing pills to keep his arm loose. It was as though several walking drug-stores had taken the field.[37]

What had created a scandal in Newhouser's time was common practice by McClain's. McClain recalled the medical pharmacopeia at his disposal. "A few pills—I take all kinds—and the pain's gone." Cardinals team doctor I. C. Middleman acknowledged, "We occasionally use Dexamyl and Dexedrine [amphetamines] . . . We also use barbiturates, Seconal, Tuinal, Nembutal . . .

We also use some anti-depressants, Triavil, Tofranil, Valium." "But," he added cryptically, "I don't think the use of drugs is as prevalent in the Midwest as it is on the East and West coasts." If St. Louis's medical arsenal included all of those drugs, one can only wonder how the coastal teams could possibly exceed it.[38]

The widespread use of preventive medicine was arguably the most significant baseball trend of the 1960s. The use of painkillers in baseball had proliferated with the discovery of new effective medicines, the increasing sophistication of team medical staffs, and the changing nature of the ballplayers. Numerous teams began to keep two or more doctors, orthopedists, and internal specialists on their staff along with trainers. It was increasingly important to maintain the health of players in which owners had made such significant investments. Training rooms began to feature whirlpools, diathermy, ultrasound, and X-ray machines.

To some degree the advent of the new medical sensibility in professional baseball was part of a widespread national movement toward medicalization. For example, alcoholism and homosexuality had once been described as "social" problems stemming from moral weakness. By the late 1960s and early 1970s, the medical community, which saw it as their national responsibility to help alleviate these problems, and the pharmaceutical corporations, which saw it as their job to sell drugs, had helped redefine these as "medical" problems. In other words, and to put it rather simply, there was a transition in definition from moral weakness to medical disease, from "badness" to "sickness."[39]

The passing of certain elements in the game's old masculine code symbolized this transition in the baseball world. Most players who had been in the game before the 1950s saw hypermedicalization as a sign of weakness. It was tradition that old timers saw theirs as the "best" era, but modern players, they charged, really could not measure up; they were hothouse lilies who sat out because of hangnails. In their day, players didn't need shots and pills to take the field. In the early 1950s, veteran Indians infielder Ray Boone, even though he was suffering from painful bone spurs in his knees, consistently refused X-rays and treatment with the "wonder drugs" of the cortisone family. Only after Cleveland's team doctor gave him assurance that the drugs "will either fix you up in two days . . . or it won't work at all. And it can't hurt you in either event" did Boone finally consent to treatment. Boone was living by an older code. In 1969 old timers watched in wonder as games were stopped after a batter was hit with a pitch, the player was sprayed with ethyl chloride, and his bruise slathered with some agent, even the controversial analgesic DMSO (Dimethyl sulfoxide). It was all a far cry from the days of just rubbing dirt on the wound.[40]

Older players' tendency to simply toss out their hurts was regarded by the 1960s as representative of "guts baseball," certainly something to be admired, but also something that was undeniably foolhardy. Team doctors and trainers pointed out that modern athletes were bigger, stronger, and often far better trained than their forebears. As their physical capabilities advanced, treatment had become more effective. It was all quite evolutionary and altogether natural. Besides, modern players, they said, were more sophisticated and therefore more apt to appreciate all the new medical advances. Nowadays, recalled the Los Angeles Dodgers' crew of trainers, "we get ballplayers of the caliber of Ron Fairly, Wes Parker and Ron Perranoski. They are well-educated, cultured, gentlemen. The ballplayers used to come directly from high school; no matter how much money this type of boy would make, he'd have a high school intellect all his life." Obviously sophisticated and educated gentlemen players knew better than to shirk a helpful injection or pep-up pill.[41]

Not every expert was certain that such a widespread reliance on painkillers was really necessary in baseball. In fact, Dr. Jacob R. Suker, an orthopedist with the Chicago Cubs for over twenty years, suggested that the long schedule and day-to-day pressure of baseball, rather than an excuse for using amphetamines or painkillers, was actually a good reason to shun them. "A ballplayer doesn't have to get 'up' every day," he said. "In fact, he can't be. So if you don't feel great at times, do the best you can." Suker went even farther, suggesting that self-administering drugs should never be condoned and that "a trainer should never inject a painkiller." Of course, nobody believed any players administered their own drugs, and all sports physicians agreed that painkillers administered under the team doctor's supervision were perfectly acceptable.[42]

If veterans of some bygone era were far from impressed by what they perceived as soft, overmedicated players, the availability of painkillers did not entirely eliminate old notions of machismo and heroism on the diamond. In fact, the most pressing ethical questions about using painkillers to play were often directly related to the desire to "man up" and perform heroically—or just perform at all. The medical specialists working with the Los Angeles Dodgers in the 1960s vividly remembered Don Drysdale, a pitcher notorious for his intimidating tough-guy attitude on the mound. Drysdale, insisted one trainer, was a hero. He had pitched with a broken finger, cracked ribs, terrible colds, and even a severe case of shingles. It astonished the training staff that Drysdale had been able to stay on the mound; how he pitched with shingles, an especially painful affliction, was almost beyond understanding. He simply could not have done almost any of it without regular shots of painkillers.[43]

If the ubiquity of medicine suggested that the traditional masculine nature of the game was changing, if only barely, there was also a significant economic factor at work. Management had invested millions of dollars in players, so it only made good financial sense to protect those players by whatever means necessary. Players were expected to return the investment through strong performances; painkillers made it possible, and as Drysdale showed, you could still meet the expectations of the game's macho code—be a hero—even while using painkillers. During the 1960s era of expansion, and of new, cavernous stadiums, pitching defined the game. In fact, many baseball trainers of the time suggested that the game of the 1960s was almost 90 percent pitching. A team's medical staff was convinced that the most important job they had was keeping their pitchers healthy. And in the 1960s there was no more valuable or fragile pitcher than Sandy Koufax.[44]

*   *   *

Sandy Koufax cast a long shadow over the baseball world of the 1960s. The quiet southpaw, thin, elegant, and ever so graceful despite a reputation as the most overpowering pitcher of his generation, towered above the pitcher's mound at Los Angeles' Dodger Stadium. It actually did not matter where he took the mound; whenever Koufax pitched it was never a question of whether he won or lost, but only of how many men he would strike out. Although it took him several years to harness his power and hit his stride, between 1961 and 1966 Koufax forged a legacy as one of the greatest pitchers in the history of the game. In 1966, still only thirty years old, he won twenty-seven games. Over the previous four seasons he averaged twenty-four victories and 307 strikeouts. He had four no-hitters (including a perfect game) to his credit. With an annual salary of $125,000, he was the highest paid pitcher in baseball history. However, just one month after leading the Dodgers into the 1966 World Series, Koufax shocked the baseball world by announcing his retirement. "I don't know if cortisone is good for you or not," he told the gathered writers, "but to take a shot every other ball game is more than I wanted to do, and to walk around with a constant upset stomach because of the pills and to be high half the time during a ballgame because you're taking painkillers, I don't want to have to do that."[45]

It was widely known that Koufax was in pain. The story of the best years of Koufax's career was the story of playing through pain. Every year he seemed to hurt more, and yet still he dominated. There was always a sense of concern, regret, or foreboding with Koufax, though. After clinching the pennant with a victory over the Phillies on the final day of the 1966 season, he had greeted reporters in the locker room. "How much were you hurting?" one writer asked. "I was hurting," he replied, "but I don't know how much. I don't know how much because I was full of codeine. It was the only way I could pitch."[46]

Koufax's career spanned baseball's medical revolution. When he was a rookie in 1955 there was really no such thing as sports medicine—not like it would become just ten years later. Rehab was virtually unheard of. You lived with injuries. Ice was for after-work martinis. In 1962, just as Koufax was beginning his run of greatness, his career was almost ended by a rare disease known as Reynaud's syndrome. A blood clot in his arm, perhaps caused by his hard grip on the baseball, had led one of his fingers to become cracked and purple. It made pitching nearly impossible. Saving the finger became the primary concern of the Dodgers' resident physician Robert Woods and team orthopedist Robert Kerlan. Using cutting-edge medicine, they administered four separate drugs to Koufax: Coumadin (an anticoagulant), fibrinolysin (used to dissolve clots in blood vessels), and Ilidar and Priscoline (both used to dilate arteries). The finger was saved, but only barely. It was only the beginning of his pain-filled journey to greatness.[47]

On August 8, 1964, Koufax had taken a big lead off of second base during a game against the Milwaukee Braves and barely managed to hurry back in time to avoid being picked off. Sliding into the base, he jammed his pitching arm. Two games later, after his nineteenth win of the season, he awoke to discover that he could no longer straighten the arm. He finished the 1964 season with nineteen wins and a case of traumatic arthritis. It was not a condition he could ever hope to cure; it would only worsen if he kept pitching.[48]

Over the next two baseball seasons, Koufax became "America's favorite medical project." Concerned letter writers, hoping to help Sandy out, wrote to Kerlan and Woods suggesting their favorite home remedies for arthritis: rub the arm with brake fluid, visit a uranium mine, or pour a teaspoon full of sulfur into Koufax's shoes each day. Eschewing brake fluid, Koufax adopted a soon to be infamous regimen to keep his arthritic arm in shape.[49]

Koufax relied most heavily on a substance known as Capsolin, an analgesic containing capsaicin, a heat agent derived from chili peppers. It was known throughout baseball as "atomic balm." Capsolin, applied straight, was too hot for most players in the sports world, so they cut it with cold cream or Vaseline. Not Sandy, though. He took it straight and in abundance. The Dodgers' clubhouse attendant always made sure he washed Koufax's laundry separately because his clothes were covered with the painful heat agent. One time, however, the Dodgers donated used jerseys to a local Little League squad.

Pity the young player who received Koufax's number 32 jersey. No amount of washing could fully remove the Capsolin or mute its effects. Then there was Carroll Beringer, one of Sandy's teammates. He accidently put on one of Koufax's sweatshirts during a hot day game at St. Louis's Busch Stadium. Beringer broke out into sweats, his skin blistered, and finally he vomited.[50]

After games, trainers fitted Koufax with a rudimentary rubber sleeve that he was to wear while holding his arm in a bucket of freezing ice water. The cold usually managed to reduce the swelling in his elbow, which on some days grew as large as his knee. Coupled with his use of Capsolin, Koufax's routine could be summed up as fire and ice. But he also ingested a variety of painkillers, including codeine. Struggling through pain with "every pitch," he was occasionally injected with cortisone (though never with Novocain), and most controversially, toward the end of his career he was administered oral doses of Butazolidin. "It killed a few people," Dr. Frank Jobe admitted of the drug that was primarily used in horse racing—often illegally.[51]

In 1968, just two years after Koufax retired from baseball, Kentucky Derby winner Dancer's Image was stripped of his victory after testing positive for the drug phenylbutazone (of which Butazolidin was the brand name). The "bute" had been administered to the colt in order to ease soreness in his ankles; this was the same purpose it served in baseball, where the absence of any doping policy stood in stark contrast with horse racing, the only sport of the time with rules, albeit inconsistent and convoluted, regarding doping. "If baseball had the same rules as racing about these things, you'd have a lot of pitchers disqualified," said Dr. Sidney Gaynor, chief physician for the New York Yankees. "The drug is administered quite commonly to relieve inflammation and cut down swelling." The Yankees' own Whitey Ford once used it. In football it was used by Redskins quarterback Sonny Jurgensen. And it was used by Sandy Koufax.[52]

The experimental use of Butazolidin on Koufax was approved by Dr. Robert Kerlan, the orthopedic specialist who worked not only with the Dodgers but also with most of Southern California's major professional sports franchises and their premier athletes. Kerlan knew that the "bute" relieved inflammation and stiffness associated with arthritis, but that if it was not carefully monitored it also killed bone marrow—he essentially had to treat Koufax as though the pitcher were a cancer patient, monitoring his blood count regularly. Kerlan was never entirely comfortable using the treatment on Koufax, but Sandy's insistence on being able to pitch, and agreement to cut his workload and eliminate throwing the pitches that put the most stress on his arm, convinced him. Besides, Kerlan used Butazolidin on himself as well.[53]

Only forty-three, but with arthritis in his shoulders, spine, and hips, Dr. Kerlan was bent and misshapen like a much older man. He sometimes relied on thirty aspirin a day just to keep going. If anyone could empathize with Koufax's situation, Bob Kerlan was that man. He loved working with athletes, especially Koufax. It was his fondest hope that medical schools, impressed with the work done by Kerlan and other doctors associated with sports teams, would begin to develop subspecialties in treating athletes. And sometimes it was just nice to bask in the glow of an athletic superstar. "You see," admitted Kerlan, "I'm kind of a hero worshiper."[54]

Because Sandy Koufax was risking so much, his very arm in fact, and because he was baseball's biggest draw, he was seen as exceptionally heroic (and even more exceptionally valuable). Nobody at the time considered the somewhat hypocritical position that baseball was going to be in when it celebrated Koufax, who was clearly unable to pitch without the assistance of numerous drugs and analgesics, and who retired when he grew weary of being "half-high" on the mound, but vociferously condemned the entire concept of enhancement, chemical or otherwise. Economics almost certainly had something to do with it, if only to a very small degree.[55]

Whatever long-term questions that Koufax's story raises, he was celebrated as a hero for his courage in playing through crippling pain. For his part, Koufax always scoffs at reports of heroism. "My heroism is greatly overstated," he would say. On occasion, when confronted with what he might have done to himself had he pitched any longer, he has admitted, "Maybe I just didn't want to think about how bad it was."[56]

Ultimately Koufax was representative of the traditional baseball hero. If he was baseball's most recognizable figure in the 1960s, he was also an intensely personal player, fiercely competitive but not particularly outspoken. His drug regimen was celebrated because he was popular, and because he was using drugs to do something courageous.

* * *

In so many other ways, beyond Koufax, the world of baseball medicine remained behind a unique veil. One of Koufax's contemporaries, Jim Brosnan, changed that. In a later foreword to his groundbreaking book, *The Long Season*, Brosnan recorded:

> As an active player on a big-league team I had seemingly taken undue advantage by recording an insider's viewpoint on what some professional baseball players were really like. I had, moreover, violated the idolatrous image of big leaguers who had been previously portrayed as models of modesty, loy-

alty and sobriety—i.e., what they were really not like. Finally, I had actually written the book by myself, thus trampling upon the tradition that a player should hire a sportswriter to do the work. I was, on these accounts, a sneak and a snob and a scab.[57]

Jim Brosnan turned thirty in October of 1959. He had been playing professional baseball for a dozen years since joining the Chicago Cubs in 1954. After spending several years in the minor leagues, he was traded to the St. Louis Cardinals in 1958. At the start of 1959, Brosnan had a career mark of twenty-two wins and twenty-two losses. Never much of a starter, he had transformed himself into a relatively effective relief pitcher, the job he would hold throughout the remainder of his career. Well liked for his clever wit and irreverence, Brosnan had also earned a reputation as a baseball intellectual because he actually read books. He even kept books in his locker, sometimes referred to as a small clubhouse library. It was, therefore, not simply because he wore glasses that he came to be known as "Professor."

Brosnan was one of the first athletes to publish an unshackled personal account of the baseball season. Before Brosnan, baseball nonfiction tended toward the sort of "gee whiz!" sports page reportage that helped create and protect baseball's closed culture and unique red, white, and blue mythology. Hagiographic biographies of star players were written for adolescent readers and numerous superficial histories of the game were penned by otherwise talented writers like Fred Lieb. The majority of baseball books supposedly written by athletes were actually written with the assistance of a ghost writer—the relationship between Ford Frick and Babe Ruth being perhaps the most famous pairing of this sort.

The Long Season was Brosnan's account of his 1959 season, in which he was traded from St. Louis to Cincinnati at the midway point. After it hit the shelves, it was widely criticized by those who believed that Brosnan had violated the sacred sanctity of the clubhouse, breaking the unspoken rule that "what you see here stays here when you leave here." To be fair, however, *The Long Season* primarily dealt with the emotional aspects of the baseball season and rarely delved into salacious detail. Nevertheless, former players like Joe Garagiola, just emerging as a famous celebrity in his baseball retirement, slammed the book, characterizing Brosnan as a loner or rebel so as to imply that his views were aberrational and his account slanted and untruthful. Veteran writer Red Smith celebrated the book, however, reviewing it for the *New York Herald Tribune*—"it is a cocky book, caustic and candid and, in a way, courageous, for Brosnan calls them as he sees them, doesn't hesitate to name names, and employs ridicule like a stiletto."[58]

Despite the bellowing of critics, Brosnan never did quit writing. In fact, when his baseball career ended in 1963, he went on to a relatively prominent career as one of baseball's most literate commentators and even a short stint as a broadcaster. His second book, *Pennant Race* in 1962, was even more controversial than *The Long Season* because it actually dealt with the sticky issue of drug use in Major League Baseball. Of course, Brosnan himself was a chronic tobacco chewer, admitting that he couldn't kick the nasty habit until his baseball playing days were over. Everyone knew that baseball players used tobacco. More shocking was Brosnan's recollection of a conversation with the Cincinnati Reds' trainer:

> "Where's the Dexamyl, Doc?" I yelled at the trainer rooting about in his leather valise, "there's nothing in here but phenobarbital and that kind of stuff."
>
> "I don't have any more," said Doc Rohde. "Gave out the last one yesterday. Get more when we get home."
>
> "Been a rough road trip, huh, Doc? How'm I goin' to get through the day then? Order some more, Doc. It looks like a long season."
>
> "Try one of these," he said.
>
> "Geez, that's got opium in it. Whaddya think I am, an addict or something?"[59]

Although *The Long Season* and, to a somewhat lesser degree, *Pennant Race* are the most honest and still arguably the best examples of the sports-diary genre they bred, Brosnan's revelations, even the casual discussion of addictive painkillers, were for some reason far less stirring upon their publication than similar allegations, by a different, albeit highly indebted, author would prove in less than a decade's time.

For one thing, the baseball establishment of the early 1960s largely ignored Brosnan's books. Let the media criticize. Let retired veterans criticize. Let Brosnan's own teammates hold him accountable. The commissioner, the laconic Ford Frick, and other league officials simply chose not to make an issue of potentially controversial revelations. Then, too, Brosnan's books may have suffered for being bluntly honest, but not provocatively so. The stories he told, even about the drugs, were about the game and the season, not about off-the-field peccadilloes, recreational malfeasance, or extramarital sex.

In the wider context of the times, drug use (and abuse) may have become something of a passé topic. While radicals such as Timothy Leary encouraged young Americans to "tune in, turn on, and drop out" and while recreational drug use proliferated across the nation, baseball remained remarkably apart. It was, by reputation and image, a staid and square sport. Baseball had no answer to the colorful, politically combustible athletes who were starting to dominate that particular scene—boxing's Ali, or larger-than-life football star

Joe Namath, who picked up the mantle, no pun intended, of owning New York City's nightlife as the drink-hard Yankees were descending into obscure mediocrity.

By 1969, drugs, both licit and illicit, were an unavoidable reality of the sports world. The 1968 Mexico City Olympics had been the first in which drug testing had been a serious issue. Already troubling stories were emerging from the world of professional football about coaches and trainers who not only forced players to use amphetamine to inspire aggressiveness but who also discovered the utility of steroids. Baseball, despite the prominent role of painkillers in the highly publicized career of Sandy Koufax, operated under the powerful illusion that there was no drug problem in the ranks of the sport.

Perhaps unintentionally, baseball's spokesmen—players, writers, owners, officials—had endorsed a tension-filled twin narrative in regard to drug use. If you used drugs solely to enhance your performance, and in the 1960s this was regarded as highly unlikely by most sporting establishments, then you were a cheat. But Reno Bertoia's short affair with tranquilizers, which complicated this position, was conveniently forgotten. Hal Newhouser pitching the Tigers to victory while doped with Novocain—and numerous other occasions in other cities and with other players where this undoubtedly occurred—was ancient history and best forgotten as well. The official rule of thumb, as "Happy" Chandler laid out in his 1949 dealings with 20th Century Fox, was that baseball would tolerate no cheaters. It could sometimes overlook them, though.

However, if players were using drugs in order to play through pain, in a fashion that made it impossible to ignore the effort, then they were deemed to be performing heroically. And the player's courage was to be celebrated. It was a hopelessly inconsistent position: to all at once draw a hard line against cheating, while ignoring many obvious forms of what was technically cheating (the rules of nature if nothing else), and then celebrating the results of those efforts as the very pinnacle of performance.

So this was the curious position—which was really many positions and no position at all—that baseball held in the spring of 1969. It was that year that *Sports Illustrated* published a three-part series of groundbreaking articles by Bil Gilbert that, for the first time, exposed and questioned the use and misuse of drugs in the sporting world. Casting a critical eye on the sports officials who still insisted on pretending that "the most stimulating thing you got at a drugstore was a soda," Gilbert instead wrote about how athletes in many sports were "popping pills for more purposes than are dreamt in almost anybody's philosophy—or pharmacy."[60]

Baseball, having welcomed a new leader in February in the person of former legal counsel Bowie Kuhn as commissioner, was aiming to recover some of its lost prestige while also trying to avoid an imminent strike. The short version of immediate events looked something like this: Kuhn would work with MLBPA chief Marvin Miller to ward off a labor stoppage. To recapture the fans' interest with an expanded postseason, a new divisional alignment debuted, along with four new teams, in 1969. Despite these changes, baseball in 1969 was very much as it had been for most of the century: a conservative game, cloaked in a rich mythology, its eyes planted firmly on the past as it stumbled into the future. The game had a long, even celebrated, tradition of ignoring or celebrating alcoholism. Its economic foundations included unbreakable ties to the brewing and tobacco industries, a relationship at best regarded as a necessary evil, but mostly hailed as something charmingly American. But drugs?

Warren Giles, president of the National League, explained why there was nothing in baseball's rules about prohibition of drug use. There did not need to be. "Nothing has ever come to my attention that would require a special ruling," he said. "It never has come up, and I don't think it ever will." Bob Holbrook, an assistant executive in the American League, was even more unequivocal. "The American League has no rules regarding pep pills, painkillers, etc.," he intoned. "Baseball players don't use those types of things."[61]

When Robert Kerlan, who knew a great deal about baseball's drug culture, and who had been a prominent pioneer in it, warned that "the excessive and secretive use of drugs is likely to become a major athletic scandal, one that will shake public confidence in many sports," baseball ignored him. In the spring of 1969, no professional American sports league, and no sports league really beyond horse racing, had established any sort of antidoping rules.[62]

A year earlier, in 1968, the writer Leonard Schecter approached former New York Yankees pitcher Jim Bouton and asked him about following in the path of Jim Brosnan, writing down his experiences during a full-length Major League Baseball season. Perhaps offer something a little more irreverent, more provocative, and funnier than Brosnan. Bouton, whose career was on the skids, had been toying with keeping a diary during his final year in New York, having been impressed with *The Long Season*. Schecter's collaborative idea sounded like a good one. And so, as the expansion Seattle Pilots opened training in the spring of 1969, Bouton was there, pen in mind if not necessarily always in hand. The long spring of baseball's innocence was almost over.[63]

PART 2

This Is Your Game on Drugs

4

Pitching around the Problem

We have had no serious drug-abuse problems in Baseball
and the objectives of our program are to keep Baseball
free from any drug problem and thus protect the
enviable record that we have, to protect the honesty and
integrity of our game, and to protect the health
and safety of our players.

—Office of the Commissioner of Baseball,
Baseball vs. Drugs

"I'll decide what's good and what's bad for baseball. That's my job, not your job." Righteous indignation animated Bowie Kuhn, the commissioner of Major League Baseball. His ironclad statement of authority, though delivered as if he were addressing an unruly gang of children, belied the fact that the meeting over which he presided was definitely not going as planned. Proclaim the powers of his office though he might, Bowie Kuhn had not managed to fully grasp, much less control, the situation wherein he now found himself. For one thing, the meeting was supposed to be a secret, so naturally everybody knew about it. Instead of the select few that he had envisioned, an unexpected crowd had descended on his New York City office. His own aides were present, but so too were Players Association chief Marvin Miller, a perpetual thorn in the commissioner's side, as well as association attorney Dick Moss. Those two men had come to support and protect Jim Bouton, lately pitcher for the Houston Astros (in New York to play the Mets) and author of the forthcoming baseball "diary," *Ball Four*. It was that book, its potentially damaging revelations, and Bouton's perceived intransigence against traditional baseball codes that were the focus of the day's meeting.[1]

Had Kuhn desired absolute transparency and openness, he could not have asked for a better setup. Reporters from several papers had gotten wind of the meeting and were waiting outside, pens in hand. Bouton's publisher was there as well and, according to Kuhn, would in days after the meeting weave for the media a sensational (and exaggerated) tale of suppression and book banning. Bouton, facing the commissioner, was confident but kept his responses close to the vest—Miller had warned him before entering the meeting that he should keep relatively quiet and let Commissioner Kuhn hang himself. Bouton's assertion, in defense of *Ball Four*'s candid revelations, that fans were tired of the "phony, goody-goody" image baseball was perpetuating, had inspired Kuhn's steely reprimand. Kuhn, for his part, was already wishing that he had simply ignored both Bouton and his book. The gallows were raised.[2]

Ball Four, the irreverent book about Bouton's 1969 campaign with the expansion Seattle Pilots, featured what was then startling insight into baseball's sophomoric, often crude, seemingly contradictory culture of boyish immaturity masked by excessive masculine posturing. Many of the book's juiciest segments had already been excerpted in several *Look* magazine articles. Nobody was yet accusing Bouton of discovering a new genre—a decade earlier Jim Brosnan, a fellow pitcher, had written two very good diary-form books giving fans an insider's view of the game. The Detroit Tigers catcher Bill Freehan had his own diary, *Behind the Mask*, headed toward release at that very moment. Unlike his peers, however, Bouton's approach was less serious. He seemingly took delight in exposing the sexual hijinks (sometimes of the extramarital variety) of baseball players, offering a full report on the popular ballplayer hobby known as "beaver shooting"—a pastime where ballplayers attempt to get a look up the skirts of female fans in the stands above the dugout. More problematically to many critics, including Kuhn, drugs featured prominently in Bouton's story. Jim Brosnan had described, in brief, what had seemed a benignly therapeutic drug culture emerging in 1960s clubhouses. Bouton, on the other hand, asserted that the use and abuse of uppers was widespread in baseball and that "many players could not function without them."[3]

Both Bouton and Miller argued that modern fans wanted this taste of reality, not saccharine artificiality. The Rockwellian image that baseball had crafted out of its own past was, in fact, myth. Players were *not* paragons of purity. They smoked, drank, and had sex just like everybody else in the country. Could Kuhn deny the long-standing romance with players like Grover Cleveland Alexander or Rube Waddell, bourbon connoisseurs from way back, whose excesses were an inherent part of their charm? Youngsters growing up in the age of Babe Ruth knew the Bambino was fond of tobacco, women (not always his own wife), and drink, but such revelations did not stop him from becoming not only the idol of his own age but also the very embodiment of the pastime for all ages.[4]

Kuhn was unmoved. Having reminded the audience that he, the commissioner, was arbiter of what was best for baseball, he now wanted answers. In particular, he wanted to know about the use of drugs in Major League Baseball. How widespread was it? *Ball Four* suggested that "greenies" had infiltrated all levels of the game, that they were practically as common as Cracker Jack. How much truth was there behind that assertion? Who, Kuhn asked, was using amphetamine? Bouton responded that it was all there in the book. Don Mincher, one of Bouton's teammates, had claimed half the guys in the league used them, "almost the whole Baltimore team . . . [and] [m]ost of the Tigers" were taking them. Jim Bouton was in no position to doubt Don Mincher. As far as he knew, a lot of players took "greenies." He had taken them.[5]

Unable to cow either Bouton or the Players Association people, Kuhn tried to save face. He told them he was not going to take any action at this time, but that he wanted the meeting to serve as a warning. The canny Miller jumped into action. "A warning against what?" he asked in his forthright way. Miller, the "quiet, mild, exceedingly understated man," who had once gone toe-to-toe with the heavies of big industry while working for the steel union, was not intimidated by Kuhn's Ivy League air or empty pronouncements of power. Was it, he asked, a warning against writing? How could the commissioner police writing? Was that not a tyranny anathema to values baseball supposedly symbolized? Kuhn blustered, claimed that he could not get specific, and that everybody understood what he was talking about anyway. In truth, there was nothing he could do. And he knew it. The entire episode was practically a microcosm of Bowie Kuhn's commissionership.

*   *   *

Bowie Kent Kuhn was the antithesis of Jim Bouton: staid and conservative where Bouton was liberal and irreverent. Bouton, the iconoclast, challenged the myths of Major League Baseball. Kuhn believed in what he called the Rip Van Winkle Theory: "that a man from 1910 must be able to wake up after being asleep for 70 years, walk into a ballpark and understand baseball perfectly." The game, much less its sacrosanct myths, was and should remain changeless. The very picture of a baseball establishment figure, Kuhn would have been ideally suited to the commissionership in an earlier age. Now, with the establishment in America everywhere under assault, Kuhn was destined to play the role of an increasingly beleaguered defender of an outmoded vision of both the national game and the national life.

When the lords of baseball dismissed the pathetically incompetent General William D. "Spike" Eckert from the commissioner's office at the end of 1968, eyes immediately turned to Kuhn. His résumé was impressive. A native of the Beltway, Kuhn had graduated with an economics degree from Princeton and later had taken his law degree from the University of Virginia. He joined the prestigious New York City law firm of Willkie, Farr & Gallagher. That firm represented baseball's National League, and Kuhn served as counselor to the league when the city of Milwaukee brought suit after the Braves moved to Atlanta at the end of 1965. Some critics later said he was chosen because he was a puppet of Los Angeles Dodgers owner Walter O'Malley, the perceived lord of the lords. Others rightly noted that Kuhn was bright, loved the game, and had a good working knowledge of the industry, something Eckert woefully lacked.[6]

Kuhn was both a logical and interesting choice to assume Major League Baseball's highest office. He was, although his subsequent reputation would never suggest it, a relatively young man, having turned forty-two in 1969. He looked like a commissioner. At six foot five, Kuhn was physically imposing and impossibly straight; he cultivated the image of a man rigidly devoted to baseball's integrity. Although often depicted as a tool of the owners, and a feckless enemy of the Players Association, Kuhn was, so far as any commissioner could be, his own man. He had grown up loving the hapless Washington Senators—and, in fact, he worked as a scoreboard operator at Griffith Stadium for several seasons. Few men to sit at the top of the baseball hierarchy could honestly claim more sincere passion for the game. But Kuhn also regarded the commissioner as the absolute arbiter of baseball's image, protector of the virtues the young Kuhn had so eagerly associated with the game, an impartial judge of players who stepped off that traditional path. Kuhn believed in the totality of the commissioner's powers. Ignoring the reality that his predecessors had established a mostly laissez-faire commissionership, Kuhn intended to be an activist chief, a commissioner-as-absolutist.[7]

"The commissioner exists to tell the owners what to do and not the other way around," Kuhn once claimed. Convinced that the ideal model of commissionership had been Kenesaw Mountain Landis, one of his boyhood heroes, Bowie Kuhn struggled for fifteen seasons to match the judge, perpetually locked in a chaotic tug-of-war between obdurate owners, unwilling to let Kuhn exercise power as he saw fit, and the Players Association, insistent on breaking down ancient economic barriers and remaking the sport's labor relations. Kuhn was described by Marvin Miller as a man haunted by both an adversarial press—they called him a "dunderhead" and a "stuffed shirt"—and his own unrealistic expectations about the possibilities and limits of his own office.[8]

Historians have typically, and not without good reason, emphasized the labor struggles of Kuhn's tenure and the personal strife that marked his relationship with union chief Marvin Miller. The two men were never close, often firing barbs at each other in both the press and later in published personal memoirs. The labor wars of Kuhn's tenure, marked by devastating strikes in 1972 and 1981, as well as the landmark 1972 Supreme Court decision in Curt Flood's infamous reserve clause case, grabbed the big headlines. It is easy to read the story of baseball under Kuhn as one of labor strife alone, but it was actually the evolving struggle to deal with drug abuse that best illustrated Kuhn's vision of the commissionership. Labor activism remade baseball despite Kuhn's best efforts to keep the game staid. The fight against an emergent drug problem provided the means for Kuhn to counter those changes by consolidating power in his office.[9]

In confronting baseball's nascent drug crisis, Bowie Kuhn would routinely exercise power in a Landisian manner (akin to that of Judge Kenesaw Mountain Landis, the game's most powerful commissioner, who towered, dictatorially, over baseball from 1920 to 1944), only to watch as opposing forces, either from within his own establishment or from without, in the MLBPA, confounded him. In an abstract sense, Kuhn's struggle to rule drugs out of baseball while concentrating absolute power in the commissioner's office connected the game more closely to the transformative political culture of the 1970s, linking baseball not only to the escalation in the war on drugs but also to a broader sports establishment in a seemingly perpetual state of crisis. In the course of the struggle, Kuhn would establish a crucial legacy in the highest office of the game: the fight against drugs was never really as much about drugs, about player health, or about integrity as it was about power and keeping the forces of social change at bay.

The June 1970 meeting between Bouton and Kuhn in the commissioner's New York office was just a small flashpoint in a growing crisis that involved not just Major League Baseball but also professional and amateur sports around the globe. By the end of the 1960s it was increasingly obvious that drugs, both performance enhancing and recreational, had become a significant problem in the world of sport. The International Olympic Committee (IOC) instituted drug testing, not always effectively, at the 1968 Mexico City games. Professional soccer leagues in Europe moved to crack down on doping. Rumors that the

Italian national team was using pep pills had surfaced at the 1962 World Cup and had become louder in the years after. FIFA was now encouraging the national leagues to do their utmost to eradicate the use of drugs. Horse racing instituted complex testing routines and harsh penalties for chemical abuses. Bil Gilbert's series of groundbreaking articles for *Sports Illustrated* in 1969 exposed a problem far more pervasive and dangerous than most spectators would ever have dreamed. Then, suddenly, insiders in all the major American sports began to come forward with a bevy of tales to horrify the God-fearing, Chevrolet-sporting, virtue and apple pie crowd.[10]

Ball Four was just one of a number of popular books that emerged from the crisis of what Robert Lipsyte aptly called "Sportsworld." Former St. Louis Cardinals footballer Dave Meggyesy shocked readers with his exposé of the violent, drug-riddled culture of the gridiron. Jack Scott, Paul Hoch, Harry Edwards, and Arnold Mandell published, or were about to publish, works that exposed racial and financial inequalities, savaged the culture of exploitation, and lamented the growing reliance on drugs in both pro and amateur leagues. Tom Meschery's *Over the Rim*, a book of poetry published the same year as Bouton's diary, implied rampant amphetamine use in the basketball world. *Ball Four's* revelations, and the publicity engendered by Kuhn's hapless attempt to muzzle Bouton, were the primary catalyst that drew professional baseball into this dizzy maelstrom. Baseball, as were all other sports, and indeed all of society, was facing a growing drug problem. Something had to be done, but what?[11]

This was the question that Bowie Kuhn inherited, the question that perplexed him through the remainder of his tenure as commissioner. During the 1970s, Major League Baseball, along with other major American sports, took its first tentative steps toward comprehensively addressing the abuse of drugs in the game. These efforts, particularly on baseball's end, were complicated by the game's traditional laissez-faire position on matters of personal privacy and performance, by rapid and confusing changes in American society and culture, and by the looming shadow of congressional action should the league fail to act.

* * *

Baseball, more than any other sport, struggled against the social upheaval of the late 1960s and early 1970s. Baseball, particularly in the age of television, was a tightly packaged product, one that had become a symbol of the stodgy "silent majority" of Middle Americans that Richard Nixon was courting. Baseball lived in the past, relishing golden memories of more meaningful yesteryears. It lacked the violent thunder of football and the funky urban flow of basketball. Unlike those sports, baseball had no truly flamboyant black leaders—no Ali, no Walt Frazier, no Johnny Sample. At the dawn of the 1970s, baseball was content to be as white and studiously square as it had been in the 1950s. In a sense, Bowie Kuhn was helming a ship built of century-old timbers, stately, proud, but creaking badly as it steered into the howling winds of a storm it was not rigged to survive. Critics suggested that the game was losing relevance. *Ball Four* was just a warning shot across the bow.

Kuhn's bumbling attempt to exercise absolute power was not the sole reason that *Ball Four* became a sensation. *Ball Four* was truly a book for its time. Forces throughout American society were challenging the establishment. In 1970 shots rang out and four students died when the National Guard of Ohio confronted demonstrators against the Vietnam War on the campus of Kent State. Questions, heated questions, were being raised about the choices made by American leadership. Vietnam had become a quagmire, and certain now that the administration of Lyndon Johnson had been less than honest as to why they had escalated the conflict in Vietnam, many Americans wanted to know why the administration of Richard Nixon not only stayed there but had also carried the war into neighboring Cambodia. Elsewhere, the macho subculture of major professional sports was being assailed, if only peripherally, by varied personal liberation movements born in the social tumult of the 1960s. Wave after wave of feminism, black liberation, and gay liberation movements all threatened the traditional notions of manhood and masculinity that thrived in the big leagues.[12]

The jock mentality that Bouton exposed in *Ball Four* still dominated the sports world in 1970. The modern player might be a creature part playboy and part athlete, but sport was still regarded as essentially a character-building exercise. It was a contest in which exhibition of manly potency was paramount. One did not need a Vince Lombardi speech to affirm that successful athletic performance was the best measure of real, healthy masculinity in a fractured world. Defenders of tradition, confronted by liberal critics, celebrated this intensely competitive image of sport. Ohio State football coach Woody Hayes suggested that the purifying wars of the playing field were a last glimpse of what was right about America. Paradoxically, it was this celebration of machismo that had been the catalyst for decades of drug abuse. Now, in the 1970s, the same cult of machismo was mistakenly deemed to be a last shield against the same threat.

The illusion of the Major League player as a macho paragon was an extension of the game's anachronistic values and politics. Journalists, whose livelihood depended on the game, helped polish a veneer on players who, in reality, were mixed up in drugs, were hopeless drunks or womanizers, or were just plain mean. Writers outside of the baseball establishment more readily caught on to the game's singular contradiction. Rock music critic Robert Christgau noted the dominant theory in baseball: a player should only be judged by his performance. What happens *on the field* is *the* thing. But baseball, Christgau explained, was very different from other, more outwardly exciting sports. Baseball required fans to invest emotion not just in the game but also in the players. So while baseball might preach the performance ethic, it simultaneously created and protected illusory visions of heroics, purity, and masculine vigor. By revealing unfortunate truths about some of the most iconic players in baseball, writers like Bouton were threatening one of the traditional foundations of the game.[13]

Jim Bunning, the Phillies pitcher and future U.S. senator from Kentucky, charged that what was flawed with *Ball Four* was what was wrong with the country. It was too much sex and too many drugs. Jim Turner, pitching coach for the Yankees, said that the book would go over brilliantly in the Soviet Union. Jimmy Ray of the Astros, according to Bouton, was less concerned with appearances or tradition than he was with preserving the availability of uppers. "If the commissioner cuts off greenies because of your God-damned book," he allegedly said to Bouton, "I personally will snipe your ass."[14]

* * *

Although Richard Nixon would share photo-ops with celebrity antidrug spokesmen and deliver stirring admonitions honoring those who performed public service announcements in his new war on drugs, it was ultimately the U.S. Congress that took the lead in the fight. Their first step was to pass legislation restricting the availability of amphetamine—clearly a drug that tempted misuse not only in sports but in domestic life as well, but a drug that President Nixon virtually ignored. In June 1973, as Nixon and his henchman grew mired in the Watergate debacle, Indiana senator Birch Bayh, chairman of the Senate Juvenile Delinquency Subcommittee, targeted the sports world and opened hearings focused on the improper use and abuse of drugs by athletes. Although the primary focus of the hearings was drug use in high school and college, the discussion ranged widely into both amateur and professional athletics. Its findings were dramatic and troubling. Whatever notion existed that drug use was a phenomenon of the counterculture was quickly put to rest. "So often, people isolate freaky kids when it comes to drugs," said one witness. "But using drugs in sports is not just something so-called freaky kids do."[15]

In the House of Representatives, the Subcommittee on Investigations, chaired by Rep. Harley Staggers (D-WV), was already one year into research on the subject. However, whereas the testimony and findings of Bayh's committee would be transparent and open, the Staggers committee operated behind closed doors. Although they would also summarize their findings as shocking and troubling, they dealt in generalizations to avoid inspiring any young athletes seeking to emulate their heroes. The hope was that the major professional leagues would take the potential of further investigation and action as a warning. Staggers, in particular, hoped that league offices would police their own sports based on the findings of his committee.[16]

In a very broad sense, the massive report produced by Bayh's committee exposed a number of troubling realities. Most notable was the broad sense that the very ethic of sports in America was at the heart of the drug problem. Winning had superseded the betterment of the athlete in both mind and body, the perpetuation of a perfect masculinity, the championing of fairness, and the path toward equality. As Bayh repeatedly insisted, "I believe it is important to win, but that how the game is played is equally important." Rep. Ronald Dellums (D-CA) stated that drugs had become the most significant problem in the world of sport. "We've allowed the major sports to become more concerned with winning than the health, welfare, and needs of each individual player."[17]

The question of how each sport could best address the "health, welfare, and needs of each individual player" became the central question of the Bayh hearings. During days of testimony from college athletic directors, coaches, amateur athletes, medical experts, and social critics, the answers were varied. Some insisted that drugs were a problem that could only be dealt with through strict testing and harsh penalties. Drugs, they said, were a symptom of cultural and moral decline and excessive permissiveness rooted in the 1960s. Like the Nixon administration, they saw law and order as the obvious answer.[18]

The law-and-order crowd insisted that control must be established now, and at every level: control at the ports, control of access to pills, to cough syrup, to the entire pharmaceutical cornucopia. The entirety of American culture was problematically drug oriented. TV, they argued, tells us to take a glass of something or just take a pill. The entire nation was being oriented to take something to relieve the situation rather than using their mental capacities to fix it. "By the time they are 20," one speaker noted, "today's children will have watched approximately 15,000 hours of television. They will have seen numerous commercials telling them that drugs can calm their stomach, quiet their nerves, clear their complexion, improve their performance on the job, and relieve their aches and pains. They grow up thinking drugs are the answer. Society has created this culture, in a sense, and the medical profession has had a part in it." The drug problem was a Frankenstein's monster created by the pharmaceutical community that wanted to sell the drugs, the medical community that endorsed the drugs, and the public who—eager for wonder treatments—purchased the drugs.[19]

Others took a more provocative stance, locating the roots of the drug problem in issues of race and pervasive social inequality. Athletes were introduced to drugs before they ever left the mean streets of a ghetto home. In other instances the systemically authoritarian nature of sports exponentially increased pressure on athletes. Where there were performance-enhancing drugs, there was the constant moral pressure to avoid them, but the countervailing knowledge that competitors around you were taking them. In a sports world where it seemed athletes had many decisions to make, they actually had the power to make few, if any, real decisions. The pressure to use drugs increased along with the pressure to perform at an elite level. Therefore, any realistic answer to the problem of drug abuse in sports had to start not with testing, but with the structural problems of an authoritarian sporting universe. That meant starting at the professional level.[20]

Almost everyone agreed that testing was an ideal solution, but it was also far too expensive. And there were other concerns with testing. Where there was testing, there were new drugs specially developed to get around the tests—the East Germans were noted pioneers in the field of progressive chemical duplicity. Drug tests were a panacea. The best long-term response was, instead, an emphasis on careful self-policing and education—lots and lots of education. And the model for the response had to come from the professional leagues—the implication being that it was drug use at *that* level that served as the catalyst for drug use at all others. What the pros used, the amateurs copied. This relationship was in evidence throughout almost every story told by witnesses before the Bayh committee.[21]

Bowie Kuhn, along with Pete Rozelle of the National Football League and Walter Kennedy of the National Basketball Association, claimed in the wake of the Bayh hearings that their leagues had long supported antidrug programs. Rozelle mandated the placement of an antidrug poster in every NFL team locker room. Kuhn acknowledged the direness of the problem but insisted that drugs were not really a serious problem in baseball, primarily because his sport was not nearly as violent as football. "But," Kuhn added, "[Major League Baseball is] aware that we have to keep a constant vigil as to the dangers of drug use."[22]

For his part, Bowie Kuhn was confident that whatever problems might confront baseball in the early 1970s, they were far less profound than those accosting the other two major American professional sports. In the NBA the focus was increasingly on recreational drug use. Performance enhancement was not an issue on the hard court, although some critics raised ethical concerns about the use of carbocaine to get New York Knicks star Willis Reed through his brief, celebrated appearance against the Los Angeles Lakers in the 1970 NBA finals. Reed's presence proved to be an emotional and symbolic lift for the Knicks, who went on to secure the league championship.[23]

But the Reed issue was trivial. Dr. Stan Lorber, team physician for the Philadelphia 76ers, noted that "in professional basketball you are dealing with a community of young people. Young people smoke marijuana and take other drugs. Basketball players are people, no different from anyone else in society." Nate Archibald, a top-flight scorer for the Kansas City Kings, agreed but added that there was an important sporting dynamic behind drug use as well. Archibald explained that many players felt that getting high would relax them and ease the increasing pressure of performance. To that end, he admitted, there was "a lot of smoking marijuana going on in the NBA."[24]

Major League Baseball suffered none of the heavy public relations hits that the NBA and NFL endured in the 1970s. Nevertheless, there was a growing sense that baseball was actually just as deeply mired in the crisis as its sister leagues. Bob Bauman, trainer for the baseball Cardinals as well as St. Louis University, a man with forty-six years of experience in the sports world, suggested that professional baseball was actually the gateway by which amphetamines had entered the other sports. "They were sometimes recommended to a player with weight problems," he explained of the old days. "Maybe they didn't help him reduce, but he got the idea they gave him more pep. So he told a thin guy about them."[25]

In the end, each of the leagues acquiesced quietly with the demands of the two congressional committees, establishing sometimes convoluted systems of self-policing. In the National Hockey League former FBI agent Frank Torpey headed up "Torpey's Raiders." Jack Danahy of the FBI and Bernie Jackson, formerly of the Justice Department, served the NFL by investigating gambling allegations but also looked into issues of potential drug abuse. Major League Baseball had former St. Louis policeman and FBI man Henry Fitzgibbon on the job. It was regarded as a relatively easy one.[26]

As Bing Devine, general manager of the Cardinals, noted, Fitzgibbon could rely on the first and best education program in professional sports. Bowie Kuhn, to his credit (and he regularly gave it to himself even if others did not), had been the first major sports leader to respond to Staggers's call for self-policing. In a press release from May 1973, Chairman Staggers wrote, "based on the constructive responses and assurances I have received from these gentlemen, I think self-regulation will be intensified, and will be effective."[27]

Whatever the league offices might do, athletes from each of the major professional leagues looked dubiously at the findings of the Bayh and Staggers committees. Ernie McMillan, tackle for the Cardinals, summed up the attitude of the players succinctly: "those cats are about five years late."[28]

* * *

Bowie Kuhn had actually taken action against drug abuse *before* the congressional hearings. Perhaps baseball made so few appearances in the hearings because, alone of the major American sports, it was taking a proactive stance—minimalist though it was—against the problem. In his memoirs, Bowie Kuhn called drug abuse one of the two great nightmares of his time as commissioner, the other being the strike of 1981 (and labor woes more generally). He recalled that when he took office in 1969, he never dreamed he would see drug abuse reach the dimensions that it ultimately would by the 1980s. Mindful of the problems from the beginning, or aware of them after *Ball Four* shattered his illusions, Kuhn claimed that he initially became aware through press reports that some players were routinely using "greenies." Retaining drug expert Dr. Garrett O'Connor of Johns Hopkins University on staff, Kuhn consulted with him and the various club presidents. On April 5, 1971, Kuhn issued a directive called "Notice No. 12," which established baseball's drug education and prevention program, the first of its kind in American professional sports.[29]

Not everyone in the baseball establishment was happy with Kuhn's program. Bob Short, troublesome owner of the Washington Senators, argued that baseball was actually making itself look worse than other sports that had more serious drug problems. Short was also concerned that if Kuhn took command of the situation, as he appeared to be doing, next might come player suspensions. Should Kuhn successfully concentrate that kind of power in his office, he might then present a formidable opponent to owners inclined to challenge the establishment—and Bob Short was first on just such a list, already harboring plans to move the Senators to Texas.

By almost any standard, the 1971 program was typical of baseball's attitude toward drugs during the Kuhn era. On one hand, and to Kuhn's delight, it promised the potential consolidation of power in the commissioner's office.

On the other, and more fundamentally, it offered a relatively innocuous, much-hyped program in response to a problem acknowledged, in baseball terms, as nothing more than trivial. In other words, it was a win-win for Kuhn—good public relations and potential empowerment.[30]

Oddly enough, the primary purpose of the commissioner's drug abuse program was not to help Major Leaguers, but to educate youngsters just starting out in baseball. It was once suggested that Kuhn was inspired to act by charges of widespread involvement by baseball players with anabolic steroids, greenies, and goofballs. Many players resented the implication of widespread performance enhancement and were wary of backing Kuhn—joining the cause would be an admission of guilt. Jack Aker, player rep for the New York Yankees, explained how players quickly lined up behind the commissioner once they discovered that the target of the program was educating kids.[31]

With the Bayh hearings on the horizon, organized baseball began holding seminars during spring training camps for Major and Minor League players and administrative personnel. Said Kuhn at the time, "we have young people coming in all the time and we know they've been exposed to drugs." The league introduced an educational booklet, *Baseball vs. Drugs: An Education and Prevention Program*, which was distributed not only to players but also to public school libraries. Later, in 1978, baseball finally added alcohol as a specially abused drug and instituted another new education program involving former Brooklyn Dodgers pitcher Don Newcombe, a recovering alcoholic himself. It would prove to be a second public relations coup. It was widely held that by the end of the decade that Fitzgibbon's security personnel and Kuhn's education program had eliminated Major League Baseball's relatively small-scale drug problem. In his autobiography Kuhn wrote proudly about how seriously baseball had taken the problem, especially since free agency (one of his landmark defeats) had sent the player's disposable income (and predilection toward drug abuse) skyrocketing after 1975.[32]

Because Kuhn had acted on the drug problem before congressional involvement, and because he was quick to comply with congressional pressure, he was celebrated by the *Sporting News* for his candid response. Kuhn linked the baseball program with the wider national War on Drugs by having the league pamphlet focus primarily on dangerous street narcotics. *Baseball vs. Drugs* explained that drug use was the result of countercultural social unrest and youth rebellion. The road to manhood, best exemplified by professional athletes, necessitated hard choices. Drugs, the pamphlet explained, exploited the fear of youngsters about the hardship of growing up. Along with President Nixon, he encouraged players to become active in community action programs. Nothing Kuhn had achieved, or would achieve, reporters wrote, "rivals in significance his drug education and prevention program."[33]

Those who took a closer look at the commissioner's celebrated program proclaimed it nothing more than a well-conceived publicity stunt. Some baseball players saw the program as a sham. Lou Brock, the speedy Cardinals outfielder, called baseball's program neither preventive nor corrective. Jack Scott was emphatic when arguing that, despite every revelation since 1968, the NCAA, NFL, and Major League Baseball all launched education programs that did little to address the actual drug problem within the sports world. *Baseball vs. Drugs* was typical of the weak professional response. In its pages there was no mention of steroids, but plenty of obscure information about the opium poppy, codeine, and morphine. In the meantime, the booklet perpetuated the stereotype that drug problems were restricted to hippies, ghetto dwellers, and other so-called undesirables. It summoned young players to achieve pure masculine virtue by contrasting healthy American manhood with a feminine, dangerously extreme, drug-addled "other." It gave the public the comfortable, but useless, notion that if they "can get Johnny to cut his hair and try out for the football team, they will have the drug problem licked."[34]

* * *

George Vecsey, in his short history of baseball, quoted an anonymous player: "the funniest thing I ever saw in baseball was Pete Rose's greenies kicking in during a rain delay." In September 1979, Rose gave a provocative interview to *Playboy* magazine in which he displayed an alarming arrogance along with a vague, often coy, attitude toward the issue of drug use in the game. Pointing out his own performance and referring to himself as the number one player in baseball, Rose celebrated his ability to get hits, sell the game, and make a lot of money. Although he tried to dance around the question, Rose eventually admitted to using amphetamine as a way to lose weight and gain more energy. Although Rose suggested the effects of amphetamine were probably placebo, he never denied that the placebo wasn't useful or desirable. "There might be a night when you play a doubleheader." he explained, "and you go to the ballpark the next day for a Sunday afternoon game. You just want to take a diet pill to mentally think you are up."[35]

By 1980, Rose was one of several veteran players poised to help push the Philadelphia Phillies over the playoff hump and on to a World Series championship. On July 8, 1980, a story appeared in the *Trenton Times* reporting that Pennsylvania authorities wanted to question at least eight members of the Phillies about allegedly acquiring amphetamine pills illegally from a Reading, Pennsylvania, physician, Dr. Patrick Mazza, a fifty-six-year-old family practitioner who worked as a team doctor for the Phillies Double-A club in Reading. Mike Schmidt, Larry Bowa, Greg Luzinski, and Pete Rose were among the players identified in the story. Schmidt and Rose denied the allegations, calling them totally ridiculous, but they were still asked to testify in court. Said Mazza: "I'm angry and puzzled." He told the press that it was not good medical practice to prescribe drugs without a physical examination and claimed that he had never done so.[36]

On July 12 Philadelphia owner Rudy Carpenter called a press conference wherein he insisted that none of his players had broken any laws and that the allegations were all speculative. He added that the Phillies had continually cautioned their players against the use of drugs and that the team's trainers did not dispense drugs without a doctor's prescription. But Bill Conlin of the *Daily News* believed that the players were not totally innocent, even though the investigation focused primarily on Dr. Mazza. The veteran sportswriter, who covered most of the Reading story as it unfolded, knew all about greenies. He had watched Larry Hisle's career go down the drain because of a probable dependency on amphetamine. Now he asserted that everyone in baseball was using amphetamine, and that if you wanted to get the really good stuff, you went to the trainer or your wife (who could usually get a prescription for using the drug as a dietary aid). Dr. Mazza, suggested Conlin, supplied the drugs because he liked being around the players.[37]

The Reading scandal was the only high-profile baseball drug scandal revolving entirely around greenies. Pete Rose, who all but admitted using the pills while simultaneously denying their utility, was typical of the entire era that stretched back to the end of World War II, but that had been most famously exposed by *Ball Four* in 1970. Legal or not, baseball players had access to amphetamine. They used it regularly. It was a serious problem, one largely unaddressed by the league's much hyped drug program.

Reading was a blip on the radar. The effort on behalf of education continued. Kuhn was especially enamored with Operation CORK, the drug and alcohol abuse prevention program started by the San Diego Padres ownership group. Operation CORK financed highly trained doctors like Dr. Joe Pursch and Joe Takamme to organize seminars on drug and alcohol abuse. McDonalds owners Ray and Joan Kroc had created Operation CORK ("Kroc" spelled backward) to deal with alcoholism within their own fast-food business, and they now wanted Major League Baseball and parties from the other major sports involved.

Some of these seminars were convened prior to the 1981 season. Even Marvin Miller, the chief of the MLBPA, was impressed with the program. "The Operation CORK program urges chemical abusers to come forward to seek treatment," he explained. But there were still problems. "But what concerned me," added Miller, "is how they can come forward without putting other players in some kind of legal jeopardy."[38]

Bob Welch's appearance and commentary was the highlight of the seminar according to Bowie Kuhn. Welch, a hard-throwing pitcher with the Los Angeles Dodgers, had checked himself into rehab at the end of the 1970s in order to conquer debilitating alcoholism. Inspired by Welch's story, the assembled CORK professionals urged the creation of employee assistance programs (EAPs) by each club in the Major Leagues to deal with alcohol and other drug problems. The EAPs would provide expert professional help for baseball employees and would follow the successful pattern of such programs in other industries. At the league's annual meeting in Dallas, Kuhn, still enamored with the possibilities of education, asked the clubs to give consideration to establishing EAPs. Some did. Many did not.[39]

In early 1981, grappling with the labor dispute that would result in the June strike, Kuhn suddenly decided it was time to update baseball's aging drug program. The league presidents and Kuhn therefore announced a new program in July that provided for severe discipline for involvement with dangerous drugs or trafficking in any kind of illegal drugs. It was a dramatic switch from education toward a law-and-order paradigm. That said, the new program did provide for players such as Welch or Darryl Porter, players who came forward voluntarily for treatment, and who would not be subject to disciplinary action. While clubs were urged to impose their own discipline for drug violations, Kuhn reserved the right to pass final judgment from on high whenever he felt necessary. Kuhn showed, in reserving that power for himself, that he had little confidence in the willingness of individual clubs to discipline their own personnel. When it came to enforcing punishment, in other words, the clubs themselves *would* not do it. Kuhn soon found that, try though he might, he *could* not do it either.[40]

That the various education programs of the major American sports had failed was about to become tragically obvious. Nevertheless, most of the establishment stuck to their guns and insisted that whatever problems existed could be eliminated by more education, by convoluted and paternalistic league policies, and—in the end—by categorical denial. Mostly, big money professional sports simply could not acknowledge or address systemic drug problems in their leagues without badly damaging valuable brand images and alienating the public. NBA star Bill Walton argued that the major sports leagues "hushe[d] up drug cases because they are in conflict with what the public wants to believe about athletes." "Sports," he said, "inspire misplaced hopes in fans—or perhaps a misplaced sense of morals. They want athletes to set high standards—not to use drugs. In fact, they insist upon it to the point of refusing to see what's going on. Many pro teams are traveling pharmacies, with cocaine being the current drug of preference. So much cocaine is snorted in the NBA that if 10 players sneezed at once, you could bet that one or two of them was losing money."[41]

Art Fuss, assistant director of security for Major League Baseball, said, "Everybody knows there is a lot of cocaine use. With the obvious increase in the use of drugs (in our society), we cannot ignore the fact that our players have a kind of celebrity status and they have high paychecks. They are not immune. We do have a great concern about the situation. But we try to do it (prevent drug use) with education rather than a heavy hand."[42]

Within baseball the debate continued as to whether there was or was not a problem. Darrell Evans of the San Francisco Giants insisted that "if there is drug use, I'm not aware of it. I haven't seen it here or when I was with the Braves." On the other side, a pitcher who had been with four clubs in both leagues requested anonymity before commenting: "The commissioner is going to be very busy if he intends to take action. I guess 85% take amphetamines." Insiders claimed that there are two or three players with every club who needed help and who were not seeking it under the existing education program. San Diego club president Ballard Smith said, "I don't think there is a team in the majors that doesn't have an alcohol problem, ours included." Others admitted that the drug problem was a long festering one. "In my day," said one old timer, "I saw a former MVP go downhill because of drug use. He was hooked and he deluded himself into thinking it helped. In fact, the drugs were deteriorating his body."[43]

Milwaukee general manager Harry Dalton offered a uniquely insightful observation about the misguided notion that average fans, and most writers, and almost the entire establishment had about baseball players. "People like to think of baseball players as white knights riding down the middle-of-the-road. They're just normal, average people who have the ability to earn their living playing a sport. They still have problems just like everybody else."[44]

* * *

On the street they called cocaine "White Girl," "Flake," or "C." Sometimes they called it "Snow." The blizzard hit the nation unawares, falling softly, drifting, largely ignored until it was too late. In the summer of 1979 the House of Representatives held hearings wherein Select Committee chairman Tennyson Guyer lamented, "this is a drug which, for the most part, has been ignored and its increased use in our society has caught us unprepared to cope effectively with this menace."[45]

A relic of late nineteenth-century drug culture, cocaine had been "rediscovered" in the 1970s and by the end of that decade had become enormously popular. Cocaine's ascendance coincided with an increase in recreational drug use in America. Based on surveys from 1979, the National Institute on Drug Abuse (NIDA) found that 68 percent of those in the eighteen to twenty-five age bracket had puffed marijuana at one time or another, and 28 percent had experimented with cocaine. By 1981 those figures were much higher.[46]

A large part of cocaine's appeal, and what made abuse of the drug so tragic, was the belief that it was not deemed addictive. It was, in light of such belief, safer than cigarettes. More importantly, unlike psychedelic drugs, cocaine didn't appear to affect productivity. In the mid-1970s, University of Massachusetts professor Ralph Whitehead proclaimed that "the new morality of young America is success, the high-performance ethic." Cocaine allowed young adults to balance a desire for excitement and indulgence with the need for high performance. It seemed to be the ideal drug for the ambitious and well-to-do. A 1978 article in *People* magazine profiled a generation obsessed with "productivity" and explained that "Coke is really easy—a toot here, a toot there . . . it's a neat drug—makes you feel good, you can function on it." By the early 1980s a youthful, ambitious American "high society" was engaged in a torrid love affair with the drug.[47]

Cocaine had, in fact, become something of a status symbol in middle- and upper-class society. *Newsweek*, as early as 1971, had described cocaine as "the status symbol of the American middle-class pothead." A Chicago Bureau of Narcotics agent even extolled the drug's virtues, noting how "you get a good high with coke and you don't get hooked." Ballplayers, their pocketbooks newly engorged by late 1970s economic transformations, were drawn to this safe, stylish, drug of the new elite.[48]

In a 1977 harbinger of the coming storm, Bill North of the Oakland Athletics had been arrested on charges of possessing and planning to distribute cocaine. The next year, the *Sporting News* followed up with an editorial announcing that cocaine had overtaken marijuana as the recreational drug of choice. Cocaine, however, was exactly the kind of drug that the league's education program was designed to eradicate. Henry Fitzgibbon, the director of security for baseball, dismissed the paper's warning. Cocaine was a problem for other sports. "WE BELIEVE our drug education program has been highly effective," he exclaimed to the press. Cocaine, after all, didn't help athletes perform, so why would baseball players use it? Besides, Fitzgibbon added, "The doctors and trainers . . . have found no indication that anyone in baseball is using *any* kind of stimulant." Somewhere, Pete Rose was surely laughing.[49]

Assuming that Fitzgibbon wasn't just lying, his response illustrates how out of touch the Major League Baseball establishment—blindly secure in their public relations–based education program—was with reality. The Reading scandal showed that amphetamine was deeply ingrained in baseball culture, but the Major Leagues were no stranger to recreational drug use either. Marijuana use was widespread throughout all levels of the sport, particularly in the minor leagues. As it was with alcohol, sometimes drug-related exploits were elevated into the game's cult mythology. The most notorious example of such a story is that of Pittsburgh Pirates pitcher Dock Ellis, who allegedly threw a no-hitter against the San Diego Padres while under the influence of LSD in 1970.

Ellis, an edgy and outspoken player in a baseball era of relative conformity, didn't reveal his secret until almost a decade had passed. He quickly became something of a cult figure for people enamored with 1960s experimentation and radicalism. Ellis's career, however, was derailed by drugs. Throughout the final years of his pro career he was an often injured pitcher drowning in a deluge of acid, speed, barbiturates, cocaine, marijuana, and alcohol ("I have never pitched a game without being high," he later claimed). Beyond the mythology of the no-hitter, Ellis's career suggests the wide boundaries and quietly destructive nature of baseball's drug culture. Dock Ellis was familiar with cocaine well before the drug became a symbol of 1980s celebrity excess. Former Texas Rangers owner Brad Corbett later acknowledged how dire the drug problem was in baseball at the end of the 1970s when he recalled the Ellis story. "Everybody loves to talk about that LSD no-hitter," he said, "but come on. Stuff like that was happening all the time. Everybody was doing something. One relief pitcher we traded for, I went to meet him in New York at Studio 54. And I walk in and look over and say to myself, 'Hmm. Is that sugar?'" Oddly enough, it took a scandal in professional football to shed light on Major League Baseball's cocaine problem.[50]

Like baseball, professional football was a paternalistic culture that demanded elite performance. Coaches and owners simply did not care what players did off the gridiron so long as they performed on it. To the brotherhood of the bottle, football offered Johnny Blood and Bobby Layne to stand alongside Mantle, Martin, and Newcombe. Early in the 1970s, stimulants and steroids were front-page headlines for the National Football League while professional baseball was hardly scrutinized. Houston Ridge's case was discussed in Congress, and sordid gridiron tell-alls multiplied in the wake of Bouton's far less seamy baseball best-seller. Former Dallas Cowboys wide-receiver Lance Rentzel was a known marijuana smoker. Pittsburgh Steelers quarterback Joe Gilliam's career was wrecked by drugs, and he was eventually arrested in a 1976 heroin bust. Despite this long history, when in 1978 journalists explored the role of amphetamine in creating gridiron rage, Jack Danahy, the league's director of security, borrowed his response from baseball's Henry Fitzgibbon and insisted, despite growing concern, that the NFL had no "drug crisis."[51]

As with baseball, minor accounts of cocaine abuse filtered through the media and were quickly forgotten. That changed on June 14, 1982, when *Sports Illustrated* featured an article by NFL lineman Don Reese. "Cocaine arrived in my life with my first-round draft into the National Football League in 1974," Reese wrote. "It has dominated my life, in one way or another, almost every minute since." In Reese's account of the NFL, cocaine was as common in the locker room as Gatorade. Suddenly the press, and with them most of America's sports fans, were paying attention.[52]

In Reese's *Sports Illustrated* bombshell he suggested, "Cocaine can be found in quantity throughout the NFL. It's pushed on players, often from the edge of the practice field. Sometimes it's pushed by players." Cocaine, he alleged, controlled and corrupted the game. Nobody should have been shocked by Reese's admissions. Football insiders had known about his problem with cocaine for years. He and former teammate Randy Crowder had been arrested in 1977 for selling a pound of cocaine to undercover cops while the two were teammates with the Miami Dolphins. Like Bill North's arrest that same year, however, it was swept to the back pages of the newspapers. That none of these men were superstars mattered a great deal. They could be written off as troubled aberrations. But if an entire sport was overwhelmed by drug use, something like that could not be ignored. Could it?[53]

* * *

The easy culprit for the cocaine craze was money. Never had the old cliché about money being the root of all evil seemed so appropriate or applicable. Cocaine had become the recreational drug of choice for the affluent. Athletes, particularly in an era of free agency and exponentially skyrocketing salaries, were certainly very well paid (some would say overpaid). The blend of too much money and too little world experience was a combustible one in the underworld of American drugs. Frank Layden, the general manager for the NBA's Utah Jazz, surmised that "rich and young at the same time is the worst possible combination."[54]

But more than just money went into the sports world's high-profile coke crisis. There were some structural problems as well, not to mention the incendiary macho culture of the professional games. Harry Edwards pointed out that the sports organizations themselves "may have contributed to creating a climate for recreational drug use among athletes by indulging, if not fostering, what amounts to a pharmaceutical haven in the locker room." Drugs were everywhere and to be used for everything. Could any drug but cocaine have been better suited to the macho world of professional sport where manly performance was defined not only by quality on the field but also by the quantity of sexual conquests off of it? Football coaches Tom Landry and Forrest Gregg argued that "jocks" were highly susceptible to abuse because they believed they were macho enough to use and not be affected by the drugs. Unlike mere mortals, the warriors of the gridiron, hardwood, and diamond were used to adulation and had grown to see themselves as virtually indestructible. Gregg called the delusion "terminal uniqueness."[55]

Not everyone, however, agreed that the affluence of modern athletes was the core issue. Marvin Miller, only recently retired from his position as head of the MLBPA, had a visceral reaction to a letter charging the players' union with undermining player loyalty, fostering greed, and creating a sport played by overpaid and mediocre athletes. The arrest of pitcher Ferguson Jenkins and the consequent legal wrangling between Commissioner Kuhn and the union was, the letter charged, symbolic of baseball's decay. Miller responded that in the years since the modification of baseball's reserve system the game had enjoyed record high attendances. The salary structure that fueled greed, mediocrity, and drug abuse was not the fault of the union but rather of competition, the very lifeblood of America's vaunted capitalist system. Baseball's problem, if problem it was, was symptomatic—not just a systemic flaw in sports, but a systemic flaw in the American way.[56]

The scramble for ever-larger contracts was in part inspired by the transitory and temporary nature of an athletic career. It could end at any time, by injury or some other uncontrollable circumstance. So it was only wise to make a fortune while a fortune was there to be made. This new pressure to earn a fat contract was coupled with the traditional expectation of performance; elite performance was now not only a testament to virile manhood but also a necessity for big financial reward. This twofold reality undergirded the booming recreational drug culture in professional sports. Drugs, especially cocaine, were part of the affluent world that athletes wanted to enter. Drugs like cocaine were also a siren-like ameliorative, promising escape from the pressures of that high-performance, high-pressure world.

Major League Baseball, like other professional sports in the 1980s, featured an ongoing amateur psychological discussion. Why were drugs in sports? Why did athletes choose to use recreational drugs, which not only do not help them perform, but may actually hinder their performance? In many cases the questions about cocaine in the 1980s were the same asked about alcohol in prior decades. The answers were, as then, varied. Some suggested that chemical abuse stemmed primarily from loneliness. "That's what it was for me," said catcher Darryl Porter. "When I went to baseball, I had never been away from home at night. That was the killer, the loneliness. One night I got drunk. I found my answer. No more loneliness. Alcohol made me have a good time . . . the drugs followed."[57]

Maybe, said others, it was not only loneliness, but boredom. The baseball season was long, a flowing epic of stops, starts, and repetitive routine inaction. "When you're traveling from city to city, you get bored going to movies or window shopping or doing things like that to occupy your time," Ferguson Jenkins told correspondents. "After you've played in the big leagues for a long time, you're doing the same things over and over again and you finally say to yourself, now I want to do something different." Drugs were something different.[58]

If some athletes were driven to drinking and recreational cocaine abuse by feelings of loneliness, boredom, or professional pressures, there was also that appealing, almost sexual, aspect unique to the cocaine high. Montreal's Tim Raines described his experience with cocaine as one wherein the primary appeal was a sense of instant elation. "There were times during the season where I pretty much had to have [cocaine] to play because I remember sometimes going three or four days without getting any sleep," Raines told one interviewer. "If I went without having it, I probably would have passed out on the bench . . . there were times where I felt the only way I could play a ball game was to be high. Cocaine makes you feel like, ah, you're Superman or something."[59]

It was a feeling that some players sought not only off the field but on it as well. The pitcher Will McEnaney, a 1975 World Series hero with the Cincinnati Reds, was traded to Montreal in 1975. There, when the pressures of performance, loneliness, and a new home piled on his shoulders, a friend suggested he try cocaine. "[My friend told me] It'll get you up, it will make you feel better . . . he was right. When I was pitching, I'd go into the clubhouse between innings and do a little just to get me up."[60]

By the early 1980s it was clear, not just from exposés by insiders like Don Reese, that cocaine was very much a part of the professional sporting culture. Closer in spirit to alcohol than the familiar performance enhancers, cocaine abuse stemmed from a heady blend of immaturity, sudden wealth, and the pressures felt on as well as beyond the field of play. Author and former footballer Pete Gent summed up the cocaine crisis in professional football as "an upper class drug epidemic in a lower class sport full of instant millionaires in full-length mink and quarter-length self-esteem."[61]

* * *

Before his attention was monopolized by the cocaine crisis, Major League Baseball commissioner Bowie Kuhn's primary concerns were mounting labor troubles, the economic conflicts between the owners and the players that would result in the devastating 1981 baseball strike. Despite evidence that suggested otherwise, when it came to baseball's war on drugs, Kuhn faithfully echoed his chief security officer and reiterated the successes of his highly praised education program. When Don Reese implied a widespread culture of recreational drug abuse in pro football, Kuhn lectured about the different degrees of physicality in the major sports, linking it to expectations of drug abuse. "I honestly don't believe baseball has the chemical abuse problems of other sports; because it is less physical . . . the players lead a more normal life than those in other major sports."[62]

Even as he dodged the issue, Kuhn also began to recognize that his education program had a limited reach. Drug testing was expensive and almost impossible to sell to the MLBPA. Instead of detection and punishment, Kuhn's program as it evolved from its early 1970s roots emphasized education, assistance, and amnesty. The financial explosion of the free agency era complicated everything. "A heavy emphasis on education obviously isn't effective with everyone," said Kuhn. "But these days especially with player compensation going up the way it is, we think we can convince athletes to have a greater incentive to protect their careers." Where, on the one hand, money opened up a high-class world of drugs to players, Kuhn also insisted that, on the other hand, it might make them more open to his program's message. Kuhn would keep dangling carrots in front of the players, but he was now ready to start swinging the stick as well.[63]

On August 25, 1980, Texas Rangers pitcher and future hall of famer Ferguson Jenkins was arrested in Toronto for alleged possession of marijuana, cocaine, and hashish. When Jenkins refused to cooperate with Kuhn's planned investigation to discover how deeply baseball's emergent drug problem ran, he was suspended without pay. The MLBPA filed a grievance, and arbitrator Raymond Goetz overruled Kuhn's decision to suspend Jenkins. It was, said Kuhn, "a grave disservice, not only to those of us in sports administration, but to concerned parents and citizens everywhere. Athletes have a tremendous influence on our youth and on society in general. Baseball's policy for decades has been to establish the game as a wholesome family sport." The *Sporting News* threw its support to Kuhn. While Goetz didn't believe that public opinion regarding drugs warranted a suspension for Jenkins, the editors of the newspaper believed that Kuhn was right to build his defense around baseball's young fans. They published an editorial explaining that while the idolatry displayed by the kids "may be misplaced, unjustified, illogical and even unfair . . . few would deny it exists. That puts an extra, an extremely important, burden on the professional athletes. Kuhn recognized that in his decision. The arbitrator did not." There was, however, something comical in the fact that the *Sporting News* chose to print their "wholesome sport" letter next to a large advertisement for Seagrams Extra-Dry gin. Don't do drugs, kids. Love baseball, look up to your role-models, and drink Seagrams![64]

What Bowie Kuhn most needed, and could not find, was a scapegoat. He needed some transgressor who, being caught unrepentant in a drug scandal, would present the commissioner an opportunity to add teeth—the teeth of commissioner-sanctioned punishment—to his education program. Kuhn always disdained the word "scapegoat," instead preferring to use the term "example." Whatever one called it, every potential "example" ultimately proved an impossible target. He might have aimed at Bob Welch, the alcoholic pitcher for the Los Angeles Dodgers. But alcohol was not an illegal drug, Kuhn had previously made outreach to alcoholics a much-lauded part of his program, and, besides, Welch had sought treatment—of his own accord—at The Meadows rehab center in Wickenburg, Arizona.[65]

The Meadows, an austere outpost in the Arizona desert, gained attention early in the decade for turning directionless drug abusers and alcoholics from the sports world into newly productive human beings. Welch and six other members of the far-flung Dodger organization, Kansas City Royals catcher Darrell Porter, and Minnesota Twins pitcher Darrell Jackson were among the center's success stories. "Our goal here is to remove the chemical as a way of life," explained the center's founder. "Once we have a chemical free person, we start to repair the damages in other areas: physiological, psychological, emotional and spiritual. A baseball player wonders if his self-worth is entirely tied to his job. We taught Bob Welch to think: I am worthwhile because I am a human being, not a human doing."[66]

So Welch, the rehabilitated success story, was clearly out as a potential scapegoat. What about Darrell Porter, the catcher for the Royals? Porter had recalled to the Associated Press how he had grown convinced that Kuhn was coming to ban him because of his drug addiction. His nerves frayed, he would stay up at night, staring out the window, clutching billiard balls with which to pelt the commissioner when he arrived. Porter's reputation as a strong-armed defender of the base paths was well earned—so, too, his new nickname: "Double-Barrel Darrell." But Porter, too, was off limits. He had voluntarily entered rehab as well. "We are satisfied that Porter's play is no longer affected by chemicals; we do not think he has damaged the public image of our sport," said Kuhn, "because the public accepts and understands his problem and that he has corrected it." Porter, like Welch, was celebrated for conquering his demons. He was another example, symbolized by the Operation CORK approach, that athletes drowning in addiction could bring themselves to the surface. Porter and Welch showed that there was clearly a third way between Kuhn's preventive education program and punitive punishment from the commissioner's office.[67]

Nevertheless, Kuhn kept searching. The commissioner almost had his "example" in Ferguson Jenkins following that player's arrest north of the border. Although Fergie was punished by Kuhn, he was never convicted by the Canadian legal system and had no permanent record. Besides, Jenkins was artful in establishing great public relations after his arrest. The star pitcher donated $10,000 and gave his time to various prevention causes. He would not do as an "example." Meanwhile, the Reading Pill Probe had come and gone with no Phillies players convicted. Only Randy Lerch, a marginal relief pitcher, confessed to *actively* seeking amphetamine. To pursue the Reading case was to beat a dying horse.[68]

Other potential "examples" never turned out. When Cardinals shortstop Garry Templeton began to exhibit bizarre behavior, the commissioner thought he had his man. But Templeton was admitted to a psychiatric clinic and exonerated of all drug use allegations. In eyeing Templeton, however, Kuhn's ambitions became dangerously transparent. Union chief Marvin Miller, commenting on Kuhn's eagerness to make an example of some—any—player, was caustic:

> That's what bothers me: the commissioner hears one rumor or reads one newspaper story and immediately he wants to go off on a witch hunt. He doesn't want to find the facts and then take steps. The Templeton drug rumors,

which, in fact, were originated by a Cardinals employee, were completely false. I appreciate the fact that baseball has a potential drug problem. But it's coming to the point where anyone with a different behavior is automatically suspected of being a drug user.[69]

Kuhn, unable to find a player who would allow him to concentrate the power to punish substance abusers, continued to try to implement new policies to stamp out the drug problem. He continued to urge each franchise to establish its own employee-assistance program (EAP). Knowing that any effort on his own part to crack down on players who used drugs would ultimately set him up against the union, as it had with Ferguson Jenkins, Kuhn was left with the solitary hope that the players could be convinced to help themselves in order to avoid the threat of a penalty. Even this approach proved to be largely a failure.[70]

Then, the very same week that Kuhn and NFL commissioner Pete Rozelle testified before Congressman Leo Zeferetti's Select Committee on Narcotics Abuse and Control, Kuhn's new "self-help" policies were put to the test. On July 21, 1982, San Diego infielder Alan Wiggins was arrested for possession of cocaine. It appeared that Kuhn was about to get his "example."[71]

Wiggins entered a treatment program at the care unit of the Orange County Medical Center. It was there that Harry Gibbs, who had succeeded the retired Henry Fitzgibbon as baseball's security chief, interviewed him. The Players Association sought to stifle the interview process by insisting that all the questions be submitted in advance. Kuhn would not comply and was pleased to find that Wiggins and his agent Tony Attanasio were cooperative, as were Joan Kroc and Ballard Smith of the Padres. After receiving Gibbs's report, Kuhn suspended Wiggins without pay for thirty days. Even this seemingly slam-dunk ruling became a fiasco for Kuhn.

Two years later, as his tenure in the commissioner's office ended, Kuhn learned from Don Fehr of the Players Association that Wiggins had been paid by the Padres during the suspension. Kuhn was appalled. Ballard Smith, the Padres general manager, later admitted in embarrassment that Wiggins's checks had slipped through the payment office without the knowledge of club management. One of Kuhn's last acts as commissioner was to fine the Padres $50,000, but there was no solace in that small act of revenge.[72]

To the American press the Wiggins case was virtually a nonstory. It was as if baseball players and drug addiction had become, in a few short years, too commonplace a tale to be interesting. Kuhn believed that had it occurred a decade earlier, the Wiggins case would have caused a furor. He speculated that the press and the public had been lulled into indifference by recurrent drug problems in other sports and in American society at large. By 1984, twenty-two million Americans used marijuana regularly, and four million more were using cocaine. A new generation of writers had emerged, "more attuned to drug use" and "less concerned about the public's old-time faith in sports." What little faith remained was now challenged by a story coming out of the American heartland.[73]

*　*　*

They called it the "Cooperstown Room." In reality, it was the basement of Mark Liebl's Kansas City home. Liebl, a super fan of sorts, hosted some of the most sordid parties on the professional baseball circuit. The parties were small, private affairs. The players who descended on Liebl's basement for festivities were usually there for only one reason. Players recalled the basement as a place where "a lot of baseball was talked and a lot of cocaine was done." Liebl was the centerpiece of a league-wide cocaine network and had connected players all around the majors to the drug. "It's all over baseball," he later said.[74]

In the summer of 1983 Bowie Kuhn learned about an FBI grand jury investigation that fingered four members of the Kansas City Royals—Willie Wilson, Willie Aikens, Jerry Martin, and Vida Blue—as regulars in the Cooperstown Room. The FBI had previously implicated a number of players from New York, Cleveland, and Milwaukee, but these stories often came to naught or were hushed up. Nothing—not those rumors or the Wiggins fiasco—could have prepared Kuhn for this last dramatic act in his personal war against drug use. "It seemed all wrong," Kuhn recalled. "Kansas City was a model franchise with a wholesome environment, beautiful ballpark, enthusiastic crowds."[75]

In October, Wilson, Aikens, and Martin were each sentenced to a year in prison. U.S. District Magistrate J. Milton Sullivant, in his decision, said: "a professional athlete . . . does occupy a special place in society, and the Court realizes that the life of a professional athlete is not all roses . . . But all the Court can do is take the totality of circumstances as found in the record" and must ultimately make the choice to look out for youngsters who viewed the players as role models. This was logic that Bowie Kuhn could appreciate. He followed the court's decision by handing down his own one-year suspensions coupled with mandatory drug testing. This, it seemed likely, was the last best chance to bring the MLBPA to the table in order to establish a testing program in Major League Baseball.[76]

The MLBA was unbending. Five days after the sentencing, the Executive Committee of the MLBPA fired their executive director, Ken Moffett. Moffett was never a hard-liner and was not cast in the mold of Marvin Miller. He had even begun discussing the feasibility of a joint drug program with Lee MacPhail, one of Kuhn's trusted advisers, and had openly admitted the serious nature of the drug problem in baseball. Moffett, in short, was amenable to the idea of automatic penalties for drug use being codified by the game's ruling bodies. Refusing to consider the validity of such powers for the commissioner, the union balked. Thanks to a lenient decision by an arbitrator who sympathized with Kuhn's position but ruled in favor of the union's stance, Wilson returned to baseball after a one-month suspension. At his first game, in Chicago's Comiskey Park, a cheeky banner greeted him: "Willie: Coke is it."[77]

Kuhn might have been a lame duck by this point, but his decisions had been well received by the press. Dave Anderson of the *New York Times* blasted the MLBPA. "Until the Players Association cooperates with Bowie Kuhn and his successor," Anderson wrote, "it will only add to baseball's problem, not solve it."[78]

The venerable Jim Murray of the *Los Angeles Times* offered Kuhn his support. "So, there you have it. In Landis's day, baseball punished its transgressors irrespective of society's view of the matter or its forgiveness. In Kuhn's day," he continued, "baseball's right to do so is challenged even when society has already condemned and isolated the wrongdoers from its ranks. What is going on? Is cocaine addiction a crime on the streets but not in the dugout? Is trafficking in it none of baseball's business unless it takes place at home plate? Is Judge Landis' saving of the game's integrity just an old fashioned notion and not applicable for Bowie Kuhn? Say it ain't so, somebody."[79]

Meanwhile, Vida Blue's situation—more complicated and troubling than that of the others—remained unresolved. His hearing was postponed until December when Sullivant passed the same sentence he had given to the other players. At his hearing, Blue had professed shame at his own conduct, insisted that the debacle had led him to rediscover himself as a person—one with considerable demons—and he now realized that drug use was as dangerous to society as cancer. Drug use, he said, was a deadly disease. Commissioner Kuhn, who had visited Liebl at the correctional center in Fort Leavenworth, had learned that Blue was Liebl's primary liaison for connecting with other cocaine users around the league. He attended Liebl's parties two to three times a week. Oftentimes Blue purchased the cocaine for other players, playing an "active and central role . . . in promoting Liebl's substantial involvement with the Kansas City Royals."[80]

In 1983 Blue had also allegedly "exposed a teenage Milwaukee Brewer batboy to cocaine by inviting the young man to a party in Blue's apartment where cocaine was available." While his office launched an investigation into Blue's role in the cocaine story, Kuhn suspended the pitcher through the end of 1984 and forbade him from signing a contract or working out with any professional clubs. After that, Blue would submit to a two-year probationary period with drug testing and compliance with an after-care program.[81]

The MLBPA rushed to Blue's defense, charging that Kuhn's penalty was overly severe and without precedent. The commissioner's investigation had been late to start, it was still incomplete as the 1984 season began, and most of the evidence against Blue came from a convicted felon (Liebl) who was possibly disparaging Blue because of outstanding debts. Other players, they noted, had received lesser penalties. More problematic for the union was the fact teams were still interested in signing Blue. The San Francisco Giants wanted to put a contract together, but were unsure what Kuhn's office would do if they attempted to sign the player. The MLBPA believed that Blue had a right to make a living and filed a grievance. The case went to arbitration.[82]

Kuhn defended his position on Blue by noting that the allegations against the player were more serious than "mere attempted possession or use of cocaine." He insisted that the suspension remain in effect until his office completed its full investigation. The MLBPA argued that since Blue had already missed more time than any of the other players, he had been disciplined enough and should be able to seek work. The arbitration panel concluded that while Kuhn should be allowed to proceed with his investigation, there was no just cause to keep the Giants from signing the troubled pitcher. At the same time, the panel justified the suspension of Blue based on interviews with the player and Mark Liebl. As he had already missed more than ninety days of the 1984 season (as opposed to forty-four days missed by the other players), Kuhn would need to submit the final determination of his investigation by the 1984 All-Star break. Vida Blue was back on the mound for the 1985 season.[83]

At the same time the Blue debacle unfolded, and while another pitcher, Pascual Pérez of the Atlanta Braves, ran through a similar gamut of applied (and then revoked) penalties, Kuhn and the union were also wrangling over the case of Los Angeles Dodgers reliever Steve Howe. Before his career ended in the mid-1990s, Howe's name would become synonymous with baseball's crippled attempts at drug education, reform, and punishment. In 1983, however, the former National League Rookie of the Year was entering rehab for the very first time. When he had a relapse, the Dodgers, in coordination with the commissioner's office, fined Howe thirty days' pay and placed him on probation for three years. The MLBPA, still headed at that time by Ken Moffett, filed a grievance. Their position was that a player who "is unable to perform because of an illness should not be subject to discipline." In 1971 an independent arbitrator had ruled that players whose conduct and performance were caused by illness should be put on the disabled list. The Dodgers and Kuhn had acted in contravention of that decision.[84]

The union truly believed that Howe, who had by this point entered a second rehab unit in Orange County, was on his way to recovery. Their great concern was that punitive action by the league would hinder that recovery and might deter other players from coming forward with similar problems in the future. Although Kuhn had apparently assured the union that he wouldn't punish Howe, the decision had already been made to "sacrifice Steve as an example to other players." The Players Association believed that Kuhn's decision was motivated by personal and political considerations.[85]

The Howe case, which resulted in a one-year suspension (Howe would miss all of the 1984 season despite a constant stream of reports about arbitration hearings), clearly revealed not only the limits of Kuhn's reach but also the growing rift among the players themselves, not all of whom believed Howe's suspension was a bad thing. Ray Knight, then with the Astros, said Howe's punishment was justifiable: "Steve was given every opportunity to straighten up." While Avron Fogelman, co-owner of the Kansas City Royals, lamented Kuhn's lack of compassion and mercy in his decisions, Tom Neidenfuer, another Dodgers reliever, accepted that "the Commissioner reached the point where he believed something had to be done. It's just a tragic day for baseball."[86]

When Howe's case was reviewed in May 1984, Kuhn—still a lame duck as commissioner—upheld the year-long suspension. "Steve continues in treatment," he told the press, "and there is unanimity of feeling among us, including Steve's medical advisors, that a return to baseball this season would not be appropriate. The most important thing for this young man is his long-range recovery." Steve Howe returned to the mound in 1985. He would be suspended for cocaine use six more times during his career.[87]

As his time in office ran out, Kuhn lamented that though they had made progress and had gotten the players' attention, his office had not solved baseball's drug problem. He blamed the MLBPA. "The heartbreaking part of all this was that it could have been solved but for the resistance of the Association." Kuhn, however, suggested in his autobiography that there was little evidence of renewed drug abuse after his struggles with the players union and arbitrators. The well-publicized 1985 trials in Pittsburgh all dealt with events from the seasons preceding his various suspension rulings. "Maybe," he wrote, "a message did get through."[88]

Despite the urging of writers who still viewed Kuhn as the best man to fix baseball, the owners voted to replace him at the end of his term in 1984. As Kuhn was preparing to exit the office, he could at least take some solace in the fact that a joint drug policy, modeled after a system in place in the National Basketball Association, was finally falling into place. Unfortunately, he knew it lacked teeth. It had to in order to be tolerated by the MLBPA. It applied only to illegal hard drugs, not amphetamines, marijuana, or other prescription drugs. It did not authorize mandatory drug testing. It would not last.[89]

5

This Is Not Just a Test

The commissioner is letting everyone know he means
business. He has sent out a message, and the message
says, "Boys, you ain't gonna get away with it anymore."
—Sparky Anderson, Manager, Detroit Tigers

When individual liberties and presumptions of guilt and
innocence are violated it [drug testing] doesn't make us
happy even if players are not involved.
—Donald Fehr, MLBPA Counsel

As an eventful 1986 dawned, the specter of new baseball commissioner Peter Ueberroth, urine testing bottle in hand, hung ominously over Major League Baseball. The man who inherited Bowie Kuhn's responsibilities and with them baseball's problems was a former travel business magnate spurred on to Major League commissionership thanks to his highly acclaimed organization (garnering *Time*'s Man of the Year honors) of the 1984 Olympic games in Los Angeles. He blazed into the commissionership in October 1984 and almost immediately arbitrated a disagreement to keep the league's umpires from striking and the following season managed to limit a players' strike to one day before a new labor agreement could be worked out with the Players Association. He reversed some of Kuhn's unpopular decisions, reinstating exiled stars Mickey Mantle and Willie Mays (both banned for their connection to casinos). As a condition for taking the job, the business-minded Ueberroth had managed to win both a raise and significantly greater punitive powers—a fifty-fold increase in the maximum fine allowed by the commissioner's office.[1]

On the surface, Ueberroth was as advertised—a wunderkind businessman with a mind for money. Under Ueberroth's guidance Major League Baseball appeared to enjoy an astounding renaissance. Attendance in the middle and later half of the 1980s was up, and the league's financial picture was looking better than it had since the early 1970s. When he stepped down as commissioner in 1989, baseball teams were financially secure, the league had a $1.2 billion television contract with CBS to swell the owners' coffers, Wrigley Field had lights, and there had been significant gains in reining in crowd violence and controlling the flow of alcohol in ballparks across the country. Nevertheless, there was something illusory about the success of Ueberroth's tenure. If Peter the Great had hit an apparent financial home run, he struck out on the biggest issue confronting his regime: drugs.

Drugs dominated the first two years of Ueberroth's time in baseball's executive office. In a 1985 interview for *U.S. News and World Report*, Ueberroth was asked what the biggest surprise of his first year had been. "The size of the drug problem," he responded. "The problem is not better," he added, addressing the notion that the problem was less serious than in the last years of the Kuhn regime. Instead, Ueberroth pointed to the prevalence of drug use in society and the discussions he had with various baseball executives. The problem ran deep, claimed Ueberroth, far deeper, in fact, than even those executives had been willing to admit. "Whitey Herzog of St. Louis said 10, 11, 12 players on his team were using cocaine a couple of years ago," said Ueberroth, "I don't think any of these people tried to overstate the problem. Without question, they all tried to understate it." It was then that Ueberroth made the promise that would define the ultimate failure of his commissionership. "I'll tell you this," he said, "we're going to eliminate drugs from baseball. We'll be relentless until that is done. The commissioner has the personal obligation to families everywhere whose children idolize players, to the game of baseball and to the players directly."[2]

Ueberroth planted his flag on ground familiar to generations of baseball fans, executives, and sports writers. Drugs threatened the integrity and sanctity of a game beloved of children and ultimately threatened the children themselves. If Ueberroth had made combating the drug problem his top priority, he nurtured a sense of melodrama in urging the MLBPA to join him in establishing meaningful rules to eliminate that problem. As the problem escalated throughout 1985 and increasingly found its way into the public eye, Ueberroth prophesied ruin: "Baseball is in trouble." "A cloud called drugs is permeating our game." "The shadow is growing larger and darker by the day." "Stop this menace." "A generation of kids" is at stake, and a "decade of baseball [is going to be synonymous] with drugs." "This," he concluded, "is baseball's last chance."[3]

Ueberroth's greatest concern in 1985 was the climatic act of baseball's escalating struggle with cocaine. The crisis reached a crescendo on September 3,

1985, the day that federal prosecutors descended on a Pittsburgh courtroom to begin trying seven men on charges of possession and sales of cocaine in and around the Pittsburgh and Philadelphia metropolitan area. The defendants sitting before the Grand Jury were unexceptional men. Curtis Strong, the key defendant in the trial, was an average looking, heavy-set man who sat quietly throughout the proceedings. Strong had most recently been employed as a chef and caterer for the Philadelphia Phillies, but it was his ties to Pittsburgh and the underworld of the cocaine trade that placed him in the courtroom. Inside, he and the other six defendants were overshadowed by the testimony of several professional baseball players who had been granted immunity in return for their cooperation in the federal drug probe. What they revealed was a baseball world far more sordid than a great many expected. It seemed as though Ueberroth's dire warnings had been well placed.[4]

*   *   *

By the spring of 1985 there was no more depressing venue in Major League Baseball than Pittsburgh's Three Rivers Stadium. Though sports fans in the Steel City might still raise a cheer for the gridiron Steelers, a football franchise limping to the end of its dynastic era, the baseball Pirates were another story. Baseball crowds at the big concrete ring by the rivers dwindled. In late 1984 the team recognized a new attendance record low. One hundred losses seemed a certainty for the following season; such futility was something nobody in Pittsburgh could have imagined just five years before. Like Pittsburgh—itself like so many cities in the Rust Belt—the Pirates were decaying, crumbling from within. On the field, the one-time title contenders floundered listlessly into the cellar of the National League East. Critics called them the worst team in baseball. Outside, industry declined, steel mills closed, local corporations downsized or relocated. Downtown storefronts were vacant, and the streets virtually empty at night. In the towns around the Steel City, unemployment soared toward 20 percent. The lords of baseball, inspired by the ascendance of a bright new business-minded commissioner, talked of expansion for 1986. The Pirates, their ownership in flux, were not certain that they would still be playing in Pittsburgh in 1986.[5]

A living memory for only the oldest of Pirates fans, Honus Wagner, the "Flying Dutchman," had starred at shortstop for the great Pirates teams of the early twentieth century. Now he stood immortalized in sculpture outside the stadium. There, under Wagner's stony gaze, drug buys became routine. The spot was a notable cog in a citywide network of illicit trafficking, a festering sore spot in an epidemic that threatened to swamp the Hill District.

It was the same Hill where Pirates icon Willie Stargell's restaurant had once served free chicken whenever "Pops" launched a home run. Those days, like bygone players, were but a memory. So common was the illicit commerce in Wagner's shadow that Pittsburgh locals called drug purchases there the "Dutch Treat."[6]

The Pittsburgh trials inspired myriad explorations of baseball's historical crises. One common comparison saw the drug trials likened to the 1919 Black Sox trials. Ueberroth was compelled to "do something Landis-like." Recalling Landis's comments to the players during that complicated episode, Ueberroth quoted the man. "I want every player to feel I stand behind him," he intoned, then added, "so long as he is on the square." As the testimony at Pittsburgh unfolded, Ueberroth suggested that if a substantial drug policy did not emerge in the wake of the trial, "baseball will have lost control of its own problems." He drummed up the traditional scare tactic: Congress would not allow the game to retain its sacred antitrust exemption if the drug problem was not solved.[7]

The stories pouring out of Pittsburgh cannot have swelled Ueberroth's confidence that the problem could easily be eradicated. Lonnie Smith explained how coke was wrapped in pages from "girlie magazines" and was sometimes sent by express mail. At least four players named Curtis Strong specifically as the matchmaker in their love affair with cocaine. Twenty-one other former and current players were alleged to have used cocaine sold by Strong. The old specter of amphetamines resurfaced in shocking fashion when several witnesses, including Dale Berra, the twenty-eight-year-old son of Hall of Famer Yogi Berra, implicated retired Pirates captain Willie "Pops" Stargell. Berra claimed he could get a "greenie" from Stargell "on any given day that I asked him for one." While Stargell denied Berra's accusations, they were made again a few days later by former Pirate batting star Dave Parker. Baseball fans were stunned and incredulous, and largely disbelieving. Stargell was an institution who had led the Pirates to their last World Championship in 1979.[8]

Greater still was the disbelief in the baseball world when Hall of Famer Willie Mays was implicated by retired Pirate John Milner. Milner claimed that he not only had "greenies" placed anonymously in his locker, but he saw a red juice-and-amphetamine concoction in Mays's locker when both had played for the New York Mets in the early 1970s. "*The* Willie Mays?" asked defense attorney Adam Renfroe. "Willie Mays—the great one," confirmed Milner. Mays, for his part, angrily told CBS that the liquid had been cough medicine.[9]

While names were flying out of Pittsburgh, baseball's guardians and critics in the press worked furiously at their typewriters. Coverage ranged from the absurd—the story of how the Pittsburgh mascot, the Pirate Parrot, had served as the primary connection between the Pirates locker room and cocaine dealer Dale Shiffman (Shiffman also dealt cocaine to the NHL Penguins)—to the sublime. It turned out, the *Los Angeles Times* reported, that Kevin Koch, the man who had played the role of the Parrot until 1985, pronounced his last name as "coke." In a more serious vein, opinions were split over whether the players or the dealers were the real villains in the story. Defense attorney Renfroe cast his client, Strong, as a little guy who had been made the scapegoat for the sins of the game. The players, particularly popular Mets star Keith Hernandez, he insisted, were rich "hero junkies" who had secured immunity while Strong faced a trial and imprisonment. In one shouting match with Dave Parker, he had yelled, "How is it that once you get immunity that you're not going to jail and won't lose your $20,000 diamond rings, that you now remember?"[10]

There was a sense that the Pittsburgh scandal marked a turning point in the public understanding of sports. Traditional notions of "play" were now complicated—and part of what made the cocaine scandal so unbearable was that fans and critics associated the athletes with the concept of "play." What they did was fun. Was the fun not enough? Did they need to seek solace in illicit drugs as well? There was a sense of bitterness in the reaction to the drug trials that one did not see in similar cases involving doctors or lawyers. Those professionals were workers. Fans and critics could summon empathy for the "hard working." It was more difficult to sympathize with men whose careers involved "playing." It was no stretch to suggest that baseball's drug problem had become, in many ways, an extension of—and escape from—the '80s cultural zeitgeist, defined by excess and a win-at-all-costs mentality.[11]

Perhaps the most striking debate to emerge in the writing about Pittsburgh was that between liberal and conservative forces, echoing those early arguments about the meaning of *Ball Four*. The *Nation*, the self-described "flagship of the left," focused on the trial as a "cautionary tale in the heroic saga of sport." In the view of one editorial, "consumers of heroism need a balanced diet: they want to told [sic] not only whom to venerate but whom to despise." In this conception the players taking the witness stand were being set up by the system, because the "system needs bums." After all, these players were victims of the second largest industry in the world, an industry that sustained the economies of several small countries and of vices that were prevalent among all sectors of American society. In the end, according to the *Nation*, the players were dupes not unlike the political suspects who faced congressional committees in the 1950s. "This time," the editorial concluded, "the dupes are dopers, the radicals are rockers, and the subversives pose nude for *Penthouse* rather than give secrets to the Russians." In short, while baseball players had exposed the danger of cocaine and spurred national concern about drug abuse, they were also being abused by a repressive society looking for ways to tear down once exalted role models.[12]

While the *Nation* suggested the necessity of symmetry in the world of heroes and villains while implicating, though somewhat backhandedly, the repressive elements in society, other writers laid into the *Nation's* readership. Foremost among them was the brutally honest, occasionally abusive, Dick Young. Pulling no punches, Young blamed the sordid Pittsburgh affair—and baseball's widespread drug problem in general—on effete liberals. Noting that American League president Bobby Brown was getting involved in the fight, Young editorialized in the *Sporting News*, "That's Dr. Bobby Brown, in case the gushing liberals want to bring up that canard that medical men don't think social drugs are THAT dangerous, whatever 'social' drugs are." He concluded emphatically, "The bleeding hearts have had their time—and drugs have replaced Wheaties as the Breakfast of Champions."[13]

The *Nation* chalked the unfolding crisis up to Zen balance. Dick Young snarled at the ill effects of liberalism run amok. Tom Callahan, who along with the *New York Times's* Murray Chass wrote extensively on the trials, bled cynicism. Baseball's facade of innocence was tarnished, Callahan noted, and had been for some time. Cocaine might not spark better playing, but it definitely affected the standings. In 1982 the Montreal Expos had expected to win their division easily but "instead lost themselves and any immediate hope of advancement in a pathetic white haze." Club president John McHale recalled instances where star outfielder Tim Raines "vaguely held the ball without completing a play or momentarily forgot to run the bases." Raines had only recently admitted that he packed a gram bottle of cocaine in the hip pocket of his uniform pants for "short snorts between innings. Mostly he concentrated on sliding into bases headfirst, to protect his stash." He recalled how the drug affected his fielding: "A ball coming straight at me, I couldn't judge how close it was. With base stealing, it messes up your concentration as far as watching the pitcher is concerned. Your reactions are slower. Sometimes I thought I had started to run before I actually started to run."[14]

The fourteen-day Pittsburgh drug trial ended in the conviction of Curtis Strong, whose desire to know and be liked by important people had led him into a life of criminal drug trafficking. In addition, Judge Gustave Diamond held Strong's lawyer, Adam Renfroe, in contempt for "reprehensible behavior." Renfroe had overstepped his bounds in trying to make the baseball players—the "hero junkies"—the targets of the hearing. At the end of the trial Diamond addressed the jury, suggesting that the trial showed baseball fans that "their idols have feet of clay," but that they had "learned of the evils of fooling around with drugs in a way that no advertising campaign could have accomplished."[15]

All too briefly the Pittsburgh trial appeared to be a watershed moment. After decades of ignoring its problems, after years of overlooking alcoholics and speed freaks, baseball surely was finally awake and aware of the problems facing not only its sport, but all of American society. The players returned to the pennant race, often to the rousing cheers of their fans, eager, it seemed, to forgive and forget. Surely, though, everyone who thought of using cocaine would remember Curtis Strong, Steve Howe, the Kansas City Four, and the careers of other players across all the major sports that had been destroyed by the drug. If nothing else, it was hoped that the shock and shame of Pittsburgh would do more to deter future cocaine abuse than controversial measures such as random drug testing.

But at the highest level there was a growing sense that the game had changed and that the rules needed to change with them. Peter Ueberroth, planning to meet with the players involved in the trial, pledged that he was "going to eliminate drugs from baseball." Players were going to be asked to submit to drug-testing clauses, and one writer suggested that "the day of the basic agreement that contains meaningful drug-testing language is close at hand."[16]

✳   ✳   ✳

Not long after the trials concluded, the commissioner sat down for a *60 Minutes* interview alongside several other baseball notables, including retired pitcher Dock Ellis and the *New York Post* veteran writer Dick Young. Together, they discussed what baseball should do with the players who admitted drug use during the Pittsburgh hearings. Ueberroth, facing interviewer Harry Reasoner, adopted what seemed to be a thoughtful, albeit ambiguous, stance. He had not yet determined what he was going to do with the "Pittsburgh 11," he explained to Reasoner, but he was contemplating what might prove the most significant action of his tenure. "I'm not going to pre-publicize it," he said, "but I'm going to look at all the information, I'm going to meet with each one and I'm going to look at them eyeball-to-eyeball, and the detrimental effect this has had on baseball."[17]

The acerbic Young, whose editorials over the course of 1985 had increasingly become curmudgeonly screeds against "druggies" and "liberals," suggested that players "be thrown out the first time they use [drugs]." Why wasn't the commissioner willing to protect the great American game by adopting a hard line against drug use? Ueberroth patiently replied that he could adopt such a position, but "it would be thrown out immediately in the courts. . . . It's a throwback, and I think he's [Young] thinking like you could 30, 40 years ago. And there's a fairness thing. I think people's rights are an important thing and I don't believe someone should be all powerful."[18]

Instead, Ueberroth issued another call for mandatory drug testing, a plea he had made several times in the months leading up to the trials. At the time of the *60 Minutes* interview the tension was still thick between the Player Relations Committee (PRC)—the wing of the establishment that represented the owners in talks with the union—and the MLBPA. Ueberroth's ambiguity disappeared, along with any pretense of doubt. "Without question. Unless there's that as a deterrent, you're not going to stop [drug abuse]. I've been tested," he told Reasoner. "It takes about 10 minutes. If they won't devote three times a year, a half hour of the year to clean up the reputation of the game, they have a problem with me." Peering into the mists of the future, Ueberroth guessed that, if everything played out as he expected, there would be drug testing in the Majors by the beginning of the 1986 baseball season.[19]

As Ueberroth contemplated what to do with the Pittsburgh gang, the owners fired an unexpected salvo at the Player's Association. During the World Series that October, an I-70 showdown between St. Louis and Kansas City, Major League Baseball unveiled a new series of commercials. Veteran stars, the men whose words ostensibly carried the most weight, whose experience in the game was most significant, starred in the brief spots. Tom Seaver, in the midst of transitioning from the pitcher's mound to the announcer's booth, and Pete Rose, the player-manager of the Cincinnati Reds, were both featured. Seaver somberly confided in the viewers. "Like every family, ours has its problems." He was talking, of course, about drugs. Although his career was almost over, Seaver still retained the honest-looking, boyish charm that defined the iconic, wholesome baseball star of bygone generations. If "Tom Terrific" said there was a problem, people would listen. Rose, on the other hand, was quite a different story. The *Nation* pointedly asked, in the wake of the new TV spots, why Rose was chosen as a spokesman. "Charlie Hustle," the magazine exclaimed, was the "exception to the rule that speed-freaked booze hounds never live beyond the age of 40."[20]

The spots served two key purposes. They were the initial effort in a new, coordinated, antidrug crusade featuring newspaper and television ads, testimonials, pamphlets, and even coloring books. It was all part of reestablishing baseball stars as good role models. The new campaign would also help fans forget—it was surely hoped—about a miserable 1985 campaign dominated by the drug narrative. Hank Aaron, who had taken an executive position with the Atlanta Braves, and who would contribute to some of the new PR campaign, lamented everything that was lost in the drug furor. "[1985] should have been a great, great year, with Pete Rose breaking Ty Cobb's record and all that, but it's been a black-mark year because of the drug scandals. It's time for baseball to move to the next chapter."[21]

The next chapter was going to include a new approach to the drug problem alongside the public relations blitz. In preparing the public and the players for the new approach, the October ads served to soften the shock from the PRC's preemptive strike against the union. Meeting in the days just after the World Series, the representatives of the owners disavowed the joint drug policy that had been in place since 1984, a policy modeled on the National Basketball Association's highly lauded program, and Bowie Kuhn's consolation prize as he left the commissionership. It was time, they said, for a new policy—one that included testing. All that was left was for Peter Ueberroth to sell the plan.[22]

*   *   *

The commissioner had the remainder of the winter to think over how he would deal with the players from the Pittsburgh drug trial. For several weeks in January, holding court in the law offices of Willkie, Farr and Gallagher atop New York's Citicorp Center, Ueberroth met with all of the players involved in the drug scandals of recent years. The meetings were described as "civil and upbeat." Members of the press were unsure as to what approach Ueberroth would take, but that did not stop them from making predictions. Some figured that the commissioner might suspend a few of the lesser players for the entire year. Such a move would assure that no team's pennant chances were hurt but would also satisfy fans outraged by the cocaine revelations of the past year. Others surmised that Ueberroth would exact harsh discipline on most of the players, knowing that such punishment would almost certainly lead to grievances by the union and would then be overturned by an arbitrator. Taking that path, Ueberroth would manage to look good in the eyes of the public, would come across as a defender of the game's integrity, and would be able to say he had tried to do what was right and proper—but the union had blocked him.[23]

On February 28, 1986, Ueberroth was finally ready to exact punishment. For the seven so-called "facilitators" of drug use, players like Keith Hernandez and Lonnie Smith, Ueberroth declared a year-long suspension from baseball that his office would lift if the players agreed to several terms. They could play if they donated 10 percent of their 1986 salary to a worthwhile drug rehabilitation program, provided one hundred hours of community service for at least two years, and agreed to submit to random drug tests for the remainder of their professional careers. For the other players, Ueberroth declared a sixty-day suspension that would be lifted if they gave 5 percent of their salary to the rehabilitation cause, provided fifty hours of service, and submitted to random testing.[24]

The lynchpin of Ueberroth's punishment was the employment of mandatory random testing. The commissioner hoped that forcing the Pittsburgh Eleven to accept the tests would be the first step toward making players throughout the league accept a testing program. Some clubs had already begun writing "testing clauses" into new player contracts. The MLBPA remained adamantly opposed to any testing and urged the Pittsburgh players to file grievances. Despite the union's urging, few players would do so. Player Representative Terry Kennedy summed up the bind in which the players found themselves. "They're [the Pittsburgh players] stuck between a rock and a hard place. I can't say I like it, but there's nothing we can do. The order has come down."[25]

Joaquin Andujar believed he was singled out by the commissioner for behavior that had nothing to do with drug abuse. He had a reputation as an outspoken eccentric and during the World Series in October had been ejected from Game Seven, a game his Cardinals would lose, after throwing a berserk fit at the umpires. Keith Hernandez was also outraged by the implications of the punishment decision and issued a statement wherein he claimed the he had been "incorrectly categorized as one who facilitated cocaine use. The facts, I feel, do not justify this position." Hernandez willingly admitted that he used cocaine in the early 1980s, but he never sold it. He did not turn other players onto the drug. The only person Hernandez hurt, he said, was himself. Initially pushed toward filing a grievance by the union, Hernandez, like his peers, ultimately chose not to. Marvin Miller lamented the softness of the players. "Apparently we don't have players with enough guts to defend themselves. If the players had lost the grievance they would be no worse off."[26]

Elsewhere, especially among the owners, Ueberroth's decision was celebrated. Sports attorney Bob Wolff called it a "tempered ruling. The things [Ueberroth] suggested are not unreasonable. He had every right to do it to preserve the integrity and maintain confidence in baseball." Bowie Kuhn, who fought his Quixotic antidrug crusade in the name of the game's integrity, was thrilled with Ueberroth's plan. "Good," he told the press in the wake of the announcement. "I support it all way . . . I particularly like the emphasis on drug testing. That's the key to the solution."[27]

For a very brief moment in early 1986 Peter Ueberroth appeared confident, assured, and proactive. With random testing as his clarion call, he was off across the metaphorical Rubicon to do battle with the union. He was widely lauded as an even-tempered and judicious leader ready to restore baseball to its pristine past, restore honor to the owners, and give worthy role models back to the baseball-watching public—a mission that even the Reverend Billy Graham said was of the utmost importance. Still, there was some reason to worry about the path Ueberroth was taking. Some rightly feared that Ueberroth's testing scheme might turn out to be grandstanding, preparing Ueberroth for a jump to the United States Senate. It was not clear, in those early months, as the wreckage of the Pittsburgh trial was still being cleared away, whether the commissioner had launched a game-changing coup or an outrageous, disingenuous, public relations sucker punch against the deeply entrenched union.[28]

The union, and other critics outside the MLBPA, wanted to know what kind of substance Ueberroth had behind his policy? If eliminating drugs was really so important, why had the owners eliminated the joint drug policy agreed upon by the agents of the players alongside the representatives of the owners? By what process would Ueberroth enforce testing? How could he ensure its reliability? He surely knew that the union would fight him every step of the way and that his grand scheme was doomed to bog down before any serious gains were made. Ueberroth's scheme, critics lamented, was not about fixing the game or saving the integrity of anyone other than, maybe, Peter Ueberroth. Maybe the commissioner thought he was steering the game out from under the shadow of drugs, but he was instead blindly tacking into the lightning-struck storm clouds of the sports world's most contentious and tragic year.[29]

*   *   *

In the long history of the sports world's struggle with drugs, 1986 was in no uncertain terms the nightmare year. No sport, professional or amateur, was untouched by the drug problem. Hardly a day passed that some new revelation about recreational or performance-enhancing drugs was not sprung upon the public. In January, as Ueberroth was still contemplating his response to the Pittsburgh Eleven, fifty-five college seniors at the National Football League's draft evaluation camp in New Orleans tested positive for cocaine or marijuana. Twenty-six of them would eventually be drafted. Then came revelations about the New England Patriots and cocaine use during their Super Bowl season of 1985. In June, as the baseball season and the battle over random testing heated up, Ueberroth and his crusade were driven from the front pages by tragedy that transcended sport. That month, Maryland basketball star, and nascent Boston Celtic, Len Bias collapsed and died after using cocaine at a campus party. Eight days later Cleveland Browns safety Don Rogers followed him to the grave under similar circumstances. "God sometimes uses our best people to get our attention," said the Rev. Jesse Jackson. "On a day children mourn, I hope they learn."[30]

Drugs were a plague not only in the professional ranks, but throughout all levels of sport. Three players on the Brigham Young University football team were arrested after they attempted to use forged prescriptions to obtain painkillers. Antoni Niemczak, the runner-up in the New York City marathon, was disqualified when his urinalysis test—designed to reveal marijuana usage—revealed the presence of performance-enhancing drugs in his system. Performance-enhancing drugs such as steroids were suddenly front and center in the minds of track-and-field watchers as well as NCAA officials.[31]

Nobody had a surefire answer for the drug problem. A quick survey of the sports world's various drug policies in February 1986 illustrates the disparate approaches of the organized leagues. Major League Baseball, arguably the highest profile sport in terms of its drug problem at that point, featured a policy in a state of limbo. You could hardly call it a "policy" at all. Only slightly more organized, the National Football League was in the midst of reworking a policy that had been in place since 1982. Drug abuse among the gridiron pro set led to fines, suspensions, or probation at the discretion of league czar Pete Rozelle, but only if a player was actually convicted of possession, purchase, sale, or use of illegal drugs. In the absence of a crime there was no punishment at all. The 1982 collective bargaining agreement called for urinalysis testing at the start of training camp (but players were given plenty of warning beforehand), whenever a player switched teams, or whenever a team had reasonable cause to test. Rozelle wanted to add more teeth via the implementation of random testing during the season, but like the MLBPA, the NFLPA was ready to fight increased testing at all costs.[32]

The National Hockey League, loudly insistent that it did not feature the serious drug problems of other major sports, had no rehab or testing program at all. However, NHL president John Ziegler had the power to ban or suspend players at his discretion, as he had done very recently in the case of Don Murdoch (forty games for possession of marijuana and cocaine) and Ric Natress (thirty games for possession of marijuana). The Men's International Professional Tennis Council conducted random testing at two major tournaments to be selected from the Grand Slam events and the Lipton International Championship.[33]

The model program, in the eyes of almost every pundit, belonged to the National Basketball Association. In the NBA, if a player voluntary sought treatment, he was referred to a rehab center in Pasadena, California. He would receive his full salary while undergoing treatment, and the league would provide after-care. A second-time offender was again referred to Pasadena, but this time was suspended without pay. Borrowing the useful baseball metaphor, a third strike (or *any* conviction based on drug use or sale) led to a ban from the league, which could be appealed after two years. The NBA program was widely celebrated as a workable and effective system developed by the players for the players. Of course, the popular NBA plan had been the model for Major League Baseball's short-lived joint drug policy, the one that the baseball owners charged was ineffective and unworkable.[34]

In all instances the major professional leagues were more concerned with recreational drug use than with performance enhancers. Only at the amateur level were stimulants, amphetamines, and anabolic steroids a focus. The United States Olympic Committee not only tested for all of these at sanctioned events, but it had also gone so far as to outlaw blood boosting.[35]

* * *

"The silence is terrifying," remarked CBS-TV commentators as Ronald Reagan signed a new antidrug bill at the White House Rose Garden in October 1986. It was time, at last, to open the door to a national discussion about the drug plague. Children, said critics, were ruining their lives with drugs. Some were dying. Sports vividly reflected the problem. Len Bias and Don Rogers were proof of that. Because of those athletes' high-profile deaths, the catastrophe of drug use was now a top priority in the highest offices in the land. As Ueberroth steered baseball toward random drug testing, his counterparts in Washington, D.C., were doing the same. There was now a concentrated public relations effort featuring President Reagan and his wife Nancy. Together from the White House they addressed the concern about drugs in the workplace and home, announcing the largest escalation in the history of the War on Drugs. The key PR element in the new antidrug offensive would be the First Lady's "Just Say No!" program.[36]

Over the next two years, the Reagan administration heavily promoted drug testing in the workplace as a critical component in the War on Drugs. Issuing Executive Order 12564, Reagan required federal agencies to develop programs and policies to achieve drug-free workplaces. Then, later in the year, the Drug-Free Workplace Act was passed through both houses of Congress. It led to the creation of new regulations by federal agencies requiring random testing of contract workers wherever there were concerns related to public safety. With the government leading the way, between 1985 and 1991 the percentage of companies conducting drug tests increased from 18 percent to 40 percent.[37]

Reagan even carried the escalation of the War on Drugs into his 1988 State of the Union Address, issuing what was deemed a clarion call at the time. "The war against drugs is a war of individual battles, a crusade with many heroes." In saying this, it was never doubted that Reagan, a lifelong sports fan, would look to the world of athletics for the heroes to carry his antidrug banner. Professional sports leagues would, in fact, become the model for all American businesses. If drug testing worked in sports, it would work anywhere. Athletes would join the fight by appearing in ubiquitous public service announcements stressing the drug-free lifestyle. From baseball's ranks Hank Aaron and Jim Palmer joined together to warn Little Leaguers about the evils of drug use. In the video where they relayed their message, Los Angeles Dodgers star pitcher Orel Hershiser joined them to stress the path to clean, honest, manhood. He did so in a strange sequence wherein he warned a young boy away from marijuana use during a bizarre bedside dream-visitation. Ueberroth was eager to put baseball squarely on the side of the national antidrug effort, and Major League Baseball lent its imagery to antidrug programs publishing pamphlets and a coloring book to send the message to its youngest fans.[38]

But for all the hokey charm of athletes coming out to urge youngsters away from a life of drugs, and despite Mrs. Reagan's well-received effort to take her message to the nation's schools, the thorny issue of drug testing continued to draw criticism. Drug testing would not go down easily simply because President Reagan endorsed it. Chuck Shumer, one of the congressional critics of the testing legislation, joked about various administration officials having to undergo these "voluntary" drug tests. Shumer allowed that people were probably OK with White House staffers getting tested, but if drug testing should become widespread it would "become a bubbling and boiling cauldron of controversy." For Shumer, as it was for so many in the world of big-time sport, the problematic issue was accuracy. "How many people know that the standard test has a 2 to 11 percent inaccuracy rate?" People who had never touched drugs in their life, said Shumer, faced a one in twenty chance that the test would reveal they had used drugs in the previous six months.[39]

* * *

In March, not terribly long after Ueberroth's announcement regarding the punishment of the Pittsburgh Eleven, the New York Yankees were preparing to face the Toronto Blue Jays in a spring training tilt. Dave Winfield, the million-dollar Yankees star, stood in the batting cage. "Education is the answer, not testing," he argued. "I don't think it has any place in sports. I tell kids 'if you want to get any place in life, leave drugs alone.' But testing isn't the way to do it."[40]

Outside the cage stood Dick Young, the elder statesman of the baseball writers, his leonine mane of white hair unruly as ever, his eyes narrowed. Drugs had become a singular obsession of Young's, a problem he had not imagined would become such a huge part of baseball life when he led the way in personalizing baseball writing in the 1960s, fathering the "chipmunk" style. Now, no longer a pioneer, Young had evolved into the arch-conservative voice of the establishment, who was jokingly seen by younger peers as opposing change simply because it was change. He was against free agency, against expansion, and against the designated hitter. One colleague aptly called the cranky Young "an ink-stained, hot dog-munching, Lyndon Larouche," a controversial conservative political figure. On this day the famously crabby *New York Post* reporter was edgy. "Why not? Why not try [drug testing]? What's it hurt to try it?" He pointed out, perhaps with a touch of sarcasm, that drugs were *illegal*. They weren't talking about booze. "If it doesn't work, then go back."[41]

"We all got opinions, Dick," replied Winfield, preparing again to take some cuts. "This is like the players and the owners. What we all need to do is sit at a round table and work this thing out, instead of sitting at a long table across from each other."[42]

Winfield surely knew, as did Young, that baseball had tried that route once already. The recently scrapped Joint Drug Policy was the fruit of long talks between the players and owners. Getting that agreement in place had been a struggle. Early in 1984, while Bowie Kuhn was still commissioner, the Drugs Study Committee, the group in charge of hammering out some sort of workable policy, had not yet done so. Kuhn was eager to leave some system in place before he left office, but an informal survey of club officials by the *Sporting News* indicated that any prospective course of action would prove difficult. The committee ultimately planned for season-long spot testing of Minor League Baseball players (they were unprotected by the collective bargaining agreement) and stepped up the drug education program at both Major League and Minor League levels. They urged teams to retain psychologists and psychiatrists on staff throughout the season. All of this was largely in keeping with the Kuhn era's singular focus on educating athletes about chemical abuse while simultaneously looking for a useful example to illustrate the punitive powers of the commissioner's office.[43]

In the end it fell to Montreal Expos president John McHale, Oakland A's president Roy Eisenhardt, PRC executive director Lee MacPhail, and PRC attorney Barry Rona to lead management toward some coherent policy alongside the union's acting director, Don Fehr, and his adviser, Marvin Miller. Hank Peters, an executive with the Baltimore Orioles, pointed out that the "battle against drugs" could be divided into three areas: education, identification, and rehabilitation. "The first and last are relatively easy to implement," he said. The EAPs, psychiatric staff, and pretty much everything else that baseball had done since the early 1970s were built around those facets. "Detection," explained Peters, "is by far the most difficult." Detection would almost certainly require testing of some sort—and no players' union member was going to agree to it.[44]

The exact method of detection ended up being the primary stumbling block in the talks between the PRC and the MLBPA. The union was adamant that *random* testing was a violation of the players' civil rights (they said nothing, on the other hand, about the civil rights of minor leaguers already being tested). And beyond the issue of detection, there were still questions about what to do with those caught abusing chemicals. Hanging over the proceedings was the memory of Ken Moffett, the recently fired union chief. Moffett had been highly, and openly, critical of drug abuse among the players and had apparently been ready to support random testing.[45]

While the PRC desperately wanted some sort of testing clause, the union repeatedly pointed out how dangerously unreliable testing was. In the mid-1980s urinalysis was a "highly inaccurate science." Inaccurate results, argued the union, could all too easily destroy careers. The only test known to be close to 100 percent accurate was the GC/Mass Spec—but it cost roughly $85 to $100 a "pop." Cheaper ($5 to $10) tests like RIA (radioimmunoassay), EMIT (enzyme multiplied immunoassay technique), and TLC (thin-layer chromatography) did not require a licensed technician to administer them. One out of four results of those tests showed the possibility of being a "false positive." It was unconscionable that for every twenty Major Leaguers tested, four might wrongly be associated with drug use—and it was almost impossible to ensure that even false positives would not be leaked to the media. "Each measurement and each drug may require many steps, and each step may provoke error," wrote Dr. John P. Morgan in his 1984 article "Problems of Mass Urine Screening for Misused Drugs" in the *Journal of Psychoactive Drugs*. "Drug measurement is not easy. Precision drug measurement is even harder."[46]

There could be problems with contaminated equipment, carryover from previous tests, or operator error (especially where unlicensed technicians were involved). A study conducted by the Centers for Disease Control and Prevention (CDC), published in 1985 by the *Journal of the American Medical Association*, checked the performance of thirteen drug-testing labs servicing 262 drug treatment facilities. Error rates for those facilities, usually using EMIT or TLC tests, often hit 100 percent—they were *always* wrong. Results for 6 percent of cocaine tests, 66 percent of methadone tests, and 37 percent of tests for amphetamine were false positives. Five out of thirteen cocaine tests had a zero percent correct-response rate.[47]

Dr. Morgan discussed how the United States Army was reviewing the results of 100,000 tests after it emerged that almost 30,000 military personnel might be facing disciplinary action. The U.S. Navy concluded that out of 6,000 positive tests, 2,000 could not be substantiated. Another 2,000 lacked key documentation. More than 65 percent of the tests were essentially useless. This was the type of disastrous scenario the MLBPA envisioned when it adopted a hard line against random testing.[48]

The PRC tried, as best they could, to assure the union that testing could work. The system used by the minor leagues, actually more thorough than that used by the armed forces, used a pre-screen with EMIT, and if that test turned out to be positive, then the league sought confirmation through the use of the more reliable GC/Mass Spec. But the use of EMIT was another stumbling block. It was little better, suggested Morgan, than a faulty lie-detector test. "Technology traps people," he said. "Such entrapment is aided by a refusal to be critical in the face of flawed technological approaches." Drug testing was an unreliable panacea, even when layered with the most reliable test then known. Besides, reliability aside, the notion that innocent players had to prove their innocence via testing was ridiculous. Some even called it "un-American."[49]

Al Rosen, president of the Houston Astros, scoffed at the often-cited civil rights argument. He wanted to know about the rights of the owners. "Everyone agrees we're talking about curing an illness," he said. "But drugs, unlike cancer, are an illness of choice. And baseball owners should have the right to try to protect themselves against loss from players who choose to become ill." In other words, this was as much about money and legitimate business concerns than anything else. When high-priced players burned out on drugs, the owners lost financial assets and big investments. As the talks bogged down, the only real point of agreement was that the NBA's new "Three Strikes and You're Out" approach was the best existing policy in the sports universe.[50]

The Joint Drug Prevention and Treatment Program as finally adopted provided two key means of dealing with drug use in baseball. It first set up a procedure whereby an impartial three-person Joint Review Council, with members selected by both the owners and the union, could order a player to submit to drug testing. Second, it established a rehabilitation list on which teams could place a player while he was undergoing treatment.[51]

There was no random mandatory testing. The owners wanted it badly, but the players would not agree to it. Nevertheless, the PRC was proud of the policy. So, too, was outgoing commissioner Bowie Kuhn. "It's no panacea," said Lee MacPhail of the joint drug policy, "but it's a good start." On the other side of the table Don Fehr was glad that the two sides were finally adopting a unified approach rather than the "scattergun approach" of recent years whereby members of various organizations lectured the players about drug use but did little else. That approach clearly had not worked.[52]

As soon as the joint drug policy went into effect, clubs that suspected a problem would be able to discuss it with the player. If that player did not acknowledge a problem or agree to some course of treatment, then he and the club would go before the Joint Review Council. The council had the power to determine whether the club had valid cause to suspect the player and how best to deal with the problem. If the player entered a treatment program during the season, he received full pay for the first thirty days of the treatment. If he needed more time, he was then given half-pay for the next thirty days, after which he was to be paid at a rate based on the minimum league salary. Players who entered rehab during the offseason would lose no pay.[53]

Unless a player was convicted of a felony or misdemeanor, or used or distributed drugs at the ballpark, there was nothing in the joint drug policy that allowed for further disciplinary action. Dick Young lamented the lack of a drug-testing procedure and the absence of any real punitive element. When the policy was scrapped in late 1985, he was ecstatic. "It wasn't any good to begin with . . . It had no drug testing procedure. It had no teeth."[54]

On September 24, 1985, shortly before the joint drug policy was eliminated, Peter Ueberroth called a press conference where he read from a letter asking players to agree to volunteer for three unscheduled drug tests via urinalysis. The tests would focus on recreational drugs and would not screen for amphetamines. "Baseball is in trouble," the commissioner explained. "The shadow that drugs have cast is growing larger and darker by the day." Don Fehr saw the ploy for what it was. "This is an attempt to bypass the union. It is possibly unlawful. It is entirely inappropriate." Ueberroth had erred badly.[55]

The players, it turned out, were not necessarily opposed to drug testing, but they were deeply troubled that Ueberroth's suggestion had not been routed through proper channels. The growing suspicion that almost everything Ueberroth did was a slickly designed public relations gimmick colored their perception of the letter now circulating through league clubhouses. It was clear that something new was in the offing and that the short-lived, unified approach to the drug problem was not long for the world.

Ueberroth had been building toward this moment since early in 1985. In May he announced that all front office personnel in baseball would be screened for drug abuse. Four days later, during a commencement speech in Los Angeles at Loyola Marymount University, he promised to accomplish the elimination of drugs in baseball. "Somebody has to say 'Enough is enough' . . . We're going to remove drugs and be an example." For Ueberroth the specter of the Tulane University men's basketball point-shaving scandal (Tulane was the punch line to the sports joke of 1985: "what's green and white and shaves twice a year?") was a frightening possibility of what might happen to baseball. "Illegal drugs provide a far better opportunity for gambling to find its way into sports than anything," he explained. He felt it wasn't a big jump from drug abuse to gambling and game fixing.[56]

It was quickly established that all players in the minor leagues and other Major League personnel—groundskeepers, stadium workers, clubhouse attendants—would be tested. Ueberroth was operating under the assumption that the fans wanted to see a more rigorous approach taken to the drug problem. A *New York Times*/CBS poll conducted between July 16 and July 21 showed that 78 percent of the fans polled believed that drug use among baseball players was a serious problem. Still, even as Ueberroth was edging the establishment away from the joint drug policy, others continued to promise that the policy would work.[57]

That summer, in the run-up to the Pittsburgh trial, Ueberroth made it clear that he planned to expand his mandatory testing program outside of the United States, targeting the winter leagues in the Latin American countries. "There are places where players play where people look the other way. I don't know how much leverage I'll have. I'm running into resistance. But I'm getting a steady flow of information that some of the root causes are there." Many believed the winter leagues were where young players got their first taste of cocaine. "I think a lot of it starts in winter ball in Venezuela; you're right next to Colombia," said Joel Youngblood of the Giants. "If you don't speak the language, what else is there to do except play ball and hang out by the pool. A lot of players were exposed to [cocaine] and it was cheaper. If we're going to shut down drugs in baseball, we have to shut them down everywhere." Dock Ellis, who knew as much about drug use in baseball as anyone, laughed at the notion: "They have as much cocaine here as they do in the Dominican or Venezuela."[58]

Despite the fact that the joint drug policy was still, technically, the rule, Ueberroth was talking more and more about testing. When it came down to it, everything about testing hinged on the thorny issue of privacy rights. Ueberroth likened it to airport security. Urine tests weren't any different than players having to go through metal detectors. Pitcher Larry Sorensen appeared bitter when he discussed Ueberroth's new testing obsession. "In the country we live in, you're supposed to have freedoms," he told one reporter, "but evidently, because I throw a slider, I don't have the same freedoms."[59]

Those who supported Ueberroth and testing contended that the union was more interested in preserving the right to snort a line in private than it was in preserving the great American game. On the other side, supporters of the union position saw Donald Fehr as a lonely but righteous fighter against public opinion. "Public perception is important; you want people on your side," Fehr once admitted. "But you don't negotiate on the basis of public opinion. Let me give you an example. If you hire me as your lawyer—you're charged with a crime—what would you have me do, take an opinion poll, and if 64% of the people said you should go to jail, then we give up? We forget about what's right? No, or you'd fire me in a hurry."[60]

Ueberroth's proposed solution was met with criticism and concern in the league's clubhouses. Gene Mauch of the Angels was concerned about drugs, but he opposed Ueberroth's solution. "I believe that drugs are a greater danger to our society than any other country is. More people in this country have died from drugs than died at Hiroshima. Two or three times as many.

But this thing from the commissioner's office . . . it isn't going to accomplish anything."[61]

On October 22, the night of the third game of the 1985 World Series, the owners scrapped the joint drug policy. "In my mind," said Ballard Smith of the Padres, "there has to be testing next year. I think the issue is going to be forced one way or another. It has to. The integrity of the game is at stake. It cannot be ignored."[62]

In reality, scrapping the joint drug policy probably had less to do with finding a better way to fight drugs than it did for the owners scoring a public relations coup against the players. By using the high-profile drug crisis to illuminate the seeming ugliness of the modern game, including (and primarily) the huge contracts of drug-abusing players, the owners believed they could lure fans to their side and establish a new modicum of control on the game and on salaries. In other words, scrapping the joint drug policy was less about fighting drugs than it was about rolling back the clock and neutering the union.

As much as he detested the joint drug policy, Dick Young had no faith in the motivation of the owners. "The Lords of Baseball trade druggie ballplayers," he wrote in one scathing editorial. "This amounts to selling drugs after the fact, concealed in the human system, after the stuff has been sniffed or smoked or swallowed by the players." The owners really had no problem with drugs as long as it didn't hurt their pocketbooks.

The liberals and their civil rights argument were even more absurd, as far as Young was concerned. "As the great progressives say, 'Hey, if a player wants to do it, it's his arm, isn't it?'" Who knew what players would be shooting up with next? Pitchers with needle tracks on their valuable arms would become a not-too-uncommon sight. The "insipid" joint drug policy, Young continued, had given "the druggie solace" and convinced him "he was only hurting himself by being naughty."[63]

Young echoed a conservative contingent that wanted to let players who dabbled in drugs suffer the worst consequences of their actions. "Don't stop to clean up his vomit or his bloody nose," said Young. Just kick him out of the game. Young recalled all of the times baseball players had demanded to be treated like "men." Now was the time to do it. The "druggie" was "no innocent babe. He's a man. God knows we've all heard that a thousand times from ballplayers: 'I want to be treated like a man.'" But men in baseball were really just boys. When Dick Young was a boy he kept out of trouble because, on one hand, he feared punishment and, on the other, he feared breaking his mother's heart.[64]

"For some inexplicable reason, kids and ballplayers no longer think that way." Players, caught up in the aftershocks of the 1960s, had become too interested in immediate self-gratification. Worse, and especially under the joint drug policy, there was no punishment to fear.

Young reserved an especially visceral broadside for Lee MacPhail, primary author of the failed joint drug policy. MacPhail was baseball's "Mother Theresa," sneered Young, "who goes through life uttering the homily: 'There is no such thing as a bad boy.' And he will say it as he lies dying on some Manhattan street with the shiv from a teenaged druggie in his chest."[65]

* * *

Early in 1985 the Los Angeles Dodgers had tried to pioneer mandatory drug testing in the Major Leagues. They inserted testing clauses into the contracts of players Mike Marshall and Bill Russell. The Players' Association contended that the clauses violated the joint agreement, and, because they still believed in the joint drug policy, the PRC concurred. The Dodgers, with no backing whatsoever, eliminated the clauses from the contracts. At the same time, players on other teams had actually agreed to the insertion of testing clauses. Almost always these were players who had, in some way or another, been implicated in one of the cocaine scandals of the early decade. Rich Dauer of the Orioles, for example, submitted to testing after he was involved in the investigation of a Baltimore area drug dealer in 1983. So, too, did Pittsburgh trial notable Dale Berra.[66]

If testing at the Major League level was unlikely to come about, a number of clubs instituted minor league urinalysis testing even before Ueberroth announced his 1985 plan. Clubs responded dubiously to the charges that this constituted an invasion of privacy. Edward Kenney, director of player development with the Boston Red Sox, emphasized the emerging stigma that most athletes were on drugs. Surely players would want to fight such a stigma. "If someone comes in to me and says we think you are on drugs, I want to prove them wrong. If an athlete is not on drugs he will be happy to submit. I don't think it's an invasion of privacy." Jim Baumer, vice president and director of player development for the Philadelphia Phillies, added, "we want to head something off that's bad early on and weed out those kind of people." The "kind" being what Dick Young sneeringly called "druggies." Of course, most critics of the minor league testing system noted that at the minor league level kids were usually afraid to use anything. More importantly, since cocaine was the high-profile drug of the age, kids in the minor leagues didn't have the money to buy it anyway.[67]

As testing proceeded in the minors and in the Major League front offices, it was only a matter of time before another club attempted to follow in the Dodgers' footsteps. Hank Peters, the general manager of the Baltimore Orioles, couldn't remember a meeting that he'd been to in the last several years wherein drug use had not been discussed. It was hardly surprising, then, when the Orioles were the first club to advocate voluntary testing for players signing contracts in the winter of 1985 and 1986. Obviously the Orioles' drug plan would be superseded by any deal agreed upon by the union and management—if and when that happened. And that seemed unlikely given the owners' October surprise.[68]

In his discussions with player agents, Peters explained that most of the contracts yet to be signed were for young players. They would be for only one year. Twenty-six of the Orioles' thirty-eight targeted players had agreed to the clauses. To critics he offered assurances. There was nothing being "forced" on Orioles players. The system was entirely voluntary. "It's for the player's benefit," Peters explained, "because it gets him out from under the clouds, and, more important, if a guy has a problem, we can discuss it and talk of it in a counseling program." The Orioles' program would provide testing through the Johns Hopkins Hospital and Medical School under the supervision of three Johns Hopkins physicians. The Orioles called it a "hands off" program because once every player was involved, it was all between the players and physicians.[69]

Voluntary and "hands off" or not, it was not clear whether the Orioles' contract clauses were legal. Ron Shapiro, the legal counsel who represented about twenty of the players looking to sign contracts with the Orioles (including superstars Eddie Murray and Cal Ripken Jr.), supported the clauses, and yet even he admitted his uncertainty about their legality. "We want the game to be clean," was all he said. "There are a lot of players who don't use drugs and feel guilt by association."[70]

When the union began to voice concerns about the clauses, Scott McGregor, a prominent pitcher with the Orioles and the club's player representative to the union, explained how the club was trying to pioneer a model drug-testing program for all of baseball. "We can't keep going to war over everything," he said. Although the union's early position was not to involve itself with what was a voluntary program, other representatives began to pressure the Orioles pitcher. When the union finally did come out against the appearance of testing clauses in the contracts of other clubs, an exasperated McGregor declared that he was up "against the union."[71]

One of the union representatives who fired a broadside at McGregor was former All-Star Ted Simmons. He replied to McGregor's plans to create a model testing program, concluding that a "poignant assault of those efforts is in order." Simmons wanted to know what made McGregor think he could propose policy: "by what authority you selectively, autonomously, and presumptuously act out of accord with the executive policy making group with the MLBPA." McGregor, Simmons pointed out, was acting outside of the collective bargaining process. What role, he asked, did Ron Shapiro play, and shouldn't he, as a legal expert, be included in discussions between the MLBPA and PRC? McGregor and Shapiro's activities "were made manifest through arrogant indifference to the collective bargaining process and the executive policy making board." The MLBPA, Simmons explained, operates "on a democratic and simple majority basis. These precepts are girthed by open debate and reason. If you cannot function within this structure, as you most recently have not, then I will continue to most stridently respond to your activities."[72]

Despite the pressure applied by union representatives, other clubs rushed to follow the Orioles in the wake of Ueberroth's decision regarding the Pittsburgh Eleven. San Diego Padres outfielder Tony Gwynn, who had a firsthand view of the Alan Wiggins drug debacle, volunteered himself for drug testing and predicted that it would eventually become mandatory. Union chief Don Fehr suggested, conversely, that the arbitration he had just filed in opposition to the rash of testing clauses would make drug testing a dead issue.[73]

"Either arbitration is going to decide that a drug policy has to be negotiated through the union, or it will allow them (the owners) to make policies," the union counsel said. Fehr alleged that drug-testing clauses were being used to gain leverage on contract talks, offering long-term deals only to players who agreed to the clauses. The test case on which the MLBPA was focusing involved arbitration filed on behalf of San Francisco Giants outfielder Joel Youngblood, who had reached agreement on a contract with the Giants but had then seen the contract withdrawn when he refused to sign a drug-testing clause.[74]

Even before players hit the field for the 1986 season the contentious issue of drug testing had created rifts between the front office and the clubhouse, exacerbated the rift between the union and management, and provided plenty of fodder for the press. Management tended to acknowledge the clauses as being reasonable protection for the investment made in players by the owners. Jack McKeon, the Padres general manager, said clauses would be put in the contracts of any players who wanted guaranteed salaries. "Hey, if you want your guarantee, if we're going to put out some amount of dollars, we're going to want that drug clause in there. We need a way of knowing that you're staying clean."[75]

Dallas Green, president of the Chicago Cubs, insisted that all Cubs contracts would include a drug-testing clause. Leon Durham, the team's star first baseman, who signed his contract in the winter of 1986, was typical of the new approach being taken by Major League clubs. "I think when you guarantee millions and millions of dollars," said Green, "the club has to have some protection."[76]

The Dodgers, who had tried this approach and had been rebuked, were now eager to apply it once again. Steve Yeager, the club's veteran catcher, signed a one-year deal, the first Dodgers contract to include the new clause. "Our philosophy won't change," said General Manager Fred Claire. "We believe in testing. We've seen it work at the Minor League level. We also think there are a lot of players who share our feeling."[77]

More than a few did. Scott McGregor was, of course, a proponent of the testing clauses. So, too, was Chicago Cubs outfielder Keith Moreland. Kansas City Royals pitcher Brett Saberhagen, a young hero for the newly crowned World Champions, asked the club to insert a testing clause into his new $925,000 contract. "I have nothing to hide. We need to get the bad image out of baseball." Garry Templeton, the Padres shortstop, remembered how everyone had believed he was on drugs in 1981. Tests at the hospital had disproved it. "The only thing that saved me," he said, "was going into a hospital and having tests."[78]

Vida Blue, whose story was well known around baseball, sent a letter to the Giants, the MLBPA, and Peter Ueberroth. "My probation will be completed in March 1986. Nonetheless, I intend to continue to be tested for drugs so long as I am an active player in the major leagues. I want the fans who have been so supportive of me in my comeback to be confident that any failure or success I have on the field is that of a well-conditioned, fiercely competitive ballplayer who gave all he had to give for as long as he had it to give." Blue claimed that he did not adopt this pro-testing stance to enhance his position with the Giants and that his views shouldn't reflect on any other players. It was then pointed out that he was likely to have to insert a clause into his contract not because of his past indiscretions but because the Giants had every intention of doing this for *all* players who signed guaranteed contracts with them.[79]

There were, of course, concerns about the reliability of the tests. John Tudor, the Cardinals' twenty-game winner, worried about the effectiveness and confidentiality of the tests when he sat down over the winter to discuss his contract with GM Dal Maxvill. "If you'd asked me a month ago, I would have said I was ready to put in a drug-testing clause. I felt it was time that this stuff stops. But in doing research, now I agree with the Players Association for the reason that testing isn't 100 percent accurate."[80]

While baseball quarreled over drug testing, the NBA, whose drug program had been on the books since 1984, banned its first three-time offenders, most notably Michael Ray Richardson and John Drew. But baseball, unwilling to adopt the ready-made "three strikes and out" policy of their basketball brethren, instead left the power of punishment in Ueberroth's hands, to be levied as he saw fit given the circumstances of each case. This had not worked for Bowie Kuhn, and it was not working for Ueberroth either. The union filed grievances against the random drug-testing clauses suddenly appearing in player contracts. The final decision on the legality of the clauses would fall to arbitrator Tom Roberts, whose decision, it was widely held, would prove the most important in baseball since Peter Seitz's landmark 1975 decision that opened the doors to free agency. Roberts's decision would determine not only the course of baseball's future drug policy, but drug policy throughout the world of American professional sports.

*   *   *

Bob Stanley was a relief pitcher for the Boston Red Sox. When he was asked to submit to voluntary urinalysis tests, he was upset. "I don't take drugs and I don't believe I have to prove it." In expressing his displeasure with baseball's new path, Stanley put himself on the side of what one reporter called one of the oldest of American values: general searches of innocent people are unfair and unreasonable. Ira Glasser, a representative of the American Civil Liberties Union, explained that Ueberroth's proposed testing scheme and the mandarins of the modern National Pastime were analogous to the hated redcoats of King George III searching colonial Americans indiscriminately "in order to uncover those few who were violating the Stamp Act or otherwise committing offenses against the crown."[81]

It was exactly those transgressions, Glasser explained, that led the country's founders to adopt the Fourth Amendment to the U.S. Constitution, striking a key balance between the privacy of the citizenry and the needs of law enforcement. As far as Glasser was concerned, the basic right that all people possessed, the right of the many to avoid searches in order to discover the guilty few, was directly challenged by random, mandatory urinalysis tests and those who supported them. A host of civil libertarians joined Glasser in condemning across-the-board drug testing as a violation of the spirit of the Fourth Amendment. Richard Emery of the New York Civil Liberties Union called random mandatory testing "a practice that would be tolerated only in

Yugoslavia or Argentina. It is fundamentally un-American." Gene Orza of the MLBPA likened testing to Japanese internment or the Hollywood blacklist.[82]

Those who took their stand on the Fourth Amendment rushed to marshal support for their position. There was some significant legal precedent in their corner. In 1968 the U.S. Supreme Court had supported the view that compulsory blood and urine tests were bodily searches and, as such, could only be conducted if there was a "clear indication that in fact . . . evidence will be found." The Fourth Amendment's search and seizure rules, of course, technically applied to search and seizure by *government entities*. The ACLU firmly believed, especially when looking at the lay of the baseball landscape, that it should apply to *all* citizens. All men, after all, were innocent until proven guilty.[83]

Some took what is today an almost cliché position: the innocent had nothing to fear from searches of this sort. Critics fired back, echoing John Tudor of the Cardinals, that the urine tests used by Major League Baseball were unreliable at best. The tests couldn't distinguish between certain types of drugs or confirm how recently the drug had been used. Innocence was, at best, uncertain in all cases and even for the cleanest players. Besides, pointing at the hypocrisy of the game's economics, critics suggested that if baseball was as concerned about its public image, and Ueberroth had made his drug-testing push in the name of cleaning up the game's image and restoring its integrity, then owners would not be encouraging baseball's ties to endless beer commercials and the lucrative sale of beer at the ballpark.[84]

Baseball was stepping over the line. Employers certainly had the right to expect sobriety on the job, but they did not have the right to monitor their employees while they were off the job. Defenders of sacrosanct civil rights complained that baseball's owners and management were all too willing to "sacrifice the rights and interests of the majority of players, who are innocent of any misconduct," in order to deal with what they saw as a public relations problem. They were, in fact, just like people who defend "warrantless wiretapping . . . by suggesting that people shouldn't mind being wiretapped if they have nothing to hide." But, critics of Ueberroth's policy proclaimed, people should have the right to hide their private lives.

Defenders of player privacy even borrowed some of the popular lines from the antidrug forces. Sports, they pointed out, like to talk about role models. Perhaps, they concluded, the establishment should consider the role model they are providing when they abandon basic American rules of fairness, subjecting not only the guilty but the innocent as well to intrusive procedures.[85]

In the wake of President Reagan's call for implementing drug testing in the War on Drugs, workplace testing had proliferated enormously. Some said that baseball had played a part in pushing the American workplace toward a new era. Sure, the NBA's policy was the most progressive and admired in the professional sports world, but baseball was, well, baseball. The National Pastime carried more weight. And now that Ueberroth was going to institute spot testing, other businesses and school districts were inclined to follow suit. "Baseball has made drug testing very popular. We're getting more calls than ever [in support of it]," said one school district administrator.[86]

Between the ACLU and civil libertarian defenders of the "right to privacy" and Ueberroth's public relations–minded supporters there was a third way. Joel Kirsch, a former team psychologist for the San Francisco Giants and director of the American Sports Institute, pointed out that the drug tests did not address the most "crucial and complex issue: Why do people take drugs?" Instead of getting down to the root of the problem, Ueberroth and the Major League establishment were endorsing a policy that Kirsch believed was short sighted and simplistic. Major League Baseball was trying to use testing to scare players away from drugs rather than discover (and combat) what is was that caused them to use drugs in the first place.

Kirsch's argument echoed decades of national dialogue on American drug culture. He described a world where ads promised a pill-shaped ameliorative to back pain, or headaches, or whatever problem one faced. But the pills and the ads were not to blame either. Why, asked Kirsh, does one's back hurt in the first place? If you could answer that question and solve the problem, then you might get somewhere. But Ueberroth's plan didn't ask the right questions or seek to deal with the real problem. It was like "putting a Band-Aid over a malignant tumor."[87]

Kirsch hoped that baseball would come to its senses and use its unique visibility and cultural cachet to make a leap forward in the war against drugs. Baseball, he explained, "has a unique opportunity to deal with the drug problem in a manner that benefits players and society at large." If the Major Leagues approached the War on Drugs in the right way, it "may be the best thing to happen to sports in some time."

For Kirsch, the problem was this: players used drugs to re-create a natural "baseball high," that moment when years of dedication to the game came together on the diamond with new, overwhelming media attention and a high salary. Rather than some quick-fix, public-relations testing program, Kirsch hoped Ueberroth would produce a series of programs that would help players rediscover that natural high outside of baseball by applying new concepts and practices to their lives—making them not only healthier and happier, but better role models for America's youth.[88]

* * *

Ultimately, the test case for the MLBPA's position would stem from the proliferation of contract clauses requiring voluntary testing, and specifically the case of Giants outfielder Joel Youngblood. Fehr and his associates notified Barry Rona and the Player Relations Council of their grievance—the clauses violated several articles and provisions in the Basic Agreement. An arbitrator, they concluded, must rule the clauses unenforceable, and any player who had suffered "damages" as a result of the clauses would need to be compensated by "such relief as will fully and completely remedy any damage suffered by him."[89]

Thomas Roberts, the arbitrator assigned to the Youngblood case, agreed with Fehr. On June 30, 1986, he declared that the voluntary testing clauses in the contracts of more than four hundred Major Leaguers were to be thrown out because the owners had not negotiated their inclusion with the union. In the absence of collective bargaining, the clauses were, indeed, a violation of the 1985 Basic Agreement. Arbitrator Richard Kashner would make the same decision for the National Football League where the NFLPA was challenging the right of Pete Rozelle to implement a drug program without union approval. "Obviously, we are pleased with the arbitrator's award," said Don Fehr. "It reaffirms an important principle in this industry. Management cannot bypass the association and use individual negotiations to change the player's terms and conditions of employment."[90]

Dave Anderson, an infielder with the Los Angeles Dodgers, articulated the player's position. "The issue is not drug testing. It's the clause in the contract. The players probably will take some negative flak on this. People may even say we're against drug testing. That's not the point. The point is that we want [the owners] to go through the union."[91]

On the other side, the owners and establishment were disheartened by what was clearly a significant defeat. "I'm very disappointed by the decision," said Barry Rona. "It's clear that the real losers are the players." Bill Giles of the Phillies prophesied even worse fallout. "I feel bad for the players, the game and the country."[92]

Others were less sure of the threat to America. "I think it sounds pretty American to me," said Kansas City Royals relief whiz Dan Quisenberry. The red-headed submariner, always a sharp and amusing interview, echoed Anderson in noting that the problem was not the effort to address the drug problem. That was no mistake. The dubious end run around the Player's Association, on the other hand, was.[93]

What had happened? Hadn't the clauses been voluntary? Mike Stone, an executive with the Texas Rangers, blamed Donald Fehr for their ruin. The union chief was looking for some excuse to justify his existence. Assaulting the drug clauses was that excuse. "I'll be damned if we're going to risk several million dollars and have no guarantees," complained Stone. Roberts's decision would lead to fewer long-term contracts. Embittered, the owners would concentrate more fully now on Ueberroth's other great scheme—fixing contract prices via collusion. Just days after the drug clause decision the owners fired arbitrator Roberts, who was in the midst of hearings regarding collusion.[94]

The owners groused about the defeat, prophesied shorter contracts, and complained that the players weren't interested in eliminating drugs from the game. The union pointed out that it was the owners who had backed out of the perfectly good joint drug policy. That system, which relied on voluntary acceptance of testing or resort to a council hearing, was "not what Ueberroth wanted," explained Mark Belanger, a former player with Baltimore and now Don Fehr's assistant. "He couldn't use it for publicity. It wasn't his baby. He's on his way someplace. I don't know where, but he's going to try to use the players to get there."[95]

* * *

After the wars of 1986, Peter Ueberroth's focus on removing drugs from the game was increasingly nothing more than a superficial public relations campaign. Donald Fehr always insisted that the owners' position under Ueberroth was "public relations related and not substantial." They knew there was never going to be random drug testing. Instead, Ueberroth concentrated primarily on the matter of collusion and locking up a record television deal for Major League Baseball. The latter effort fattened the pocketbooks of the owners, wheras the former lightened them considerably.[96]

The MLBPA, as usual, filed grievances when the owners launched their plan to artificially lower player contracts by colluding not to bid on free agent players and thus fix contract prices. The arbitration decision on "Collusion I" favored the union, calling for owners to recoup the players for $20-$30 million in lost wages. Then, instead of meeting face-to-face to discuss free agent bids as they had been doing in the past, owners went to work within Ueberroth's newly contrived system wherein bids were entered into an information bank shared around the front offices of the league. Although some salary raises were clearly being considered, there was still evidence of continued price fixing. In the summer of 1988 gates were growing, fans were coming out in droves, and baseball seemed to be enjoying a renaissance. Arbitrator George Nicolau dropped the hammer in his decision on "Collusion II." The owners had to recoup more than $270 million in potential damages.[97]

Meanwhile, Ueberroth proposed yet another drug plan, to be implemented in 1989. It was little different from his previous attempts. It was in part a response to a 1987 season that was almost as bad as the previous one. First there were more congressional hearings, reminiscent of the Bayh meetings in the early 1970s—and equally inconsequential: lots of talk about heroes, morals, sport, and spectacle. There was nothing in the way of pragmatic answers to the "Sportsworld" drug crisis. In baseball more specifically, the headlines of 1987 were dominated by the tragedies of Mets phenom Dwight Gooden, his bright young career untracked by cocaine abuse, and LaMarr Hoyt, whose exploits turned baseball's inability to deal with drugs into comic absurdity.

Hoyt, despite his beefy frame and unkempt style, was one of the most successful pitchers of the early 1980s. He parlayed excellent control and stamina into the 1983 Cy Young Award while with the Chicago White Sox. Hoyt was traded to the San Diego Padres in 1985 to be their new workhorse (the Padres were coming off a World Series appearance in which their pitchers had performed poorly; closer Goose Gossage took one look at Hoyt and happily proclaimed him not a "workhorse" but a "Clydesdale"). Despite a fine first year in San Diego in which he turned in a 16–8 record and was the All-Star Game winner for the National League, Hoyt's 1986 year was symbolic of the game's travails in that year. It was truly a dismal season.[98]

He was detained by authorities and paid a $620 fine on February 10 when he tried to sneak Valium and marijuana across the Mexican border at the San Ysidro port of entry. Eight days later San Diego police found marijuana and an illegal switchblade in his car during a traffic stop. He was given three years' probation for the misdemeanor. After a stint in rehab, and a poor performance on the playing field, he was arrested again at San Ysidro on October 28 when a customs agent noticed a bulge in Hoyt's clothing. The border guards confiscated two bags containing nearly five hundred pills—Valium and Propoxyphene. Sixty days in prison and a suspended sentence did little to put Hoyt on the right path. He missed all of 1987 when Ueberroth suspended him after he was arrested for attempting to sell cocaine. He would never pitch again.[99]

If collusion was a disaster, and the continued drug fallout an embarrassment—especially when the commissioner asserted the need for extra security to protect his family from Colombian drug cartels and suggested using the air force to bomb Colombian drug fields—Ueberroth saved some face before suddenly leaving office in 1989. His final gift to the owners was a $1.1 billion contract with CBS for the televising of the All-Star Game, World Series, and twelve regular season contests. Another $100 million came from ESPN in return for 175 cable telecasts. It was a massive windfall to the owners (who would put it, in the wake of collusion, into ever more massive player contracts). The price-fixing and behind-doors wheeling and dealing did little to help Ueberroth's reputation with the union men. The long-term legacy of his tenure was the nearly complete demolition of whatever trust existed between the establishment and the union.[100]

This would be felt nowhere more strongly than in the game's effort to eradicate drugs. That problem, and especially the contentious issue of testing, would fall to Ueberroth's successor, A. Bartlett Giamatti, the former president of Yale University. Whatever Giamatti's position on the drug issue, his tenure in baseball's highest office was overshadowed by the Pete Rose gambling affair (which eventually overtook drugs as the major baseball scandal in the headlines). On April 1, 1989, not long after banning Rose from the game, Giamatti, a chain-smoking Red Sox fan, Renaissance scholar, and passionate devotee of the game, suffered a massive coronary. Baseball's would-be philosopher king died before he could even begin to tackle the nagging drug problem. But even before Ueberroth left, celebrated for his courageous stand against drugs and success in making baseball so profitable, there were signs of darker days ahead.

In October 1988 the American League Championship series pitted the Boston Red Sox against the explosive young Oakland Athletics. Manager Tony La Russa's A's were driven by a pair of young power hitters in the heart of the batting order, their ball-crushing exploits having earned them a catchy nickname: the "Bash Brothers." Mark McGwire, tall and relatively slender, was a former Olympian who settled in at first base, led the American League with forty-nine home runs as a rookie in 1987, and generally eschewed the limelight. Cuban-born outfielder Jose Canseco, on the other hand, had Hollywood good looks as well as a freakish combination of speed and power. In 1988 he had led the league in home runs with forty-two and had also stolen forty bases. He was hailed as the prototype of the next generation of superstar players. Before the first game of the series, however, Canseco took time out to respond to allegations about performance-enhancing drugs made by *Washington Post* reporter Tom Boswell during a televised interview. Every time Canseco came to bat in that game a unified chant echoed around Fenway Park: "Ste-roids! Ste-roids!" There was trouble ahead.[101]

6

Summers of the Long Ball Frauds

It's like the big secret we're not supposed to talk about.
I think we all have our suspicions who's on the stuff, but
unless someone comes out and admits to it, who'll ever
know for sure?

—Tony Gwynn, *Los Angeles Times*, July 15, 1995

Do you want to know the terrifying truth, or do you
want to see me sock a few dingers?

—Mark McGwire, "Brother's Little Helper,"
The Simpsons, October 3, 1999

On March 17, 2005, the Steroid Era crisis hit critical mass as a handful
of players sat before the House Government Reform Committee to answer
questions about drug use in professional baseball. Mark McGwire was there.
So was Sammy Sosa. Also there were Rafael Palmeiro and Curt Schilling.
Jose Canseco, the era's most infamous informer, was conspicuous, a pariah
practically reveling in the glare of public scrutiny. Frank Thomas, the slugger whose biceps, if not so obviously real, could only have been devised in
the unbound imagination of a comic book illustrator, was a friendly witness
speaking from afar via telecom.

Strangely absent was Barry Bonds, the man who had by then become
the Steroid Era's public enemy number one. Committee cochair Tom Davis
(R-VA) suggested in a March 13 *Meet the Press* interview, firstly, that Bonds'
absence was due to the fact that Bonds was still the subject of the ongoing
Bay Area Laboratory Cooperative (BALCO) investigation and, secondly, that
had Bonds been called in for questioning, the entire meeting would have lost
sight of the real problem. "You bring Bonds in," said Davis, "it's going to be
just about Barry Bonds. It's more widespread than that."[1]

With Bonds out of the picture, most of the attention that day was focused
on Mark McGwire with a searing intensity for which the retired slugger was

clearly not prepared. McGwire had been out of the limelight since his 2001 retirement but remained, thanks to the allegations in Canseco's tell-all, *Juiced*, a prominent poster boy for performance enhancement in baseball. Although it is clearly what the committee wanted, McGwire was not interested in offering a confession. His opening statement, a milquetoast public relations plea, was a disaster. He readily admitted that "there has been a problem with steroid use in baseball." He even offered to be front and center in any effort by Congress and the league to clean up the game and to warn young players in all sports away from the drugs. But when William Clay, the representative from St. Louis, asked McGwire if he could assure his fans that he had played the game with "honesty and integrity," the slugger visibly shrank.[2]

Tension was evident in McGwire's eyes, magnified by a pair of thin-rimmed glasses that added a serious and sober intellectual air to the former slugger. His red hair was graying. Just forty-one, McGwire looked old and tired. Several times he appeared on the verge of tears. Weariness suffused his response to Clay. "I'm not going to go into the past or talk about my past. I'm here to make a positive influence on this."[3]

The committee, however, was not interested in do-gooder promises. They were hunting for skeletons and scapegoats. They wanted to know if the allegations in Canseco's book were true. Did McGwire use performance-enhancing drugs? Who else used them? When did this begin? McGwire hedged. He was frightened. "My lawyers have advised me that I cannot answer these questions without jeopardizing my friends, my family and myself," he said. This response nettled the questioners, but McGwire was unflinching. Each time McGwire was asked to respond to allegations of steroid use, he retreated behind the increasingly bizarre and embarrassing defense that, while he wanted to help, he was not going to talk about the past.[4]

The past, however, was the entire point for some of the speakers at the hearing. Senator Jim Bunning (R-KY), who had enjoyed a Hall of Fame career as a pitcher during the 1950s and 1960s, set the tone for the day. Baseball's past was sacred. It was valuable. It needed protecting. Referring to the expanding physiques of behemoth sluggers like McGwire and Bonds, Bunning recalled how different the game had been in his day. "When I played with Henry Aaron, Willie Mays and Ted Williams, they didn't put on 40 pounds . . . and they didn't hit more home runs in their late thirties as they did in their late twenties. What's happening in baseball is not natural, and it's not right." Bunning insisted that users of performance-enhancing drugs be blasted from baseball's record book, erased from the history. "If they started in 1992 or 1993 illegally using steroids," Bunning said, "wipe all their records out. Take them away. They don't deserve them."[5]

Despite its high profile, the hearing was mostly farce. Tom Lantos, congressman from California, called it a "theater of the absurd." Canseco, truth-teller to Congress, stool pigeon to his peers, insisted that steroids were not a recent problem. Steroids, said the retired slugger, were "as acceptable in the '80s and mid-to-late '90s as a cup of coffee." They were, however, a problem that required government intervention. If Congress failed to act, claimed Canseco, drugs like steroids would never be rooted out of baseball. It would be a terrible mistake to let Major League Baseball police itself, even though Bud Selig, the commissioner, was already vowing to implement a zero-tolerance policy. "I will suspend any player who tests positive for an illegal steroid," Selig said. "There will be no exceptions. The union is aware of that, and they accept it."[6]

Unsavory character or not, Canseco was clearly getting the best of the hearing while McGwire appeared evasive and out of touch. Canseco had asked for immunity from prosecution before agreeing to come to the hearings. His request had been denied, but there he was just the same. His accusations about drug use by Rafael Palmeiro and Sammy Sosa were met with incredulity. Sosa hid behind a mostly fabricated language barrier and the pretense of innocent naïveté. His opening statement was read aloud by his lawyer: "Everything I have heard about steroids and human growth hormones is that they are very bad for you." Palmeiro, the veteran Baltimore Orioles first baseman and television Viagra pitchman, was especially steely. In a much-repeated segment of the hearings, he looked into the camera and wagged his forefinger. "I have never used steroids. Period. I do not know how to say it any more clearly than that." Later events would suggest that Palmeiro was not being entirely honest.[7]

While McGwire's meltdown would feature prominently in the evening news segments, there was nothing remarkable to emerge from the questioning of the other Major Leaguers. The committee's leaders, Davis and Henry Waxman (D-CA), forestalling critics, explained why such a hearing was even necessary. Baseball had failed to take care of itself. "There's a cloud over the game that I love," said Davis, sounding eerily like Peter Ueberroth peering into the cocaine blizzard of the mid-1980s. "There's a cloud over baseball, and perhaps a public discussion of the issues, with witnesses testifying under oath, can provide a glimpse of sunlight."[8]

Congress was seeking the sunlit diamond of a halcyon past. More than just following the age-old quest for a symbolic Eden, lawmakers were worried about the impact of Major League steroid abuse on young fans. Steroid use at the highest level created a perception of acceptance among college and high school athletes. Some studies tenuously suggested increased steroid use in that demographic. "Kids are dying from the use of steroids. They're looking up to these major league leaders in terms of the enhancements that they're using. And we have to stop it," exclaimed Waxman on *Meet the Press*.

In light of this, and despite the many topical experts called to join the players before the committee, it was Donald Hooton of Plano, Texas, who offered the most passionate and personal testimony. His seventeen-year-old son, Taylor, had used steroids and later killed himself in 2003. Hooton was convinced that the steroids had been the culprit in his son's death. "Let me implore you to take steps to clean up this mess," he begged the panel. "Please help us to see that our children's lives were not lost in vain." He called players who had taken steroids "not only cheaters, you are cowards." Hooton's testimony was visceral and moving, but some wondered if the lack of scientific grounding in his allegations might not be worrisome.[9]

As with other hearings of this nature, there were calls to action. The first step toward cleaning up the game would come with the formation of an advisory panel. Two of the most outspoken steroid critics, Schilling and Frank Thomas, agreed to join. Palmeiro also volunteered his services. The message was obvious: baseball could still police itself. The players who did not use steroids were eager to see users exposed and embarrassed. "I think the fear of public embarrassment and humiliation upon being caught is going to be greater than any player ever imagined," Schilling said. Canseco, for his part, agreed that the kind of public shellacking the players received in hearings such as this might prove to be a significant deterrent.[10]

Meanwhile, the commissioner, suddenly under siege, insisted to the committee that steps were already being taken, that baseball had finally come to its senses and was on the right track before the hearings were even convened. The "cloud" that so troubled Representative Davis was an illusory creation of unreasonable critics "who, although well-intentioned, are not well informed about baseball's multifaceted campaign against such substances." Selig and his fellow officials hailed baseball's new drug policy as the "gold standard" in sport. Davis and Waxman were not convinced and pointed out that MLB's supposedly lofty new standards actually fell well short of standards set by the IOC and most other sports as well.[11]

According to Selig, the MLBPA had taken an "unprecedented step" in December 2004 when it reopened the current labor agreement in order to discuss an even stronger policy on performance-enhancing drugs. Union chief Don Fehr, hardly under less duress than Selig, explained that the MLBPA did not support or condone "the use of any illegal substance." "We are committed to dispelling any notion that the route to becoming a major league athlete somehow includes the taking of unlawful performance-enhancing substances," he said. Committee members grilled Selig, league officials Rob Manfred and Sandy Alderson, and union chief Fehr over what they saw as flaws in the sport's drug-testing policy, which was instituted for the 2003 season and strengthened over the winter to include, for the first time, penalties for first-time offenders. However, baseball's policy called for a ten-day suspension for first offenses, as opposed to two years under the IOC policy.[12]

In the end, the hearings of March 17, 2005, provided great copy for the sporting press, but it was unclear in the aftermath whether the public shaming would lead to any substantive changes. It seemed just as likely that, like most every effort of Congress to get involved in professional baseball, these hearings were nothing more than a terrific opportunity for moral grandstanding. As evidenced in the testimony of both Jim Bunning and Jose Canseco, there was a significant disconnect between the perception of baseball's sacred past (it was clean in Bunning's day!) and the reality of its long-standing problems (it actually was not!). Commissioner Selig promised to take steps (had not every chief baseball executive always done so?), and the union appeared, as always, to have finally seen the light. There was an air of fabricated hysteria about the entire affair. Children were in danger. Sacred records were under assault. The entire National Pastime was threatened. Dick Pound, the head of the World Anti-Doping Agency, lamented: "How would you like to take your son to a baseball game and you've got your hot dog and you've got your Coke and you say, 'Son someday if you fill your body with enough shit, then you can play in your country's national game.'"[13]

Seven years earlier, with baseball at the height of a glorious home run–fueled renaissance, nobody could have envisioned such a grim predicament for the great game.

* * *

It was September 8, 1998. The sixty-second home run, the ball that would set the new single-season record, soared down the left field line at Busch Stadium. It carried baseball back into the hearts of a suddenly rapt American audience. No majestic, towering blast, this was instead a 341-foot laser beam cutting through a thousand flash-born explosions. On the mound, Chicago Cubs pitcher Steve Trachsel became a footnote to history. The hitter, St. Louis Cardinals slugger Mark McGwire, a red-headed Goliath at six foot five and 250 pounds, lifted his fist in the air as the ball cleared the fence. "I was sure it was going off the wall," he later admitted. The surge of euphoria that came with realization caused him to miss tagging first base. Fans watching on television heard announcer Joe Buck, son of the Cardinals' legendary radio broadcaster, urge McGwire to go back and touch it. In the radio booth Mike Shannon had no time to start his apoplectic home run chant—"Get up baby, get up!"—instead providing a surprisingly pithy exclamation point for the historic moment: "We have a new Sultan of Swat!"[14]

This was much more than a just a home run. It was something else entirely. It was bigger and more significant. At her house, watching the game with two children from next door, *San Francisco Chronicle* writer Joan Ryan captured the meaning of the historic moment:

> I looked at the two children from next door. They'll know baseball only in the era of musical-chair rosters and autograph auctions. They'll hear the old timers, even as we did growing up, talk wistfully about the good old days, when heroes were heroes and the game was pure. "These," I said out loud, "are those days."[15]

McGwire's blast was a time machine, providing a brief moment of Golden Age magic for baseball fans inclined now to cynicism about the game's stultifying commercialism. "The buzz about baseball is amazing now," remarked one St. Louis fan on hand to witness the feat. This was the moment that the baseball establishment had been waiting for since September 1995, when Baltimore's Cal Ripken Jr. first began chasing away the ill will created by the 1994 strike. Ripken, a stoic throwback, had been replaced by a captivating new hero who was, as Joan Ryan suggested, part Paul Bunyan, part George Bailey, and 100 percent American. Of course, McGwire was a stoic character in his own way, but in his person, too, there was bombast and power, elements to which Americans have always been attracted.[16]

After the game, Major League Baseball commissioner Bud Selig was on hand for a less spontaneous, official, on-field ceremony. He called the moment "one of the most historic nights in baseball history" while presenting McGwire with the very first Commissioner's Historic Achievement Award. Selig had been waiting a long time for the moment. In celebrating McGwire and his accomplishments he was also announcing that baseball was well and truly back, more popular than it had been in all but increasingly distant memory.

It was the perfect capstone of a summer that nearly every baseball writer in America celebrated as the renaissance of the National Pastime. Tom Verducci of *Sports Illustrated*, later one of the era's most erudite critics, proclaimed that "America is a Baseball Nation again, and Mark McGwire is the head of state." Mike Lupica, the New York journalist who chronicled the amazing season in *Summer of '98*, linked McGwire's moment to Cal Ripken's in that first difficult post-strike season. "The country stopped for Ripken," wrote Lupica; "now it stopped for McGwire."[17]

The happy moment ended all too soon. It was already an established fact that the heroic McGwire was using supplements—legal but controversial—during his hunt for Roger Maris's record. Debates about the uses and side effects of androstenedione ("Andro" to its muscle-bound converts) were, within fewer than two baseball seasons, dwarfed by endless allegations and relentless rumors about steroids and other designer performance enhancers that were fueling baseball's powerful new home run–stroked engine. In short order Major League Baseball's renaissance was perverted into the Steroid Era. Instead of celebrating them, Major League Baseball would try to separate itself from those golden seasons, apparent forgeries, which McGwire had momentarily evoked.

It is nearly impossible to say exactly *when* the so-called Steroid Era in Major League Baseball began. Jose Canseco, McGwire's former teammate, grandly claims to have pioneered the use of steroids and other performance enhancers when he came into the Major Leagues in 1985. Tom House, one-time relief pitcher for the Atlanta Braves, claims that pitchers were using steroids (and just about anything else that promised to improve their performance) in the late 1960s and early 1970s. Eventually, baseball historians could even confirm that Pud Galvin, a star pitcher of the late nineteenth century, had experimented with the famous Brown-Sequard elixir—one of the earliest testosterone derivatives.[18]

Nevertheless, bookends for the Steroid Era can reasonably be placed on the 1994 labor stoppage at one end and on the release of the Mitchell Report in December 2007, thirteen seasons later, on the other. But to mark the Steroid Era as unique and aberrational—as so many did, threatening to mark every record set during those thirteen seasons with an asterisk—is to ignore the evolutionary quality of baseball's drug culture. The Steroid Era was the inevitable conclusion of a long process. Baseball's unique mashup of competitive masculinity, negligent paternalism, internal economic strife, and public relations–themed drug policies was the perfect recipe for what became the Steroid Era. Throughout the process, Americans marched right along with their diamond idols, eagerly greeting each new medical miracle that promised to smooth away age, restore vigor, or enhance masculine virility. The real story of the Steroid Era is, ultimately, about what price Americans, at the end of the twentieth century, were willing to pay to win (on the field of sport, in the workplace, against the relentless forces of nature) and what effect that all-consuming attitude had on them, their games, and their lifestyles.

*　　*　　*

Baseball's premier spectacle, the World Series, survived two world wars (absent some players, of course) and a global economic catastrophe. Discord, depression, death—even the violent earthquake that rattled the contestants of the 1989 Bay Bridge series between Oakland and San Francisco—all failed to stop baseball's annual culmination. What neither natural nor man-made cataclysm could conspire to do, the decades-long cold war between baseball's owners and players finally accomplished. The strike of 1994, baseball's eighth labor stoppage since 1972, ended that season prematurely and, as management and the union adopted equally rigid stances, led to the shocking cancellation of the World Series. Numerous polls taken at the end of the 1994 season all suggested that fans were convinced that unabashed greed had finally killed the National Pastime.[19]

Baseball as it had existed prior to the labor stoppage—economically and stylistically—was gone forever after the strike. On a purely structural level, the owners had already determined to realign the Major Leagues before the strike, adopting a three-division setup and introducing a wild card playoff participant. Interleague play was on the horizon. Bucking tradition meant, theoretically, bringing in *more* fans who could now hope that their team might win that extra playoff spot. More fans might come to see teams play that, because of the old schedule, had never played in their city before. This was the owners' game plan to bring their seemingly stodgy league back into competition with the wildly popular National Football League and the hip, fast-paced National Basketball Association. Even as they tried to push baseball into the future, however, the owners still dreamed of pushing the clock back on the expanding salaries of their employees. Pursuit of that futile dream led, as it had in every past instance, to a strike by the Major League Baseball Players Association.[20]

The 1994 strike ripped much of any remaining nostalgic gloss off the game. Fans and writers spent their bile and disappointment in editorials and letters published in papers across the nation. They swore themselves off the game forever. They wondered where it had all gone so badly wrong. "The players and owners can both go to hell," exclaimed one bitter fan. "I'll find other outlets for my time and money." Columnist Bill Gallo suggested, in a fit of hyperbole, that the baseball strike was "as grim and tragic" as Verdun, the most brutal bloodletting of World War I. "Never again will baseball occupy the cherished place in the American imagination that it once held. Never again will we believe . . . the essential joy of the game is gone."[21]

The strike figures prominently in the traditional Steroid Era narrative, that story of innocence lost, restored, and then lost again. It is a simple tale. Baseball, brought low by the strike, badly needed an icon in the grand old style. It needed a player—as Babe Ruth had done in the wake of the Black Sox debacle—to lift the game above its own self-inflicted injuries and to recapture the hearts and minds of a dubious public. Looking over the Steroid Era we can see how several different players become repositories of certain social or cultural values, how each image was shaped (and sometimes distorted) by the media, and, in all but one case, how the introduction of the troubling chemical variable transformed the initial quest for heroes into an even more fervent hunt for villains and scapegoats.[22]

The baseball strike officially ended on April 2, 1995, when a federal court led by Sonia Sotomayor issued an injunction that restored the old, expired collective bargaining agreement. Baseball was back, but in ragged shape. The cost of the labor stoppage had been prohibitive in terms of both finances and reputation. The owners, for their efforts, had lost nearly $700 million. Their employees had lost $250 million. A total of 921 regular season games had been cancelled. Fans abandoned the National Pastime en masse. Polls such as those run by ABC News suggested that baseball's popularity had sunk to a thirty-five-year low as a result of the strike.[23]

When baseball finally returned in 1995, it was a crippled sport derided by fans and critics alike. Tom Verducci of *Sports Illustrated* wrote that "the return of the game was greeted with anger, derision, mockery and—the worst of all—indifference." Americans just did not care anymore. It would take something special to draw them back to the old ball game.[24]

Cal Ripken Jr., the star shortstop for the Baltimore Orioles, was something special. He hadn't missed a game since entering the Orioles starting lineup on May 30, 1982. On one level he was spectacularly modern, a productive offensive player at a traditionally defensive position. Ripken combined steady defensive play with powerful batting, making him a forerunner of the early twenty-first century's slugging shortstops. On a less tangible, less quantifiable level, Ripken was a compelling throwback. Haywood Hale Broun described Ripken as a figure emerging from a time machine: "You half expect him to be wearing a baggy flannel uniform and using a skimpy glove."[25]

Most importantly, after a decade of cocaine scandals, Ripken was a clean star. Curry Kirkpatrick of *Newsweek* hailed Ripken for his wholesomeness.

"Ripken stands out as the ideal role model—an anti-Mantle who, rather than abuse his family and body over the span of a distinguished career, has held them along as the twin citadels of his success." Ripken was unfailingly honest; a player who drove and drank the very products he endorsed—the Chevy Suburban and milk. It seems rather funny, sad, and absolutely crucial to note how the dying Mantle was held up as the negative point of comparison to Ripken's wholesomeness.[26]

September 6, 1995—the night that Ripken finally surpassed Lou Gehrig's consecutive game record—was remarkable. The FOX network had scrapped its entire slate of prime-time Thursday season premiers to telecast the record-breaking game. Forty-three million Americans tuned in. Upon the conclusion of the fifth inning (making the game against the California Angels official) fireworks lit up the night sky around Baltimore's beautiful Camden Yards. Time stopped while Ripken and his accomplishment were feted. President Bill Clinton was on hand and explained to the press that Ripken's night would "help America fall back in love with baseball." Newspaper headlines suggested the president had hit the mark. "CAL, THANK YOU FOR SAVING BASEBALL," one blared.[27]

Unfortunately, the lesson that the league's power brokers took from the celebration surrounding Ripken's record-breaking evening was that fans most hungered to see record breaking (as opposed to all the intangible qualities that had been hailed in Ripken in the months leading up to the celebration at Camden Yards). As Edward Bennett Williams, the owner of the Orioles, allegedly suggested, "we need dingers. Home runs are how people will return to the ballpark." Blunt as it was, this was actually a reasonable conclusion.[28]

One of the sad side effects of the 1994 strike was that it aborted a quartet of record-challenging campaigns. San Diego's Tony Gwynn was on pace to become the first player since Ted Williams (in 1941) to hit over .400 for a season. Chicago's Frank Thomas was contending for the American League's Triple Crown. Fans were especially excited about the first sustained challenge to Roger Maris's single-season home run mark of sixty-one. Both Matt Williams of the San Francisco Giants and Ken Griffey Jr. of the Seattle Mariners were on pace to challenge the mark as the season floundered. Fans and players everywhere seemed devastated not just by the premature closure of the baseball season, but by the denial of history making. Records, even sacred ones, were meant to be challenged.[29]

The work begun by Cal Ripken Jr. was, so the narrative goes, completed by Mark McGwire and Sammy Sosa during the summer of 1998. That summer was a rebirth of baseball in every sense; thriving attendance, endless media coverage, and restored cultural relevance could not have better suited the owners or players. One almost had to let his or her memory travel back to the immediate post–World War II era to recall a time when baseball seemed so *alive*, so important. Veteran writer Frank Deford trumped Verducci when he proclaimed 1998 the "greatest year in sports history" almost entirely on the weight of the National Pastime's home run epic as authored by Mac and Sammy. The writer Dan Okrent read the McGwire story and rediscovered baseball's social relevance. "In no other sport is [the Puritan work ethic] more visible than in baseball. The other sports . . . never isolate the hero quite the way baseball does—especially when it places him alone in the batter's box and challenges him to perform the most difficult feat in all of sports." Writing for *Time*, he later added that McGwire "couldn't banish the stain of sleaze that leached through our public life this year, nor could he restore civility to our discourse or turn the media's attention to rotten schools or Serbian brutality. He is, after all, only a baseball player. But what a baseball player he is, and what a year it was, and what balm he brought to a nation that seemed to spend the year flaying its flesh."[30]

Mark McGwire was a hero, an extension of American power, and he was also the poster boy for a culture that increasingly embraced the restorative miracle of supplements and pharmaceutical wonder drugs. It was not so easy, however, to conclude that he was a creation of that culture. While his body was a Jekyll and Hyde study in growth, his production on the diamond had always been defined by volcanic power. McGwire had *never* been a slap hitter. In 1974, a ten-year-old McGwire launched a home run in his first Little League plate appearance. Despite his power, the young McGwire was initially a pitcher, the position usually reserved for the biggest and strongest players. Just the same, he had undeniable power potential, once hitting a ball so hard that it slammed into a building nearly five hundred feet away from home plate. After scout and University of Southern California assistant coach Ron Vaughn helped turn McGwire from a pitcher into a "fearsome power hitter," McGwire set a then Pac-10 single-season record with thirty-two home runs while playing for the Trojans in the early 1980s. He starred on the 1984 U.S. Olympic baseball team. In his first full Major League season with the Oakland A's the rookie slammed forty-nine home runs to share the Major League lead with Chicago's Andre Dawson.[31]

Along with Jose Canseco, McGwire helped change the fortunes of the struggling Oakland Athletics franchise. With the "Bash Brothers"—the charismatic Canseco, a blend of raw power and speed, and the stoic, powerful McGwire—as their bedrock, the A's were American League champions for three consecutive seasons from 1988 through 1990. They won a world championship in 1989. They revolutionized the way players trained for the game. Led by coach Dave McKay, the A's were arguably the first Major League franchise to embrace weight lifting as a developmental tool, rejecting the long-held baseball tradition that bulking up meant slowing down, that a muscle-bound swing was a bad swing. Of course, Canseco later revealed in his sensational tell-all, *Juiced*, how he (and McGwire) were pioneers of another sort, already supplementing the weight training with steroid cocktails. At the time, McGwire only acknowledged that his efforts to get better included lemonade, then oranges and Snickers bars, broccoli and—eventually—spinach.[32]

The Bash Brothers era ended all too quickly as Canseco began to struggle with injuries and was shipped out of Oakland midway through the 1992 season. The shine had worn off McGwire as well. In 1991 he hit an abysmal .201 (although he still won a spot on the American League All-Star team.) After a resurgent 1992, he appeared in only seventy-four games between 1993 and strike-shortened 1994. Foot and back injuries seemed to have completely derailed his career. And then, just like that, Mac was back, fueled by new health supplements and, more importantly, a new approach at the plate courtesy of hitting coach Doug Rader. "He's learned the strike zone better, his swing is more compact, and he's much more disciplined," explained rival manager Bobby Valentine. McGwire hit fifty-two home runs in 1996. He bashed fifty-eight more in 1997, splitting time between Oakland and St. Louis. And all the time he grew bigger. Mike Lupica remembered how his children were stunned at how large McGwire had grown. A McGwire at-bat engendered instant attention. Fans flocked to the Cardinals spring training grounds in Jupiter, Florida, to watch McGwire because "he might hit one out today. Maybe he would go deep."[33]

To be sure, McGwire looked nothing like the great sluggers of the previous generation; he physically dwarfed the grainy images of Mays, Mantle, Maris, and Aaron that resided in American memory. And unlike Maris, whose aloof and private nature rankled fans, America ultimately embraced "Big Mac." Fans wanted McGwire to become the new home run champion, wanted him to hit one out of the park every day—every at-bat. America was in love with the long ball, McGwire hit them more often and better than anyone else, and the source of his power—stance, swing, powder, or pill—was not important.

That is not to say that the story of 1998 was the story of the home run alone, but great pitching exploits paled beside the season's hitting fireworks. In some ways, barely noticed in the celebration of old-fashioned heroics, baseball had become a circus, an almost freak show dominated by a muscle-bound cadre of sluggers. "The boys of summer are bigger these days," commented Richard Corliss of *Time*. "That's the explanation for the homerpalooza. In workout rooms they sculpt their bodies like works of art and war, partly because they know the big hits generated by big muscles will earn them big bucks." The year 1998 was the first season in baseball history in which four players hit at least fifty home runs. The exploits of McGwire and Sosa overshadowed Seattle's graceful superstar, Ken Griffey Jr., the media's then anointed heir to both Maris and all-time home run king Hank Aaron. Griffey was the rare home run hitter of the era who did not look like a body double for the pro wrestling circuit.[34]

Beneath the spectacle and celebration of 1998, concern was forming amid baseball's new home run–fueled prosperity. The game's newest hero was a man with clay feet. Earlier in the 1998 season Steve Wilstein, a writer with the Associated Press, had seen a supplement bottle in McGwire's locker. America's real-life Popeye (the usage bordering immediately on cliché) supplemented his spinach with a power pill. McGwire, for his part, freely admitted that he had been taking an over-the-counter supplement called androstenedione—a substance developed in the 1970s by East German labs for enhancing state-sponsored athletic programs. Andro was banned in most other major sports, including the Olympics. A New York City physician, Lewis Maharam, upon learning that McGwire used Andro, quipped that if "we decided to send a Dream Team to the Olympics in baseball, McGwire . . . wouldn't be able to go."[35]

How would Americans respond to the fact that their new idol was using a substance that most doctors equated with steroids? Although it was technically a legal supplement, was it ethical for an athlete to use Andro? What, one writer asked, are "we supposed to make of the fact that there is an artificial flavoring inside The Natural?" It was widely assumed, as the home run totals of the mid-1990s climbed, that a juiced baseball (more tightly wound) or smaller, more intimate ballparks were behind the boom. Now, as McGwire admitted his use of not only Andro but also the muscle-builder creatine, he also insisted that "everybody I know in the game of baseball uses the same stuff I use." Sammy Sosa admitted to using creatine. Suddenly, before the celebration of the magical season could properly conclude, the nagging question was whether something *more* than the ball was juiced.[36]

* * *

The home run summer of 1998 was the culmination of two movements. One, and by far the broadest, was simply the progressive evolution of baseball's own culture of performance enhancement. For those paying attention, the shock of McGwire's secret chemical weapons should not have been much of a shock at all. Baseball's history was, after all, pockmarked with amphetamine scandals. The memory of "Steroids!" chants raining down on Jose Canseco during the 1988 American League Championship Series were no more than a decade dim by 1998. The columnist George Vecsey saw firsthand the cult of performance enhancement forming in the early 1980s, if not before. "The more that sports are built up in modern society, the more there is a temptation to produce the edge artificially," he explained. "The more money, the more adulation, the more television coverage, the more lifetime comfort . . . the more athletes are willing to juice themselves up." Vecsey recalled pitchers of decades past stumbling off the mound while his fellow reporters used hand signals (miming the swallowing of a pill) to explain the bizarre behavior of certain players.[37]

Even if one chooses to discard the long history of "greenies" in baseball, there were still early warning signs that steroids and steroid derivatives threatened the National Pastime. The National Football League had been dealing with muscle-enhancing drugs since the early 1970s. Although the league was apparently well-informed on the topic and had a testing program designed to root out abuse, almost every writer knew that steroids were a crucial part of the NFL's "gladiator" culture. The Olympics had been struggling with steroids for decades. In 1984, a major scandal erupted in the run-up to the Los Angeles Olympics when twelve Americans left the Pan-American Games in Caracas, Venezuela, rather than be tested for drug use. Eight of the medal winners from the Caracas games were eventually disqualified after drug tests detected steroids in their system. The disastrous fallout from the games led some to fear that the Olympics would become a competition between "mutants puffed chemically." It was simply naive to believe that while steroids were embraced by track and field athletes and football brutes, baseball players completely avoided them.[38]

The bad news from Caracas hit the country at the same time as baseball's Bowie Kuhn was meting out punishment to the first wave of baseball's cocaine abusers. There was a sense, however, that Kuhn and his advisers viewed the events in Caracas as being completely unrelated to their own nascent cocaine problem. Dr. Robert Kerr, a Los Angeles physician, was not quite so confident. In a 1983 interview he estimated that over the course of eighteen professional years he prescribed steroids for at least ten thousand athletes from baseball, football, basketball, and track. He conjectured that there were at least a million athletes in the country using steroids. Kerr believed that by prescribing the drugs he had actually "saved" athletes from resorting to a dangerous "dark-alley black market." After all, he concluded, "we're talking about consenting adults here. They know the risks, they know that we don't know the long-term effects yet. But if we can provide laboratory monitoring, maybe we can prevent any effects . . . the danger in the current controversy is that these athletes (steroid users) will be mentioned with the NFL cocaine users and be driven further underground."[39]

It turns out that Kerr was rather prophetic. The snowballing cocaine crisis eventually swamped the major professional sports and led, at the end of the 1980s, to the controversial engagement over drug testing. The seemingly widespread recreational drug problems, coupled with fan resentment of athletes' high salaries and constant media attention, led to a sea change in sports in those years. Suddenly, the primary focus on drugs moved from detection and care to detection and punishment. It used to be about getting involved to save athletes from themselves. Now it was about saving sports from the athletes. When the Canadian sprinter Ben Johnson set a world record in the 100-meter race at the 1988 Summer Olympics and was later disqualified for doping, he rode the first wave of that sea change into the media spotlight. Whatever he had done, Johnson was not an athlete with a drug problem. He was just a cheater.[40]

It was in the year of Ben Johnson's shame that Tom Boswell, during a *Newswatch* interview with CBS's Charlie Rose, calmly explained how Oakland's Jose Canseco was the "most conspicuous example of a [baseball] player who has made himself great with steroids." Boswell was one of the first to imply that steroids were not as unheard of in baseball circles as most pundits routinely suggested. Boswell even hinted that Oakland manager Tony La Russa knew about Canseco's steroid use when he admitted that Canseco did make "some mistakes" early in his career. Other American League players reportedly called steroids a "Jose Canseco milkshake." The Canseco allegations would eventually get buried beneath rehearsed denials, the Pete Rose gambling debacle, and the league's mounting labor woes. But that was not before David Valdes, a friend of the A's slugger, was arrested in Detroit's Metro Airport for carrying a loaded handgun, steroids, and other pills in his briefcase. Canseco, who was boarding the plane with Valdes, lamented afterward that he just could not understand why he was being dogged by questions about steroids.[41]

Oddly enough, before the Canseco rumors and well before McGwire's record-setting campaign, there was another baseball summer marked by home run mania. That was the summer of 1987 when, quite suddenly, home runs began to fly out of baseball yards at a record clip. Commentators wondered then about the potential sources of the long ball barrage. As usual there was talk of a "livelier" ball, but that seemed a dubious culprit. With baseball still buried in a recreational drug crisis, it seemed reasonable that drugs might be playing a key role in the statistical boom. "Odd that no one has yet wondered if that fresh spate of thunderstruck home runs could be even partially steroid-induced," wondered writers at the *Miami Herald*. "The homers-per-game jump from 1.82 last year to 2.15 this season—that's 18 percent—is a little difficult to blame on the livelier ball alone. Some of these guys are getting too much bigger and stronger too fast just to credit weight training, nutrition, etc."[42]

All of the talk about steroids—not necessarily in baseball but certainly in other parts of the sports community—compelled Congress to raise significant penalties in 1990 for possession of not only steroids but twenty-five other anabolic substances as well. The elders of Major League Baseball, however, did not entertain any thoughts about placing anabolic steroids on their own list of banned substances. On June 7, 1991, hoping to puncture the owner's bubble of complacency, Commissioner Fay Vincent dispatched a memo to each of the teams in Major League Baseball as well as the Major League Baseball Players' Association. It stated in part:

> The possession, sale or use of any illegal drug or controlled substance by Major League players or personnel is strictly prohibited . . . This prohibition applies to all illegal drugs . . . including steroids.

The seven-page Vincent memo did not address the contentious issue of random testing—that had to be collectively bargained with the union—but it did outline treatment and penalties for drug users. Vincent, who had replaced his good friend Bart Giamatti in the commissioner's post after Giamatti's sudden death, was himself soon to be ousted by the owners. He hoped, however, that his memo would convince clubs that steroids were illegal and dangerous, and that the clubs should not hesitate to confront players who they believed might be using performance-enhancing drugs.[43]

Vincent's hopes were dashed. "My memo was totally ignored by all," Vincent wrote in a 2007 email to the *New York Times*. "The point was to alert the baseball world to the recent inclusion of steroids as illegal prohibited substances under federal law. But the union did nothing to underscore my memo and I think the clubs ignored it as irrelevant." At the time, he explained, baseball was in the middle of the spiky labor negotiations preceding the devastating 1994 strike. The owners were concerned that unless they broke the union, the entire structure of baseball (as they wanted it to stand) was going to collapse. After a decade of headlines, drugs were purposely shoved to the back pages. At a time when baseball clearly should have been most diligent, it was utterly negligent.[44]

The second major movement that led directly to the home run barrage of 1998 was legal and political. It grew primarily out of federal deregulation of the supplements industry. In a thunderous clash of big money and science, marked by vocal grass-roots campaigning, the U.S. Congress was convinced to pass the Dietary Supplement Health and Education Act (DSHEA) of 1994. In the past, the government had granted the Food and Drug Administration the initiative to control consumer access to herbs, vitamins, and other homeopathic remedies. As New Age medicine became the vogue, there was increasing disaffection with FDA restrictions. Congress weighed the issue over the course of several months and reportedly received more mail from concerned citizens regarding regulation of supplements than it had received on any single issue in the past except for the war in Vietnam.[45]

The passage of DSHEA was clearly viewed as a sign of government capitulation to the will of a powerful majority. It allowed the unrestricted sale of herbs, vitamins, minerals, and other substances—including natural hormones and amino acids—so long as no medical claims were made by the manufacturers on behalf of the products. Supplement producers could imply the usefulness of their product, but users would have to do their own research and make their own informed decisions before purchasing them. By calling a substance a "supplement" and removing any claims that the product was a medicinal cure, almost any product (even a potentially controlled substance) could be labeled a "food."[46]

In short, the loosening of federal laws concerning nutritional supplements opened the door for products like androstenedione (which could be naturally derived from Scotch pine and the Mexican yam) and creatine (a natural amino acid powder) to become legitimate parts of the sports world. With the deregulation of supplements, the United States sporting complex was instantly changed, as was how the world viewed it. Americans were keen to purchase substances over the counter (safely, they believed) that might once have seemed extraordinarily risky. Foreign athletes, whose countries had much tighter restrictions on such substances, flooded into the United States to buy performance enhancers that were illegal in their homeland.[47]

One of the immediate results of DSHEA's passage was a massive profit boom for the supplements industry. According to the *Nutrition Business Journal*, the supplements industry had earned $8 billion prior to DSHEA,

but had $21 billion in sales the following year. A second, more nebulous re-
sult was the emergence of ethical conflict in the world of competitive sport.
DSHEA had clearly opened a Pandora's box for the entire athletic community:
athletes forever on the lookout for an "edge," black market suppliers eager
to exploit them, and the drug detection lab experts racing to keep up with
them.[48]

During the DSHEA debates of 1994, muscle enhancers such as Andro
had not really been a consideration for the act's main proponents, Senators
Orrin Hatch (R-UT) and Tom Harkin (D-IA). It was actually McGwire's
record-breaking baseball campaign that suddenly cast a glaring spotlight on
performance enhancement and the world created by DSHEA deregulation.
The supplement industry was suddenly revealed to be an ugly and shadow-
strewn wasteland of opportunism, gimmicks, and lies. Many producers of
supplements dealt in outrageous promises, improper (and misleading) labeling, and potentially deadly products. "You'll grow like a freaking weed on
Dianabol-laced-fertilizer using this NATURAL growth hormone simulator,"
one ad screamed at potential users. Other ads touted the wonders of HGH
to "wash away the disease of aging." As the supplement industry played on
the vanity of the aging and tapped the eternal human desire to discover a
fountain of youth, skeptics worried mostly about the young and tractable. In
the great tradition of decades past, it was ultimately the perceived threat to
younger fans and athletes that spurred reconsideration of the deregulatory
act and its fallout.[49]

"When you're dealing with substances that are supposed to alter the body's
hormonal balance, whose purported wonders are limited only by the imagination of the marketers, and they're selling this to teenagers, you have a formula for real trouble," said Dr. Gary Wadler, a sports medicine specialist and
antidoping advocate from Long Island. Mark McGwire chafed at the thought
that his supplements were harmful. "If it's not safe, let the FDA get it out of
here," he argued in the summer of 1998. Many agreed with him. DSHEA,
however, made things far more complicated than that. The FDA's powers
were hopelessly limited. The lack of research on hormonal precursors like
Andro meant it was nearly impossible to prove that the supplements were,
in fact, harmful.[50]

Even as it raised questions about the foundations of the home run bonanza,
the media also played a significant role in spreading the culture of supple-
mentary enhancement. Conflating sex, power, and the home run barrage,
Nike produced what is easily the Steroid Era's definitive commercial. As a
band of groupies, including television starlet Heather Locklear, surround

Mark McGwire, who is seen launching balls into the distant reaches of the ballpark, Cy Young Award–winning pitchers Tom Glavine and Greg Maddux of the Atlanta Braves clamor for attention. Spurned, but also convinced that McGwire has tapped into some great secret, the two aces embark on a heavy training routine (in their new Nike shoes) to build themselves into home run hitters. Suddenly, the groupies are attentive, and the pitchers celebrate, concluding that "chicks dig the long ball!"[51]

Both Nike and Gatorade playfully articulated the new culture of enhancement—just *wear* or *drink* this to do the same things that famous athletes do. McGwire's success was a greater, and more dangerous, pitch. Sales of Andro increased fivefold in the month after the bottle was reported in McGwire's locker. Television ads for sports muscle enhancements were usually relegated to late-night programming on fringe channels devoted to wrestling and bodybuilding. In the feverish mania surrounding McGwire's home run chase, however, ESPN was the first network to run ads for androstendione. Almost immediately high school organizations around the country fired off complaints that the ads sent a bad message to student athletes. The spots, part of a national campaign by MetRx Engineered Nutrition, had appeared during a show called *American Muscle*. ESPN defended the ads because Andro was not illegal. Secondly, the network had no plans to air them on any programming beyond the bodybuilding shows. Nevertheless, they dropped the ad the next day.[52]

* * *

It was difficult for many fans to crucify McGwire, no matter what his possible transgressions. American baseball fans, after all, had once loved the idea of Joe Hardy. His was the secret dream of many a fan, especially those who loathed the unbeatable Yankees of the Mantle era. McGwire used a legal supplement to give his already considerable skills a sharper edge. Joe Hardy sold his soul to the Devil in order to acquire skills that he'd never possessed, skills that would enable his beloved Senators to finally topple the "Damned" Yankees from their traditional spot atop the American League standings. One can only imagine what the reaction would be among baseball fans (or musical aficionados) to a story in which super-fan Joe Hardy opted for ergogenic supplements in lieu of selling his soul.[53]

McGwire benefited to some degree in being the first big-name star whose supplement practices were exposed. This was seemingly new territory for both fans and the sportswriters who conveyed the game to them. Because of this, throughout the summer of 1998 only a few prominent voices raised concerns as to whether Americans should seriously consider what role Mc-Gwire's supplements played in his assault on one of sports' golden records. Tension only really began to mark the new baseball renaissance as fingers began pointing toward the top of baseball's hierarchy. There, a rudderless drug policy—baseball had not had the foresight to ban Andro as had the NFL and the Olympics—led to fatal contradictions. Critics pointed out that Randy Barnes, an Olympic shot putter, was found to have used Andro and had been disqualified from his particular event. The standard story was that Barnes had "betrayed the spirit of fair competition." What, then, had Mark McGwire done? As John Lucas, the NBA's high-profile drug mentor, asked, "how do we know if we are watching the athlete or the drug?"[54]

Tony La Russa, McGwire's manager, responded derisively to anyone who dared suggest that McGwire's power was procured from a bottle. "You can't teach timing in hitting a baseball, especially when you're talking about hitting a 93-mile-an-hour slider," he said. "And if it was just muscle and strength generating those home runs, then you'd have every weight-lifter and offensive lineman come off the street and start hitting balls over the fences." It looked as though they already had. The aesthetics of the game changed. Baseball players began to look like pro football linebackers. Nevertheless, at the same time, the classic argument that baseball players relied on finely tuned motor skills, hawk-like vision, and quick wrists was always the first line of defense when charges of supplement use and abuse came up.[55]

And now McGwire, a player who, while with the Oakland A's, had been at the forefront of the movement that argued that the old tradition was wrong—that work in the weight room would actually *help* a player's timing, bat speed, and ability to hit consistently—was seeing the old argument trotted out in his defense. Hitting, defenders of the new era exclaimed, was a skill that eluded even the strongest and most skilled of athletes. Michael Jordan's ill-advised detour into the minor leagues was classic proof of that. Bobby Valentine, a manager and former player, explained that Jordan's inability to produce the necessary bat speed resulted from having too much upper body strength.[56]

Supplements were a non-issue as far as La Russa and a great many others were concerned. The issue was not credibility or fairness, said the Cardinals manager. This was really all about privacy. The real villain in "Androgate" was not McGwire, but the press—the nosy, antagonistic, sports media. McGwire even referred to the reporter's gaze into his locker as "snooping." A short time after the McGwire episode, a *Denver Post* columnist supposedly reached into the locker of Rockies outfielder Dante Bichette and actually read the label on the bottle of Andro that Bichette kept there. That sort of prurience was unacceptable. The veil of privacy that had become the standard defense of the players in the wars over alcohol abuse, recreational drugs, and drug testing was now the main defense against media members seeking juicy stories about supplement use.[57]

And there was widespread supplement use throughout the Major Leagues. After McGwire, a number of other players around the league acknowledged taking Andro. Among them was Oakland's Jason Giambi, a protégé of McGwire's. There was also the aforementioned Bichette of Colorado. Jose Canseco, the self-styled Johnny Appleseed of steroids in baseball, had used Andro and then stopped because he claimed that it did not really help. Two years before McGwire's record-shattering flight toward Planet Maris, the same year that Mac shed his injury jinx, a fleet-footed Baltimore Orioles centerfielder named Brady Anderson hit fifty home runs. This was truly a shocking accomplishment. Anderson had hit sixteen home runs the year before. He looked like he belonged on the set of TV soaps like *Melrose Place* or *90210*, not starring as Baltimore's new Babe Ruth. Anderson's was a singularly remarkable explosion of power that was attributed at the time to his single-minded dedication to the weight room. And maybe, if you pushed hard enough, it was also partially due to the creatine use that he eventually admitted to. No matter. Everyone seemed to be "digging the long ball" at the time. Ethical questions about Anderson's unusual, and statistically aberrational season, gained very little traction.[58]

Even players of past generations struggled to find, much less voice, outrage. They were actually rather curious about the potential benefits of Andro. "If they had made it [then], I probably would have [used it]," exclaimed Hank Aaron. "I don't see [that McGwire] did anything wrong. He's strong. Like all the other guys playing now, he hits the ball a long way, and works out in the weight room, and all that other stuff they do." All that *other* stuff, said critics, was the rub. Just what is the other stuff? Aaron, however, refused to specifically list performance-enhancing substances as a factor in the home run chase of 1998. Instead he pointed out the smaller ballparks and the effects of expansion. Expansion was always a good excuse for a home run explosion. The expansion of the American League had been a popular culprit in explaining why Roger Maris was able to break Ruth's record in 1961.[59]

McGwire, who obviously had more than a few high-profile champions in his corner, had very little to say in his own defense, relying instead on the simple assertion that Andro was legal. He determinedly announced that he would continue to use it until it was declared illegal or banned by baseball. In the heat of the home run chase he even explained to reporters that Andro actually served a more important purpose than just improving his baseball skills. He used it, he said, to improve his sex drive. "It's good for your sex life," he explained. "I'm serious. You guys think I'm joking, but I'm serious." McGwire was supplementing his masculinity, not his baseball skill. What red-blooded American male could fail to relate?[60]

McGwire's defenders took up the argument and maintained that the supplement's influence was more prevalent in the bedroom than at the ballpark. If baseball players were using it, it was likely they too wanted some extra zing for bedroom extracurriculars rather than to expand their clout at the stadium. The argument had, after a fashion, come full circle back to the baseball skills versus raw power argument. "If you don't have talent, no drug is going to make you be a better player," said Tim Raines, the former Montreal Expo who had become a productive journeyman outfielder in his later years. "Maybe you'll get muscles, it might build up your body, but it won't make you a ballplayer. You have to have talent. McGwire didn't get big last year. If there was a guarantee [that Andro helped hitting], I'd be taking it. We all would be taking it."[61]

For its part, Major League Baseball was only willing to take half-measures in order to dilute the scandal surrounding McGwire's pills. Commissioner Bud Selig along with MLBPA chief Don Fehr issued a joint statement in which they explained that they had asked their medical advisers to study the whole area of nutritional supplements. Major League Baseball promised to reach conclusions about the slippery supplements industry that had so far eluded other organizations.

It was all a diversion. Selig and Fehr were not interested in creating a serious controversy in the midst of the new baseball boom. The home run epic was a Golden Goose. "In recent days," their statement read, "there have been press reports concerning the use of certain nutritional supplements by Major League players. The substances in question are available over the counter and are not regulated by the Food and Drug Administration. In view of these facts, it seems inappropriate that such reports should overshadow the accomplishments of players such as Mark McGwire." John Hoberman, a university-based expert on European doping, recalled in his history of testosterone that "labor-management collusion on this scale for the purpose of preserving a doping subculture has long been a familiar arrangement in European professional cycling." Everyone, explained Hoberman, looks the other way, acts slowly, and wants to know as little as possible about the issue. As it was with cycling, or had been with East Germany's swim team, so it was with Major League Baseball.[62]

Major League Baseball was not willing to move in any clear direction, preferring to obfuscate and delay. Other sports, and in particular foreign sporting agencies, were appalled. Dr. Don Catlin, head of the Olympic drug testing lab at UCLA and the man who helped set up the NFL's drug protocols, remembered receiving email questions from abroad. The emails asked, "What in the world is going on in America?" It was simply impossible for outside groups to understand how a supplement like Andro, which had been banned in their countries for years, was suddenly so prevalent in America. It seemed to be a jarring contradiction for a nation with a robust reputation as a committed fighter against worldwide drug use.[63]

The men who advised the league offices as baseball's medical experts were Dr. Robert Millman and Dr. Joel Solomon. The two men had previously been involved almost exclusively in cases involving illegal drugs such as cocaine. Recalling that chaotic era of tug-and-pull with the union and the media, Millman and Soloman were to seek input from club personnel, trainers, and doctors before making any determination about the utility and danger of supplements like Andro. The general position of the league was that there were no reputable clinical studies on Andro. Its effectiveness was questionable. More importantly, baseball's leaders continually pointed out that Andro was, technically, perfectly legal. You could get it over the counter. This was, in fact, viewed as something of an embarrassment by the medical community. "Androstendione is a steroid," said Catlin. "There's no question about it. It shouldn't be available."[64]

Dr. Charles Yesalis, arguably the foremost expert on performance-enhancing drugs in America, concurred with Catlin's assessment. He did not understand how Andro could be sold over the counter. "It beats me," he said. "It makes no sense at all." "The behavior of baseball has been ignorant and arrogant," said John Hoberman. "Andro is a gateway drug to the use of anabolic steroids in the mainstream of America. Baseball's position is just irresponsible."[65]

Just the same, even if those on the clinical side of the issue were given to declaring Andro a potentially dangerous supplement, few were willing to attribute McGwire's exploits to the bottle. Dr. Stanley Field of the American Association of Clinical Endocrinologists complained that "sports stars who take supplements are 'throwing dirt in their system'" and mucking up "phenomenal body mechanics." Those who took supplements in the hope of becoming stronger or more vigorous were simply wasting their time.[66]

* * *

If you went looking for those phenomenal body mechanics, for the perfect baseball player, you would almost certainly arrive at Barry Lamar Bonds. Baseball was in his blood and in his upbringing. His father, Bobby Bonds, was a player well ahead of his time. Bobby's unique and unrivaled combination of speed and power was a combination the league was not used to. The elder Bonds became the first player in Major League history to have more than two seasons wherein he hit thirty home runs and stole thirty bases. Despite his rare on-field accomplishments, Bobby Bonds was a player whose magnificent skills were often underappreciated. It also happened that his career was impeded by a serious drinking problem. Biographers of the younger Bonds would later chronicle, rightly so, that Barry was not only driven to realize the dreams and enormous promise that his father left unfulfilled, but was also highly conscious of his father's personal demons. In the eventual furor over his alleged performance enhancement, Barry Bonds would bitterly criticize baseball's long-standing relationship with the alcoholic beverage industry. To charges that he cheated the game and was a poor role model, Barry would sneer and suggest that writers focus instead on the hypocrisy of a sport that had not only failed to protect his father, but may have actually facilitated Bobby's, and hundreds of other player's, premature decline.[67]

Bonds certainly inherited many of his baseball talents from his father, but it did not hurt that he also grew up around Major Leaguers. His was the best sort of baseball education. His godfather was the Hall of Famer Willie Mays, possibly the greatest player since Ruth. Some claimed Mays was even better than the Bambino—he just happened to be a great black player in an era of racial upheaval and social transformation. If Mays was seldom openly bitter about what limited credit he received, Barry could, and would, be bitter for him. With such guidance from above as well as inherent skill, Barry emerged as a multisport star at Junipero Serra High School in San Carlos, California, and then at Arizona State University. Although his dream was to play for the San Francisco Giants, the team where his father had enjoyed his best years, he was instead drafted by the struggling Pittsburgh Pirates in 1985's Amateur Draft. Barry would not linger long in the developmental leagues. By the end of 1986 Barry Bonds, the "Sledge-Hammer Kid," was firmly ensconced in Pittsburgh's starting lineup.[68]

Between 1986 and 1998, Barry Bonds put all of his considerable talents on exhibit—sublime skill and a dangerously all-consuming competitive fire—first for Pittsburgh, where he helped the Pirates to three consecutive division titles between 1990 and 1992, and then for San Francisco, where, in a fabled 1993 homecoming, he became the face of the Giants franchise (as well as Major League Baseball's highest paid player). Adopting his father's #25 jersey number, Barry Bonds was a baseball paragon. He combined graceful fielding, electrifying speed, and a remarkably quick, short, and powerful batting stroke. He compiled impressive home run totals, he won Gold Gloves, and he took home Most Valuable Player Awards. But for all his on-field accolades, for all his phenomenal mechanics, Barry Bonds was never loved by the press.

In fact, Bonds became a favorite foil for writers across the country. Part of this stemmed from Barry's attitude, the obvious chip he carried on his shoulder. His ego was another barrier. If there was anyone that recognized what a special talent Barry Bonds was, it was Barry Bonds himself. The chip and the ego wore thin in blue-collar Pittsburgh. Barry Bonds, the Steel City story goes, was a midsummer superstar that faded in October. However much he might see himself as the second coming of Say-Hey Willie, he was not a player who performed when it counted. He was shallow. He was indifferent. Teammate Andy Van Slyke, the kind of gritty player Pittsburgh loved, criticized Bonds for playing poorly and making mental mistakes when Pittsburgh needed him most, on the verge of a World Series appearance in the 1992 National League Championship series. Bonds bristled at the charges. He pooh-poohed his unimpressive playoff stat line. Pittsburgh disliked him, he suggested, because he was a black player who also happened to be a great player (but a different sort from the city's beloved Willie Stargell or Latino Roberto Clemente.) One writer, covering Bonds during his transition from Pittsburgh to San Francisco, suggested that "If Bonds had discretion and diplomacy to go along with his intelligence and ability, he'd be the Michael Jordan of baseball." In the meantime he was just a very good, often great, player who was also a petulant head case.[69]

Arrogant, petulant, an easy target for a cynical press, Bonds nevertheless had some reason to feel as he did. Like his father, and despite his more impressive on-field accomplishments, Barry Bonds was often underappreciated. Baseball historian Bill James wrote that Bonds was "certainly the most unappreciated superstar of my lifetime . . . [Ken] Griffey [Jr.] has always been more popular, but Bonds has been a far, far greater player." In 1999, James, a founding father of the statistical analysis that swept baseball at the turn of the century, rated Bonds as the third best leftfielder of all time. "When people begin to take in all of his accomplishments," James predicted at the time, "Bonds may well be rated among the five greatest players in the history of the game." It was clear, however, that in addition to baseball talent, Barry may have also inherited his media skills from his father. The elder Bonds could be especially prickly. "People that think Barry's got an attitude don't know Barry," explained Bobby. "They can take the attitude and stick it up their ass. End of conversation."[70]

During the summer of 1998, Bonds was typically brilliant. With the sporting world gone long-ball mad, however, his thirty-seven home runs seemed a paltry output next to the gaudy numbers being put up by McGwire and Sosa. His production even fell well short of his traditional rival. Bonds's home run total looked as pale next to Ken Griffey Jr.'s fifty-six home runs as it did next to McGwire's gargantuan seventy. Years later, once Bonds became the center of his own performance-enhancement scandal, stories suggested that Bonds was both envious of the attention given to McGwire and also highly suspect of the motives of the press—he believed they wanted to celebrate the accomplishments of a white slugger, not a black one. This made sense to Bonds. This was like Mays, or Aaron, challenging the ghost of Ruth. As far as Bonds was concerned, the lack of credit he had received during his career was due in part, he believed, to nothing more than the color of his own skin. According to excerpts from the highly controversial *Game of Shadows*, Bonds allegedly told those nearest him in 1998 that the league was letting McGwire, who Bonds suspected was using performance enhancers, tackle the record "because he's a white boy."[71]

The anger and resentment that Bonds felt regarding all the attention heaped on McGwire is evident throughout the story told in *Game of Shadows*. According to the materials turned up by the *San Francisco Chronicle*'s investigative journalists alongside leaked FBI records, Bonds determined that he, too, would use what he called "the shit" in order to break records. The slugger's frustration erupted after an injury-plagued 1999 season. When the Giants and Cardinals met for a three-game series at Candlestick Park that July, Bonds found the batting cages roped off in order to control the crowds who had descended to watch McGwire take batting practice. He reportedly began knocking the cordons down, "Not in my house!" he exclaimed. His jealousy of McGwire, rage against perceived disrespect and racism, and general all-around paranoia continued to eat away at Bonds. The best player of his generation no longer seemed to be relevant.[72]

Bonds, however, was healthy again in 2000 while the injury-riddled McGwire struggled onto the final lap of his career. That season Barry clobbered forty-nine home runs. Then, in 2001, he toppled McGwire's single-season home run record, hitting seventy-three homers. Whatever his motivation, Bonds wanted nothing less than to redraw the magical summer of 1998 in shades of his own choosing. Sadly, the coverage of Bonds's chase for the record was decidedly sober. Outside of San Francisco, it was almost anticlimactic. People were less excited than in 1998—perhaps because the record was still so fresh, perhaps because Bonds was less likable than McGwire, perhaps because of the increasingly persistent rumors of performance-enhancing drug use, and perhaps, in the final analysis, because of Bonds's race. Maybe this *was* Aaron and Mays all over again. Fans had cheered McGwire even after his Andro admissions. Although there were growing rumors—just look at his expanding physique!—Bonds appeared outwardly clean. He was breaking the record without any help. And not many, even in the press box, were cheering for him.[73]

As Bonds was taking up his chase for the single-season home run record, the press routinely referred to him as "sullen" or "peevish." Although it was McGwire's record that he was chasing, the primary point of comparison in that understated 2001 race was with Sammy Sosa. In this instance it was the color of their skin that united the two players, but it was their attitudes (toward other people, toward the game) that were so markedly different. Everyone saw it. Unlike his 1998 duel with McGwire, this time around Slammin' Sammy was definitely the favorite.

Sammy Sosa had grown up poor in the coastal Caribbean city of San Pedro de Macoris in the Dominican Republic. The press delighted in reminding readers how Sosa had been forced to use an old milk carton as a glove to field ground balls, had used tree branches or other scrap wood for a bat, and had never even felt the smooth grain of a Louisville Slugger in his hands until he was fourteen. His home was a shabby, door-less dome of cinder blocks behind a converted hospital. When he was discovered by Texas Rangers scouts in the early 1980s, they described the scrawny Sosa as "malnourished."[74]

The young Sosa struggled, however, to make it in the Major Leagues. Though slender and underdeveloped, Sosa was a violent and hopelessly erratic hitter. Coaches bemoaned his indiscriminate swinging, and soon it was a popular joke that Sosa would swing at a white paper cup if it accidentally blew toward home plate. Even after he was traded by the Rangers to the Chicago White Sox, and then from the White Sox to the cross-town Cubs, his batting stroke was wild. Mark Clark, who pitched against Sosa with the Mets (and later joined him as a teammate with the Cubs), remembered that "you could bounce a ball in front of the plate, and he'd swing at it. He'd go for high, bad slider. You knew he was going to be up there hacking."[75]

In the summer of 1998, however, Sosa—who had filled out his "malnourished" frame and become a compact, muscular outfielder—traded indiscriminate hacking for sudden, incredible consistency. It was true that Sosa had become a productive home run hitter over the previous three seasons, hitting thirty-six, forty, and thirty-six home runs, respectively. Nobody, however, considered him a competitor to take on the Ken Griffey Jrs. of the world, and certainly he was no match for the prodigiously powerful McGwire. He was not a blip on the Maris chase radar through the start of June. But in

June 1998, storming into the headlines out of the Windy City, the character of "Slammin' Sammy" was born, propelled by a white-hot month of slugging in which he hit a record twenty home runs (topping the old mark of eighteen set by Detroit's Rudy York in August 1937). With each home run the Cubs slugger touched his lips twice, tapped his chest, and pointed to the sky. When he knocked a ball out of the park, he smiled. When he struck out, and he still often did strike out, he smiled. His warm demeanor even captivated McGwire (a man Sosa referred to as "my friend"), and his good humor helped lighten the weight of "Androgate." When news of McGwire's supplement use broke, Sosa pulled a bottle of Flintstone vitamins from his locker and mugged for the cameras.[76]

For all that the media celebrated Sosa's natural warmth and Latin flair (itself a problematic concept), there was a darker side to the emerging competition. Even after Androgate, it was clear that McGwire was the overwhelming favorite of most Americans. Internet search engines found McGwire's name twice as often as Sosa's. Some argued that while McGwire's track record of hitting home runs was well documented, Sosa was a "fluke" who probably didn't deserve a shot at the record. Even the somewhat questionable nature of McGwire's power was trumped by lingering matters of race and xenophobia. The majority of Americans preferred a white user of questionable supplements to a grinning black man from beyond the national border.[77]

Now facing off with a black rival, Sosa was still portrayed as the stereotypical embodiment of Latin good nature, but he was now the baseball hero that most fans wanted to see succeed. That Bonds played with a large, highly visible chip on his shoulder only made matters worse. The *Chicago Tribune* explained how Sosa was the baseball superstar most attuned to his public despite having had a few high-profile financial disputes with Chicago management in the previous year. Bonds, conversely, was a player—in reality fiercely loyal to his hometown team—who wanted nothing to do with the public.[78]

Ultimately, making sense of Barry Bonds is a difficult task, one that no single book, much less part of a single chapter, can accomplish. Nevertheless, some clear pictures do emerge. First, Bonds was obviously treated differently than either McGwire or Sosa. At his peak, when he was probably the best player in the game, he was never viewed as a hero much less as the savior of baseball. He was just a tremendous talent with a bad attitude. He was never sanctified like Ripken. He was no match for McGwire's Paul Bunyan by way of George Bailey routine. If Ripken was everything that a baseball player should be, and McGwire was exactly the type of hero America wanted in 1998, then

Bonds was destined to play the role of embodying everything Americans despised and everything that was wrong with baseball by early 2002.[79]

Lingering issues of race aside, the tragedy of Barry Bonds is that the world of baseball changed dramatically at exactly the time when Bonds finally began charging toward record-setting heights. Although initially only the subject of dubious rumor and innuendo, eventually Barry's name was dragged into a full-blown steroid scandal that threatened to level baseball as surely—and perhaps more permanently—than the 1994 strike. Bonds had no more than set the new single-season home run mark when baseball's fabled code of silence was completely and irrevocably shattered.

By the start of the 2002 season there were growing questions among those who followed baseball about what Bonds might be doing to enhance his performance. After hitting a home run to ensure a Giants victory over San Diego early in the year, Barry was asked about steroids. "You can test me and solve that problem real quick," Bonds answered. "To me, in baseball it really doesn't matter what you do; you still have to hit that baseball. If you're incapable of hitting it, it doesn't matter what you take. You have to have eye-hand coordination to be able to produce. I think (steroid use) is really irrelevant to the game of baseball." It was about to become very relevant.[80]

* * *

On June 3, 2002, *Sports Illustrated* published an article that included former San Diego Padre infielder Ken Caminiti's admission that he used steroids in 1996. That season Caminiti hit a shocking forty-six home runs, led the Padres to the playoffs, and won the National League MVP Award. Caminiti claimed that in 1996 steroid use was widespread in baseball. "It's no secret what's going on in baseball," he said. "At least half the guys are using steroids." Jose Canseco told *Sports Illustrated* that as much as 80 percent of the league was using steroids (he later recanted and claimed to have been misquoted or taken out of context). Arizona's star pitcher, Curt Schilling, told the *Washington Post* that steroids "are incredibly prominent in the game, I don't think there's any question about that. . . . It has enhanced numbers into the stratosphere."[81]

With steroids now front and center, baseball's establishment slowly creaked into damage control. Suddenly it would no longer do to have its biggest superstars—and its biggest records—tainted by the brush of performance enhancement. Sadly, the sport tripped over the usual hurdles. Major League Baseball's testing program, eviscerated in the cocaine wars of the 1980s, was by now virtually nonexistent. The revelations of 2002 finally, after years of fruitless sparring, convinced management and the union to sit down and agree to limited drug testing. Under the new plan that emerged from those talks a player could test positive for steroid use five times before receiving a one-year suspension. Even then, after five positive tests, the league retained the option to fine the player rather than suspend him. It was clear that the sport was protecting its most marketable assets and ensuring that teams chasing a pennant would not lose a star player down the stretch. Major League Baseball's policy appeared toothless compared to the IOC policy, where an athlete caught just once was banned for two years. The new policy was a joke, reviled as "worse than terrible."[82]

If Caminiti's revelations had seemed a damaging speed bump, in October 2003 the wheels came tearing off the careening bus that was Major League Baseball. That month, the *San Francisco Chronicle* unveiled reports about an emerging drug scandal involving the Bay Area Laboratory Cooperative (BALCO). The Burlingame, California, facility was known as a producer of nutritional supplements used by athletes throughout the sports world—track and field, football, baseball. A few months earlier an anonymous source, a track coach, had provided the U.S. Anti-Doping Agency with a syringe said to contain traces of a new chemical being used by athletes. Tests confirmed that the newly discovered drug was an anabolic steroid called tetrahydrogestrinone (THG) or "The Clear." It was undetectable because it broke apart before ever reaching the subject's urine. That September, when government agents raided the BALCO facility, they found containers of steroids and human growth hormone (HGH). BALCO's owner, Victor Conte, a former musician (he played bass with the band Tower of Power) turned sports health guru, was identified as the source of the new drug. At the same time, agents raided the residence of Burlingame area trainer Greg Anderson, a close friend and personal trainer to Barry Bonds. Anderson, it turned out, was also in possession of anabolic steroids.[83]

BALCO had ties to most of the major sports, and the ongoing high-profile investigation dragged a number of big names into the spotlight. What eventually came to be known of baseball players' involvement with BALCO came from three sources: a *Sports Illustrated* interview with journeyman slugger Gary Sheffield, alleged grand jury testimony published in the *San Francisco Chronicle*, and a government memorandum obtained by the *San Jose Mercury News*. Most of these reports focused on Barry Bonds. Because of his reputation, Bonds's fellow players struggled to defend him or to find excuses for him as they had for McGwire. Jason Giambi called Bonds, whose physical growth between his years in Pittsburgh and record-setting San Francisco years was visually stunning, a "cartoon character."

Bonds, for his part, steadfastly denied any wrongdoing. This was just jealousy and racism rearing their ugly heads in a world that was out to vilify him. Instead, Bonds insisted that he had been using nothing more than flaxseed oil and a special arthritis balm, not BALCO's designer drugs.[84]

With Barry Bonds's legacy on the rocks, Major League Baseball hurtled toward a day of reckoning regarding the performance-enhancement issue. Jose Canseco helped send the entire thing over the cliff with the 2005 publication of his autobiography, *Juiced*. The book ostensibly revealed what many had speculated was true for years. Canseco had, in fact, used steroids. Now, in print, he referred to himself as the "Godfather of the steroid revolution." He also alleged that he had taught numerous teammates over the years how to integrate steroids and other chemical helpers into their training regimens. Canseco portrayed himself as a judicious drug user who first used steroids in 1984. He used them routinely throughout his career. Steroids, he explained, represented an opportunity, not a danger. Those who said otherwise spoke from "ignorance." He and Mark McGwire used them regularly during their last years together in Oakland.[85]

Canseco further revealed that he believed that Oakland traded him to the Texas Rangers in 1992, not because his performance had slipped, but because of his well-known reputation for using steroids. After joining the Rangers, Canseco wrote, he became a performance-enhancing guru to players on that club, including emerging stars Juan Gonzalez, Rafael Palmeiro, and Ivan Rodriguez. "Soon I was injecting all three of them," Canseco wrote. "I personally injected each of those three guys, many times." All three players denied Canseco's allegations at the time. All three would be mentioned in the 2007 Mitchell Report as performance-enhancement drug users.[86]

Canseco insisted that President George W. Bush, who owned the Rangers in the early 1990s, "had to have been aware" of the widespread performance enhancement taking place in his club. The White House chose not to respond to Canseco's allegations, instead pointing to the president's 2004 State of the Union Address in which he had issued a national call for the league and the union to come together to eradicate steroid use. Congress was obviously listening. The March 2005 hearing was convened. By the time it concluded, Mark McGwire's heroic reputation was forever tarnished. Now Major League Baseball went into full-on damage control. In little more than a decade, baseball had gone from the depths of strike-induced despair to glorious home-run fueled heights to despair again. The *B* in MLB may have stood for "baseball," but it also stood for "BALCO" and for "Barry Bonds." Above all else, what baseball seemingly stood for, early in the twenty-first century, was for drugs. What many failed to notice was that, to some extent, it almost always had.

*   *   *

In January 2010, two years after the sensational release of the Mitchell Report, Mark McGwire sat across from interviewer Bob Costas and, at long last, admitted what almost everyone already knew to be true. The confession tumbled over McGwire's lips. "It's time for me to talk about the past," he said, "and to confirm what people have suspected. I used steroids during my playing career and I apologize." This was surely meant to be closure, for McGwire if no one else, but it didn't feel that way. This was just one more loose end on that long, ragged, thread. Questions remained unanswered. Where did it all begin to unravel? How? Why? Mark McGwire was optimistic that those questions were no long relevant. "Baseball is really different now—it's been cleaned up." The commissioner, Bud Selig, was equally sanguine. "The so-called steroid era," Selig insisted, "is clearly a thing of the past."[87]

Epilogue

Brave New Game

"A guy this sweet," wrote Gerry Callahan in a 1996 *Sports Illustrated* profile of young Mariners shortstop Alex Rodriguez, "must be hiding some cavities." Looking back from nearly two decades later, the latent irony of this statement is stunning. Rodriguez, a player who once claimed he would rather have a Gold Glove than a silver bat, may now be the most recognizable face of performance-enhancing drug (PED) use in baseball—possibly in all of sports (although cyclist Lance Armstrong can probably stake some claim to the title). In the wake of the Mitchell Report findings, Rodriguez adamantly proclaimed his innocence when he was connected with PED use, later cried as he expressed remorse for lying about his past abuses (it turns out he *was* connected to PEDs), and then doubled down on the denials when indicted yet again, this time for transgressions related to the Biogenesis doping scandal in 2013. On January 11, 2014, Rodriguez, after a lengthy period of arbitration, was formally suspended for 162 games—effectively losing the entirety of the 2014 season. It was, at that point, the longest non-lifetime suspension in Major League history. Irony or no, Gerry Callahan was right. It turns out there were cavities.[1]

It is only right that A-Rod should stand at the center of the narrative for a moment, here at the end, because he reflects much of what has gone into defining the story of drugs and baseball over the last few decades. On one level, and the most obvious, Alex Rodriguez is the new face of the Steroid Era. He is that simply because he is the latest, the last in line, supplanting McGwire, Bonds, and Clemens. It is not inconceivable that another player will someday knock A-Rod from his perch as baseball's preeminent villain, but for now A-Rod has become synonymous with doping in baseball.

At the same time, much like Barry Bonds, Rodriguez is an almost unfairly easy target for critics. When it comes to A-Rod, it is difficult to discern where the outrage over drugs begins and the disdain for the arrogant player ends. Most of the material written (some of it left unpublished) about Rodriguez over the last twenty years paints a less than becoming portrait of the man. A-Rod tends to come across as a remarkably vapid character—when it comes to Rodriguez there is no clear moral center, no sense of strongly held beliefs. What does clearly emerge is practically parody. The meaning of A-Rod could be summed up by the infamous photograph in *Details* of Alex kissing his own reflection, or by the inexplicable "centaur painting" that made headlines in 2009, or by the many tabloid snapshots of his personal life.[2]

Put the tabloids, titillating as they may be, aside. When it comes down to it, no single player better reflects the hard reality of baseball in this troubled era than does A-Rod. Alex Rodriguez is a living, breathing metaphor for Major League Baseball (which, if baseball is as reflective as this book suggests, therefore makes him a good cipher for America in the twenty-first century). Remember, there was a time not so long ago that if Americans wanted to celebrate any reflection in the mirror that is sports, they wanted to celebrate A-Rod. His intrinsic blankness (what emerges as vapidity now was freshness and innocence then) made him the perfect canvas for positive sports narratives. As a young Rodriguez told Gerry Callahan, he just wanted to be remembered as a "good person" (he took uniform number 3 as a tribute to Dale Murphy, one of the game's most celebrated "good guys"). In an age of Nike ad explosions, outsized contracts, and overcooked hype, was there not something refreshing about a player whose greatest desire was just to be a good man?[3]

A-Rod was traditional and yet also incredibly modern. On the field, he was one part Ozzie Smith: a slick fielding shortstop with terrific range, soft hands, and a cannon arm. He was one part Babe Ruth, a slugger gifted with prodigious power. Coming up to the Major Leagues with the Seattle Mariners, Rodriguez seemed destined to become the face of the game. In 1996, at an age when most players were in college or the low minor leagues, Rodriguez was already making a case for being the best player in the American League. He was squeaky clean. He called his mom five times a week, avoided alcohol, and worshipped his veteran teammates. He was, not to put too fine a point on the word, *perfect*. When A-Rod abdicated the shortstop position to the retiring Cal Ripken at the 2001 All-Star Game, the message was clear: baseball's preeminent "good guy" passes the torch to the ascendant "good guy." Baseball, the moment said, is in great hands. This A-Rod was a player who would have fit in any era of baseball's Elysian past. One can easily imagine Fred Lieb profiling him, or a Lester Chadwick line of saccharine "A-Rod for Boys" stories churned out as homages to clean living and good behavior.

But there was another side to Alex Rodriguez, one more modern and decidedly more complicated. His awe-inspiring on-field talent was matched by a remarkably honed sense of public relations off the field. Even in his rookie campaign some teammates saw it. "[That innocent kid stuff] is an act. Don't let him fool you," explained one teammate. "He knows how good he is. And he knows how good he's going to be." His nickname, A-Rod, became his brand: every great play and every long clout added to the luster of A-Rod Corp. LLC. Not just a baseball star, he was a national celebrity—a man with model good looks and a coterie of advisers telling him what endorsements to sign, what clothes to wear, where to be seen, and what to say. He dated the world's biggest superstars (Madonna!), earned millions (especially after signing a record $275 million contract with the New York Yankees), and hit home runs, launching five hundred by the time he was thirty-two.

Traditional, clean, modern, and media savvy, A-Rod was the perceived antidote to the game's ailments. In the aftermath of the 2005 congressional hearings, the BALCO debacle, and the understandable outpouring of cynicism, Alex Rodriguez emerged as the anti-Bonds—one player with incredible public self-awareness and a positive public image to go with his scintillating baseball talent. Who could be a better representative of the game in the twenty-first century? Americans could embrace a player who so carefully defined himself—he was beautiful, successful, and powerful. In an age of drugs and cheating and superficiality, here was affirmation of the old verities. This son of Dominican immigrants was the American Dream writ in bold letters right there on the diamond. The game may have produced Bonds, but it also produced Alex Rodriguez. Most Americans despised Bonds; many of them dreamed of being Alex Rodriguez.

Then, in February 2009, the fairy tale began to unravel. Rodriguez had always denied using performance-enhancing drugs—had, in fact, denied using them on national television during an interview with CBS's Katie Couric. Now, in an unusually human moment, he told ESPN's Peter Gammons that, driven by the pressure to compete and perform, he had used steroids between 2001 and 2003. It was a perfectly staged confession. In reality, Rodriguez was launching a preemptive strike to save his brand, his name, from utter ruin. Prior to the Gammons interview he had been confronted by *Sports Illus-*

trated writer Selena Roberts with documentation that he had failed a drug test for Primobolan and testosterone in 2003—the documentation was part of a leaked "survey" from that year. The story of the failed test would break in the February 16 issue of *Sports Illustrated*. Rodriguez knew the story was true (he had been vaguely informed of the failed test by union rep Gene Orza in 2004). With nothing to lose—the story was going to break regardless—he went on the offensive. He admitted that he had been "stupid," but then focused his energies on blasting Roberts in the Gammons exclusive. A-Rod may have made mistakes (don't we all?), but this vindictive reporter (a "stalker") was practically carrying on an unfair crusade against him.[4]

When *Sports Illustrated* demanded an apology for what was clearly unwarranted slander, Rodriguez supplied that as well—if only half-heartedly. He could apologize—for using drugs, for lying about using drugs, for slandering those who exposed his drug use. Apologies came easy. A-Rod was playing the all-American game of second chances. The rules were simple: say and do whatever it takes to make the cheers come back. He would admit to being young, naive, and stupid. But he was growing up, he assured fans, just like the game, emerging from what he termed a "loosey goosey" era. He was still the player to put baseball back on the map. While grand juries were confronting Barry Bonds and Roger Clemens for their alleged lies, fans could have faith that A-Rod was telling the truth.[5]

Having apologized, Rodriguez announced that he would become a spokesperson for the Taylor Hooton Foundation, educating youngsters about the dangers of steroid use. From start to finish, the entire affair was a master class in public relations. For one brief moment, Alex Rodriguez stood as proof that talent (and good PR advice) almost always trumps wrongdoing. Although some took to calling him A-Fraud, Rodriguez, no longer a shining paragon but still lustrous, was soon back hitting home runs. Memory is short in the age of enhancement. When he homered against the Orioles to open the 2009 season, the crowd at Yankee Stadium roared in support. He sealed off the 2009 season with a strong performance in the postseason, leading the Yankees to a World Series title and putting to rest his loudest critics. Stop the tale there, and you have one of those classic redemption stories that Americans love so much.

But A-Rod's story was not complete, nor with it the story of baseball and drugs. In January 2013 Biogenesis of America stormed the headlines. In March, Major League Baseball sued six people connected to Biogenesis, accusing them of damaging the sport by providing banned substances to players. Among the players listed on Biogenesis's rolls were Milwaukee

Brewers star Ryan Braun and Alex Rodriguez. The league began meting out punishment, but it was quickly clear that Rodriguez was the primary target. Biogenesis founder Anthony Bosch even told *60 Minutes* that he personally injected Rodriguez, and he did it all in exchange for $12,000 a month.[6]

When the record suspension of Rodriguez was handed down in January 2014, it put a final exclamation point on the era of performance enhancement in Major League Baseball and wrapped up a decades-long narrative. In the end, Alex Rodriguez turned out to be the scapegoat so long sought by the Major League establishment. And for Americans who had invested so much in the A-Rod story, his punishment became their punishment—but it was cleansing, like having the veil torn away. They could come to love baseball once more, but they would never again invest the game, or any one player, with such meaning. It was all just entertainment and PR. And is that not fitting for a player with such PR savvy as A-Rod? Even in ignominy, Alex Rodriguez personified the game.

Maybe the ultimate lesson of the A-Rod story is that Bud Selig finally realized the dreams of Bowie Kuhn and Peter Ueberroth. The system as it currently exists grants the commissioner's office more power than it possessed at any point since Judge Landis was in office. Selig, at times, has managed to play fast and loose with the Joint Drug Agreement, but he also emerged as the victor in the arbitration hearing that banished A-Rod for an entire season. As he prepared to leave office, Selig's champions could point to the success of testing protocols ushered in on his watch and to the power wielded by his office in the interest of restoring the game's integrity. Forget the Steroid Era (it is in the past!)—baseball ultimately got it right. A-Rod was exiled. The game would be more vigilant moving forward. Even Rodriguez's stunningly successful comeback in 2015, following his record suspension, did little to alter the finality of the scapegoat narrative or the belief that Major League Baseball has appropriately corrected its course when it comes to PEDs.

Certainly there is a sense both in and out of the game that increased testing will ultimately solve the PED problem. Baseball's players have thus far proven willing to adapt to a new system, one with increased testing, but big questions remain. What can be done about Major League Baseball's sometimes careless treading of the line between confidentiality and public shaming as it skirts dangerously near breaking the joint drug agreement? And the critics of drug testing remain vocal. "Drug testing is still impotent, has been impotent since it started," said Charles Yesalis. "Frankly, many of these drugs work way too well and there's way too much money involved to ever see a light at the end of the tunnel." Testing cannot keep up with the designers of modern drugs; and the men with the money will always be tempted to seek advantages. The benefits outweigh the risk. It is entirely possible that even the strongest testing regime cannot permanently root drug use out of the game.[7]

The Steroid Era ended not because baseball solved the problem of performance-enhancing drug use—A-Rod's story actually illustrates how far the league was from doing so—but rather because the luster of that narrative faded into a tiresome stream of suspicions, allegations, revelations, and confessions. To put it bluntly, the narrative just became played out. Some even began suggesting that the conventional Steroid Era narrative—the story that performance-enhancing drugs had provided the spark that saved baseball from itself following the 1994 strike—was false. Major League Baseball only returned to its pre-strike attendance levels (30,964 per game in 1993) in 2006, three years after the advent of stiff penalties for failed drug tests. Attendance in what some have called the "Testing Era" has been higher than in any of the years of the Steroid Era. As home runs have declined, attendance has risen.[8]

Of course, attendance is only part of the story. If sports are where Americans sometimes debate the meaning of life, then the Steroid Era may hold a lesson about an inherent contradiction in American culture, the disconnect between the desire for fairness on one hand and the devotion to capitalism on the other. Capitalism, noted writers at the *Houston Chronicle*, "never rewarded anyone, no matter how hard he or she worked, for a product void of market appeal." If steroids didn't actually equate to an attendance boom, the "big bang" did create a sensation, created more advertising, birthed bigger endorsement opportunities, and bigger paychecks for slugging superstars.[9]

Of course, not every player in Major League Baseball was motivated to use drugs to secure a fat contract. One popular argument about the use of performance-enhancing drugs centered on the issue of job security. There are only so many Major League roster spots to go around. Superstars, the players who make the most money, feel the competition for a spot far less keenly than players on the fringes of a Major League roster. It is on those fringes where performance enhancement was most likely to be common.

The writers at *Baseball Prospectus*, advocates of deep statistical baseball analysis, suggested that steroids really did not make a big difference at the top level of the game. Players like Barry Bonds might be able to stay in peak condition for longer periods of time due to drugs, but the drug's impact on their statistical output was not going to be extreme. Instead, it was players whose jobs were threatened who were more likely to turn to steroids or other performance enhancers. If the majority of studies on the influence of steroids in baseball are to be believed, and there is always a degree of speculation to such research, the drugs do not actually contribute to massive statistical output. Just so, an extra five or six home runs, while they meant nothing to a Bonds or a McGwire, were often the difference between a new contract, reassignment to the minor leagues, or unemployment for a career backup.[10]

Financial gain and employment security are rational motives for using performance-enhancing drugs. Besides, if one looked out beyond the diamond world, were not many workaday Americans using drugs—some traditionally used in the Major Leagues—to perform better at *their* jobs? Students across America popped Adderall to get through study sessions and grueling exams (and behold, today, critics worry about the influence of ADHD drugs in the game!). Surgeons and legal professionals relied on amphetamines or other uppers to keep their edge in a highly intense workplace. When it comes down to it, few things could be more American than using a supplement to improve job performance. This is to say nothing of performance in the bedroom, a constant worry for twenty-first-century Americans, evidenced by endless marketing campaigns for Viagra (with ads boldly plastered on Major League Baseball's website) and Cialis. Performance-enhancing drug use in Major League Baseball ultimately reflects the pill-happy reality of American life in the new century.

The drugs that baseball must eradicate from the field are, today, pervasive parts of American life. Millions of Americans—none of them star athletes—are looking for performance enhancement of one sort or another; the kind that only a little pill or injection can provide. Outside of the sports world there are musicians (the rapper Mary J. Blige, for example) and actors (like Sylvester Stallone, the legendary Rocky) who were linked to HGH or steroid use. Sly even told *Time* magazine that "everyone over 40 years old would be wise to investigate [HGH and testosterone] because it increases the quality of your life." If the use of performance-enhancing drugs was not only not un-American but was, in fact, fundamentally American, why are people so bothered by the use of the same drugs in the world of Major League Baseball?[11]

That has been one of the underlying questions behind this book. The answers to that question are multifold, and some are more speculative than others. The first is based on tradition, on numbers, on history itself. What is our expectation about sports? We expect that athletes play by the rules, play fair. We expect to see a competition of *human* skill. The introduction of drugs, not to mention the possibilities presented by genetic manipulation, clearly obscures these basic expectations. It isn't just steroids or designer PEDs, either. They may tilt the field in one direction, but recreational drugs like cocaine or marijuana may tilt it in the other direction. A batter with a hangover may be at a distinct disadvantage when he comes to the plate. Of course, moving down this path risks getting into a debate about degree, but the fundamental assumption that sport is and must always be a field of pure competition is nevertheless quite clear. Drugs of any kind pervert the essential essence of sport.

More than any other sport, followers of baseball are obsessed with numbers. Baseball's historical eras are linked by statistics. The ability to compare players across generations depends on the sanctity of the game's numbers. When critics sounded their steroid-induced death knell for the old pastime, what they were really lamenting was the loss of baseball's common language, the ruin of its unique connective tissue, the breaking of the covenant between past and present. Almost anything that happens on the diamond can be reduced to a number, calculated, and analyzed in increasingly complex ways. A home run counted the same no matter when it was hit—in 1920, 1949, or 1999. Looking through the numbers, fans could compare latter-day sluggers like Mike Schmidt or Reggie Jackson with icons of the distant past: Mantle, Aaron, DiMaggio, Ruth. The intrusion of drugs, which may have the potential to inflate individual statistics, threatens to destroy these numerical bridges between generations. With performance enhancers in the mix, the fear is that comparing the numbers of Ruth and McGwire might ultimately be like translating a text from Latin to French. Drug use obscures and perverts the common language of a venerable game.

Beyond the perceived dissonance of sacred numbers, there is also an aesthetic revulsion when it comes to the outcry against performance enhancers. Part of what has often struck the common baseball fan is his physical compatibility with the players that he idolizes. This was a purely aesthetic, visual relationship. A man who watches baseball, but who might not be able to play the game very well, can still imagine himself as a slight, rangy infielder. That player could be his mirror image. Although he cannot throw a ninety-five-mile-per-hour fastball, the fact that he looks like the lanky southpaw on the mound fuels Joe Average's baseball dreams. The same man would surely struggle to imagine himself in the place of a massive, muscle-bound linebacker on the gridiron or slamming a basketball over some towering giant on the hardwood. The physical growth of baseball players into impressive, almost comically muscle-bound specimens threatens to destroy this fundamental aesthetic relationship.[12]

In either case, numerical or aesthetic, drugs threaten core elements of baseball's myth-shrouded past. The ability to weigh merit and compare greatness through the numbers is lost. The visual aspect of this "game for all Americans" is obscured. In sum, the last pure place is not pure. It is, in fact, nothing more than another modern form of entertainment cum spectacle. Seen from this angle, it could be that the slightly renewed attraction to baseball in the Testing Era is due to the sport's return to human scale.

Perhaps the answer lies not in numbers or aesthetics but in deeper, more theoretical territory. The German sociologist Norbert Elias described how a "civilizing process" drew human beings away from barbarism through the application of key social pressures. People, Elias explained, were expected to exercise self-control, to build a strong internal conscience that would ward them away from any temptations they knew to be "wrong." The rules and framework of society were in place, therefore, so that humans might lead ordered lives. The processes' insistence on "order" led human beings to seek to control every aspect of their own bodies. In time, with the new advances of the scientific community, particularly in the twentieth century, the possibilities of rigorous order—of absolute control over the body and its potential—became limitless. Nature could be improved upon. With rationalization and strict control, man could move beyond all natural limitations. One is reminded of the 1985 Stallone film *Rocky IV,* wherein the Soviet boxer Ivan Drago (portrayed by Dolph Lundgren) is hailed as an evolutionary step forward. "It is a matter of size. Evolution. Isn't it, gentlemen?" asks his trainer. "Drago is the most perfectly trained athlete ever. This other man has not the size, the strength, the genetics to win. It is physically impossible for this little man [Apollo Creed] to win. Drago is a look at the future!"[13]

John Hoberman, the professor of Germanic languages who has become a notable scholar about drugs in sports, led the way in arguing that the pharmacological advances of the twentieth century exponentially increased the likelihood that the human body would, in the future, be brought under complete control. Miracle drugs, suggested Hoberman, would eliminate dread diseases, help reverse the aging process, and promote a general state of good health. Each step taken by the scientific community, however, was felt throughout society. Soldiers on the front lines of World War II battled injury and fatigue with amphetamine; later, after the war was over, amphetamine found its way into the homes (and games) of civilian Americans.[14]

In the wake of World War II, America's obsession with good health (or the elimination of pain at the very least) was complemented by the arrival of new miracle drugs designed for the amelioration of just about *any* potential complaint. Doctor visits were rendered unnecessary as drugs became available over the counter. Suffering and minor complaints were suddenly things that should not be tolerated, but instead should be eliminated. In America, the passion for the "Good Life" was supplemented by miracle pills. One of the foundations of Christopher Lasch's culture of narcissism, which defined postwar American life, was the availability of supplements, exercise routines, and other medical marvels birthed by the science community. It was only natural that something that was so much a part of American culture would find its way into the games of that culture. There is an inherent hypocrisy in all of the media sensationalism about the horrors of BALCO and Biogenesis while anti-aging clinics continue to earn millions from average Americans wanting to look and feel younger.[15]

More than anything else, drug use in baseball could be ascribed as a direct corollary to the American obsession with winning. Americans have emphasized winning—broadly construed—all the way down to the lowest levels of their society. Young schoolchildren are taught that winning is the only thing that matters. This attitude, in the broadest possible sense, underscores most of baseball's public relations initiatives regarding drugs. When Major League Baseball claims it wants to eliminate drugs from the sport for the health of the players, one has to wonder why it has not banned tobacco. After all, no substance has as proven a track record of harmfulness. Yet tobacco remains a nostalgic part of baseball's manly subculture.[16]

What about alcohol? Like tobacco, it is legal in society, but it also has a well-documented history of physical destructiveness. Beyond Mickey Mantle, whose experience is briefly recounted in this book, there are other stories such as that of St. Louis Cardinals pitcher Josh Hancock, who was killed in an April 2007 car crash. His blood alcohol level was nearly double the legal limit in the state of Missouri. Although the Cardinals mourned and even banned alcohol from the clubhouse for a period of time, Major League Baseball remained a sport distinctly linked to the brewing industry. That a Major League Baseball game doubles as one prolonged beer advertisement is difficult to dispute.[17]

Owners were never as interested in the health of their employees as they were in the bottom line. The need to win, in every way, trumped every other concern. This all-American hunger even clouded the popular argument that sports needed to eliminate drugs if for no other reason than for the sake of American children. Players, the cry resounded, must return to being good role models. Studies, however, have proven that despite athletic doping indiscretions, there is not a runaway epidemic of drug usage at the youth level. Current adolescent rates are 1.5 percent and dropping. The claim that children model their behavior after prominent athletes is also dubious. A number of scientific studies suggest that fewer than 20 percent of young people identify any athlete as a "role model." The further suggestion that youngsters inject performance enhancers just because an athlete may have done so is even more dubious. Remember, the drugs used by athletes are often prohibitively expensive. In fact, when studies of steroid use at the high school level have been produced, it appears that young men use steroids not to mirror any professional idol, or even to improve their athletic performance. Instead, steroids are used to improve their physical appearance in order to attract the attention of girls.[18]

This is not to say that some student athletes are not using steroids for athletic gain, or that steroid use is not dangerous. Rather, the point should be that students use them deliberately because of promised rewards or due to the immense pressure to succeed—the American obsession with winning. In the end, Americans value role models only secondarily. What they really value is excellence—measured by performance in competition. Model citizens who are also marginal athletes are weeded out through the rigors of the game. Most uncommon is the athlete—a Grant Hill in the NBA, a Drew Brees in the NFL, or a Cal Ripken Jr. in baseball—who happens to be both a superb athlete and a legitimate role model. The very idea that a player is obligated to be a role model has always been a flawed one. In a society where winning is everything, it is impossible to also expect model behavior. The price of winning is too high for athletes to be role models.

If we cannot have role models, we do not necessarily want pariahs either. Of course, in today's game a failed test does not mean the permanent ostracizing of the guilty player. The eccentric but very popular Manny Ramirez was never far from the game after his transgressions. Following their failed tests both Melky Cabrera and Bartolo Colon actually earned new contracts. Cabrera got a two-year, $16 million contract from the Toronto Blue Jays for 2013. Colon, sticking with the Oakland Athletics, got a million-dollar raise. Despite all of this, Bud Selig proclaimed it a "proud day" when baseball announced the introduction of new HGH testing. That players had been caught was a victory for Major League Baseball. Every suspension following a failed test seemed to be proof that the new system was working and that cheaters were being punished. They just got new big paychecks after enduring that punishment.[19]

*　*　*

In the end, the history of drug and alcohol abuse in baseball complicates the sporting story we are telling about ourselves. Sport is the ultimate field of collective memory, and we long for that field of play to be pure, even if we know it is not. How else can we celebrate what that mirror shows us than by forging an elaborate mythology about purity, spirit, and team play while airbrushing away the flaws? Baseball is our game, imperfect as it is and as we are. In the forging of the international "American Century," professional sports grew and changed, from localized amusements into mass spectacles of entertainment—circuses for a latter-day Rome. As society advanced its wealth and its technological know-how, sports reflected the transformation. Big profits paid for the drugs, fat contracts came chained to the pressure to perform, and the pressure demanded escape. The enormous pressure to perform at the highest level, coupled with greed, negligence, and a healthy dose of ignorance in the game's establishment, led players like Mickey Mantle, Sam McDowell, and Ryne Duren down the path of alcoholic ruin—a fate they shared with millions of ordinary Americans. The same pressures that drove Reno Bertoia to take tranquilizers in 1959, or Sandy Koufax to accept injections in the 1960s, led Alex Rodriguez, in a slightly different economic context, to inject steroids early in the twenty-first century.

We can quibble over the not insignificant concept of legality to the end of days, but there is more that connects A-Rod, Clemens, and Bonds to Mantle, Koufax, and Tuttle than the game they played. Drugs, of this sort or another, were dangerous and ubiquitous parts of their professional lives. Drug use reverberated through the game on every level—advertising alcohol and tobacco underwrote the bottom line, amphetamine use was a necessary bulwark against the long grind of the season, and recreational drugs were the inevitable result of bigger contracts, bigger pressures, and greater celebrity. It was really just a small step, a logical step, from greenies and tranquilizers to Winstrol and HGH. The tracks were laid decades before the Steroid Train rolled into MLB Central.

In writing about the 1919 Black Sox scandal, Eliot Asinof suggested that baseball "was a manifestation of the greatest of America at play. It was our national game; its stars were national heroes, revered by kids and adults alike, in all areas of our society. In the public mind, the image was pure and patriotic." This was baseball as Bart Giamatti imagined it. It was a pure place, an Eden where the sun was shining, the grass was perfectly clipped, that we could enter at any time, there to see Adam at play before Eve seduced him with a sweeter fruit. Baseball was meant to be a mirror that showed us at our very best. Asinof also reminded us that "if baseball was corrupt, then anything might be—and probably was."[20]

We should be careful about making too much of the game and its problems, but we should also recognize how relevant the game still is, and what it can tell us. What must so annoy us, in this mirror of Eden obscured by alcohol and drugs, is that we *do* see ourselves, not necessarily as we want to be but as we are.

Notes

Introduction. The Last Pure Place

1. *New York Times*, 11 January 2010.

2. *New York Times*, 10 January 2013, 12 January 2014; *Miami Herald*, 30 January 2013; *Miami New Times*, 30 January 2013.

3. CBS News, *60 Minutes*, 14 January 2014.

4. See especially Stephen J. Gould, "The Creation Myths of Cooperstown: Or Why the Cardiff Giants Are an Unbeatable and Appropriately Named Team," *Natural History*. November 1989, http://www.naturalhistorymag.com/picks-from-the-past/02484/the-creation-myths-of-cooperstown; Twain quoted in Palmer, *Athletic Sports in America*, 446–447; Guttmann, *A Whole New Ball Game*, 53; Spalding, *America's National Game*, 3–4; Whitman quoted in Voigt, *American Baseball 2*: 49.

5. Giamatti quoted in Elias, *Baseball and the American Dream*, 9.

6. DeLillo, *Underworld*, 171.

7. A useful starting point for basic definitions, despite its occasionally hysterical tone, is Goldman, Bush, and Klatz, *Death in the Locker Room*.

8. Boswell, *Why Time Begins on Opening Day*, 1

Chapter 1. Time in a Bottle

1. *Dallas Morning News*, 16 August 1995.

2. *New York Times*, 12 July 1995.

3. *New York Times*, 23 July 1995.

4. Castro, *Mickey Mantle*, 176–177; Mickey Mantle, "My Time in a Bottle," *Readers Digest*, December 1994, 88; "Another Season with The Mick," 18; "Second Chance for the Mick to Inspire Us," *USA Today Baseball Weekly*, 30 March 1994, 71.

5. *New York Times*, 17 May 1957; *Washington Post and Times Herald*, 17 May 1957; Barra, *Yogi Berra*, 235.

6. *New York Times*, 4 July 1957; Castro, *Mickey Mantle*, 176–177.

7. There is a different version of the Copa incident given by almost every member of the team involved. The description here is a composite of the following accounts of the "Copa Battle": *Sports Illustrated*, 27 May 1957; Mantle and Gluck, *The Mick*, 155–157; Castro, *Mickey Mantle*, 176–177; Barra, *Yogi Berra*, 235–236; Pepe, *Ballad of Billy and George*, 61–63; Falkner, *Last Yankee*, 99; Ford and Pepe, *Slick*, 139.

8. *Newsweek*, 24 June 1957; *New York Times*, 17 May 1957, 4 July 1957; *Chicago Daily Tribune*, 22 June 1957. Most Copacabana stories assume that Edwin Jones, the delicatessen owner and diehard Yankees fan, had been hit by Hank Bauer. Bauer always insisted that it had been the Copacabana's bouncers who did the deed, but he later reportedly confirmed to close friends that he had actually thrown the punch.

9. *Chicago Daily Tribune*, 17 May 1957, *Washington Post and Times Herald*, 22 May 1957, 4 June 1957, 5 June 1957; *New York Times*, 25 June 1957. Bauer, later manager of the Baltimore Orioles, describes the mystique of the Copa incident and the eventual result of the legal wrangling in *New York Times*, 2 March 1964.

10. "The Damndest Yankee of Them All," *Sports Illustrated*, April 1956, 34; "Baseball's Roughest Players: They Brawl, Cuss, Spike, Slug—and Win," *Pocket Magazine for Men*, May 1954, 4; Vincent, *We Would Have Played*, 170; Golenbock, *Wild, High and Tight*, 118–120.

11. Falkner, *The Last Yankee*, 105; Vincent, *We Would Have Played*, 170; Golenbock, *Wild, High and Tight*, 112–118.

12. Whitey Ford recalled that the trade was the lowest moment in both his career and Mickey Mantle's. Mantle said it was "like losing a brother," in *Washington Post and Times Herald*, 4 June 1957; Golenbock, *Wild, High and Tight*, 121; players reminiscence about baseball's drinking culture in Robinson and Peary, *We Played the Game*, 144, 437–438, 602; Bob Lemon quoted in Kahn, *October Men*, 305. Lemon also famously asserted: "I never bring the losses home. I always leave 'em in a bar somewhere along the way," in *New York Daily News*, 13 January 2000.

13. *Spaulding's Official BaseBall Guide*, 1884; *Cincinnati Enquirer*, 3 November 1881; *Sporting News*, 23 January 1892, 18 April 1896; Casway, *Ed Delahanty*; Voigt, *American Baseball*, 1: 116; Bowman and Zoss, *Diamonds in the Rough*, 311. Ty Cobb once suggested drinking as a cure for "going stale" in "Ty Cobb Says, If Going Stale, Drink," *Liberty*, 20 September 1924, 41.

14. Casway, *Ed Delahanty*; Lieb, *Baseball As I Have Known It*; *Buffalo Express*, 8 July 1903.

15. *New York Times*, 22 September 1905; "Some Odd Superstitions of the Ball Players," *Baseball Magazine*, June 1922, 308; Von Borries, "Requiem for a Gladiator," 147; Scheinin, *Field of Screams*, 49; Okrent and Wulf, *Baseball Anecdotes*, 29–30.

16. Stewart and Zoss, *Diamonds in the Rough*, 316.

17. Lardner, "The Fun Loving Rover," *Newsweek*, 5 June 1939, 25; "The Lighter Side of the Game," *Baseball Magazine*, February 1939, 417; *Sporting News*, 21 October 1972; *Philadelphia North American*, 6 October 1905; "Reminiscence of Rube Waddell"; Connie Mack Discusses the Eccentric Twirler," *Baseball Magazine*, February 1912, 73.

18. For solid overviews of the social history of alcoholism in America see Lender and Martin, *Drinking in America*; Barrows and Room, *Drinking*; Musto, *Drugs in America*. For baseball's attitude toward drinkers, examples include *Sporting News*, 21 October 1972; "What 'Color' Means to a Ball Player," *Baseball Magazine*, January 1924, 349; "Baseball History Is Littered with Empty Bottles," *USA Today Baseball Weekly*, 6 December 1995, 23; "Baseball's Roughest Players," 4; "'Characters' Have Always Brightened Baseball Scene," *Baseball Digest*, September 1986, 50–51.

19. Skipper, *Wicked Curve*, 201; Sullivan, *Diamond Revolution*, 165–166; "They Walked By Night," *Sport*, February 1950, 28.

20. "Beer and Baseball," *New Yorker*, 24 September 1932, 20.

21. Sampled works on masculinity and drinking include Drucker and Gumpert. *Voices in the Street*; Wilson, *Drinking Cultures*; Rotskoff, *Love on the Rocks*; Kimmel, *Manhood in America*; *Los Angeles Times*, 16 April 1967. Billy Martin's views on education are profiled in Harrigan, *Detroit Tigers*, 100–106. On baseball culture, see "'Characters' Have Always Brightened," 50–51.

22. Veblen and Chase. *Theory of the Leisure Class*, 70; Dreifort, *Baseball History*; Kimmel, *Manhood in America*; Peary, *We Played the Game*, 602; "Characters' Have Always Brightened," 50; "They Walked by Night," 28; *Los Angeles Times*, 16 April 1967; Harris, *Southpaw*.

23. "Why Managers Hate Wives," *Saturday Evening Post*, 25 March 1950, 28; Al Stump, "Dames Are the Biggest Headache," *Saturday Evening Post*, 25 March 1950, 7; "The Gals behind the Guys in Baseball," *Baseball Digest*, June 1973, 71; Wenner, *Mediasport*; Gilbert, *Men in the Middle*.

24. "'Characters' Have Always Brightened," 50.

25. Jim Kaplan, "Alcohol Was Bob Welch's Problem: This Is the Account of His Solution," *Sports Illustrated*, 29 March 1982, 6.

26. Ibid., 6.

27. Kahn, *Era*, 165.

28. "What's Happened to Our Heroes," *Sports Illustrated*, 15 August 1983, 22.

29. Paul Waner, of Pittsburgh Pirates fame, is undoubtedly the most famous player about whom this traditional baseball story is told. See Paul Waner and Larry Ritter, *Oral History Interview with Paul Waner*, 1964, Lawrence S. Ritter Oral History Tapes; Kahn, *A Season in the Sun*; Bouton and Shecter, *Ball Four*, 30.

30. *New York Times*, 11 June 1995; *Texarkana Gazette*, 14 August 1995; Thomas Sorensen, "Mantle Was Life in the 1950s," *Odessa (Texas) American*, 8 June 1995, 18; Rader, *Baseball*, 171–173; Halberstam, *Summer of '49*; Mantle and Herskowitz, *All My Octobers*; Prince, *Brooklyn's Dodgers*.

31. *New York Times*, 2 April 1995.

32. *Lufkin Daily News*, 14 August 1995; *Arizona Daily Star*, 9 June 1995; *New York Times*, 16 August 1995; *Chicago Sun-Times*, 16 August 1995.

33. Barzun, *God's Country and Mine*.

34. Golenbock, *Wild, High and Tight*, 113–120; Prager, *Echoing Green*, 129; Mantle and Herskowitz, *All My Octobers*.

35. Prager, *Echoing Green*, 192–193; Koppett, *The Rise and Fall of the Press Box*, 85; Considine, *Toots*; Bainbridge, *Wonderful World of Toots Shor*; Jacobson, *Toots*.

36. Toots was on the cover of *Sports Illustrated* for 27 July 1959; *New York Times*, 24 January 1977.

37. Kahn, *Era*, 166; Prince, *Brooklyn's Dodgers*.

38. "I Was Baseball's Bad Boy," *Baseball Digest*, 22 May 1948, 28; "The Real Joe Page," *Sport*, May 1973, 38; "The Gay Reliever," *Sport*, February 1958, 54; S. Goldman, *Forging Genius*, 22; Rossi, *Whole New Game*, 49.

39. "Stengel, Legend and Fact," *Baseball Digest*, January 1959, 5; S. Goldman, *Forging Genius*, 22.

40. "Lindell Bombers" were dry martinis so beloved by Johnny Lindell that he personalized the name; "Lucky for Bucky Harris, He Just Couldn't Trade Lindell," *Baseball Magazine*, March 1948, 339; S. Goldman, *Forging Genius*, 22.

41. "That Fella," *Time*, 3 October 1955, 58–63; "Stengel, Legend and Fact," 5; Golenbock, *Wild, High and Tight*, 115; Creamer, *Stengel*; Stengel's quote is reminiscent of a famous saying attributed to Phillies outfielder and broadcaster Richie Ashburn: "The kid doesn't chew tobacco, smoke, drink, curse, or chase broads. I don't see how he can ever make it."

42. *Sporting News*, 16 August 1961, 25; "Fast & Loose," *Time*, August 4, 1958, 38.

43. "Eleven Years After His Fastball Last Hit a Big League Batter . . . Ryne Duren Can See Clearly at Last," *Sport*, May 1976, 73; Duren and Drury, *Comeback*.

44. Mantle, *The Mick*, 176; Peary, *We Played the Game*, 551; Shapira, "The Booze of Summer: Ryne Duren's Story," 81; *Sporting News*, 1 June 1974.

45. Ed Linn, "The Yankees Mr. Fireball," *Saturday Evening Post*, 11 April 1959, 30.

46. Ron Fimrite, "Hell-Raisers in Halos," *Sports Illustrated*, 19 July 1993, 46.

47. Fimrite, "Hell-Raisers in Halos," 46; "The Inside Story of the Angels' Success," *Sport*, April 1963, 56.

48. *New York Times*, 28 September 1991; "Sam McDowell Pitching for a New Cause," *Baseball Digest*, April 1983, 81.

49. "Don Newcombe: Baseball Great Wins," *Ebony*, April 1976," 54.

50. "Newcombe's Pitch," *Black Sports*, October 1976, 37; "Don Newcombe," 54.

51. Waterman, "Racial Pioneering on the Mound," 185; *Sporting News*, 5 April 1980; "Don Newcombe," 55–56; "Friends of Don Newcombe Shocked at Revelation about Drinking Problem," *Jet*, 20 March 1975, 45–49. Alcoholism was as much a scourge in the professional Negro Leagues as in the white league. Undeniably the most famous casualty of the bottle in black baseball was the prodigious Josh Gibson, whose tragic career is recounted in "Looking for Josh Gibson," *Esquire*, February 1978, 104, and in Ribowsky, *Power and the Darkness*.

52. "Don Newcombe," 57–58.

53. "Don Newcombe," 58–62; *Sporting News*, 17 January 1976.

54. "Sam McDowell Pitching for a New Cause," 81.

55. "The Silly Season," *Newsweek*, 12 July 1965, 64; "Can 'the Next Koufax' Finally Make It?" *Sport*, April 1967, 67; "Sam of 1,000 Ways," *Sports Illustrated*, 17 August 1970, 38; *Sporting News*, 8 August 1970.

56. *New York Times*, 28 September 1991; "Sam McDowell Pitching for a New Cause," 81.

57. Rader, *In Its Own Image*, 58.

Chapter 2. Tobacco Road

1. *New York Times*, 13 May 1996, 3 April 1997.

2. *USA Today Baseball Weekly*, 16 April 1996, 17 April 1996; *Mother Jones*, August/September 1996.

3. *USA Today Baseball Weekly*, 17 April 1996.

4. *USA Today Baseball Weekly*, 8 April 1998.

5. *New York Times*, 30 July 1998; *USA Today Baseball Weekly*, 5 August 1998.

6. Koppett, "The National Spit Tobacco Education Program," in *To Improve Health and Health Care*, 134; *USA Today Baseball Weekly*, 17 April 1996, 22 May 1996.

7. *Washington Post and Times Herald*, 8 April 1956; *Nation*, 19 April 1958.

8. *New York Times,* 7 March 1957.

9. "Radio Continuity, Pall Mall, New York Giants, June, 1957," June 1957, Bates: ATX01 0144507-ATX01 0145300, Legacy Tobacco Documents Library. http://tobacco documents.org/atc/60233299.html.

10. Ibid.

11. "Radio: Bat, Beer, and Camera," *Time*, 26 April 1954, 104.

12. Ibid.

13. "*Printer's Ink*, 29 May 1959; *New York Times*, 30 March 1958.

14. Zeiler, *Ambassadors in Pinstripes*, 19–20.

15. Sunday, "The Famous Booze Sermon," in Sunday and Ellis, *Billy Sunday*, 86.

16. "Chaws," *Sports Illustrated*, 4 July 1977, 55–56.

17. "What's Brown and Wet and Hits You in the Ankle?," *Sport*, November 1964, 7; Alexander, *Breaking the Slump*, 188; "Chaws," 55–56.

18. *USA Today Baseball Weekly*, 13 September 1995.

19. American Tobacco Co., "Bull Durham: An American Legend since 1871," 1992, Legacy Tobacco Documents Library, https://industrydocuments.library.ucsf.edu/tobacco/docs/nzly0169; *Atlanta Constitution*, 16 July 1886.

20. Voigt, *American Baseball*, 1: 41, 173.

21. A Wagner card, the "most sought after on earth," could sell for as much as $25,000 in less than perfect condition. *New York Times*, 17 November 1994.

22. Alexander, *Breaking the Slump*, 125, 141.

23. Ted Wilde, dir., *Babe Comes Home*, film, 1927, Wilde's film is one of the most sought after 'lost' baseball films in the world. Numerous lobby cards and posters for the film remain extant. Referenced in Erickson, *Baseball in the Movies*, 38–40.

24. *Colliers*, 23 April 1938, 24 August 1940; *Saturday Evening Post*, 17 August 1940; Viceroy ad man quoted in Lipsyte, *Sportsworld*, 43; *Christian Science Monitor*, 10 April 1964; *Forbes*, 15 September 1972; Cramer, *Joe DiMaggio*, 291; Alexander, *Breaking the Slump*, 188–189.

25. Voigt, *American Baseball*, 3: 272; For an overview of the ways in which ads and commercials play to fantasies, desires, and the creating of identity, see especially Ewen, *All Consuming Images*, 14, 70–71; Crawford, *Consuming Sport*, 118; Barnouw, *Sponsor*, 79.

26. *New York Times*, 25 February 1938.

27. Ibid.; *Hearst's International Cosmopolitan*, April 1928.

28. *Colliers* 25 May 1935, 2 May 1942, 3 May 1947, 1 May 1948, 23; *Life*, October 1935.

29. *Tan*, March 1952, back cover; *Ebony*, March 1953.

30. Cramer, *Joe DiMaggio*, 291; Alexander, *Breaking the Slump*, 188–189; "Chaws," 55–56.

31. Blanc, *Essential Bugs Bunny*.

32. *Colliers*, 23 April 1949; *Tan*, July 1951, back cover; *Sporting News*, 29 August 1951.

33. *Sporting News*, 4 October 1950.

34. Kell interview quoted in Marshall, *Baseball's Pivotal Era*, 347. As a Detroit Tigers broadcaster, Kell also refused to pitch beer advertisements; see *Christian Science Monitor*, 26 February 1964.

35. Voight and Veeck, "View from the Bleachers," VHS, 1982; *Colliers*, 1 May 1948.

36. *Sport*, December 1959; *Sporting News*, 11 May 1960.

37. *Sporting News*, 11 May 1960.

38. *Washington Post and Times Herald*, 15 October 1961; Baylor College of Medicine and A. Blum, "Tobacco Industry Sponsorship of Sports: A Growing Industry," 27 October 1988, Bates: 87645106-87645202, Legacy Tobacco Documents Library, http://tobaccodocuments.org/lor/87645106-5202.html; *Washington Post*, 5 May 1964.

39. *Wall Street Journal*, 24 January 1964; *Afro-American*, 28 January 1964.

40. *Chicago Tribune*, 12 January 1964; *Los Angeles Times*, 3 November 1966; Rabin and Sugarman, *Regulating Tobacco*, 84.

41. *Washington Post*, 21 July 1974.

42. *Sporting News*, 8 July 1972; Pearlman, *Bad Guys Won*, 191.

43. Skoal ad, *Sport*, May 1980; *Sporting News*, 17 April 1989; "Chaws," 54.

44. "Hold On There America," *Sports Illustrated*, 7 February 1983.

45. "Sports and Suds," *Sports Illustrated*, 8 August 1988.

46. Eaves, "Relationship between Spit Tobacco and Baseball," 437–442; *Los Angeles Times*, 11 October 2012.

47. Cooper, Ellison, and Walsh, "Spit (Smokeless)–Tobacco Use," 126–132.

48. "Informational Memorandum Regular Summary of Recent News and Editorial Comment," 15 August 1963, Bates: 2025028884-2025028952A, Legacy Tobacco Documents Library, https://industrydocuments.library.ucsf.edu/tobacco/docs/msdg0099.

Chapter 3. Where's the Dexamyl, Doc?

1. *Chicago Daily Tribune*, 29 May 1949, A3; Milland, *It Happens Every Spring*.

2. Good, *Diamonds in the Dark*, 133; Marshall, *Baseball's Pivotal Era*, 270; Milland, *It Happens Every Spring*.

3. Milland, *It Happens Every Spring*.

4. Marshall, *Baseball's Pivotal Era*, 270; Most and Rudd, *Stars, Stripes and Diamonds*, 31.

5. For a good cross-section of discussion on cheating in baseball history see "Tricks of the Diamond: Strategy, the Guiding Force in Baseball," *Baseball Magazine*, November 1911," 27; "Doctored" Baseballs in the Game," *Literary Digest*, 22 September 1923, 64; "It's O.K. to Lie, Cheat and Steal," *Baseball Magazine*, January 1949, 249; "You've Got to Cheat to Win in Baseball," *True*, August 1961, 59; "'Me and the Spitter,'" *Baseball Digest*, August 1974, 30; Durocher and Linn, *Nice Guys Finish Last*, 1.

6. "Mental Attitude, the Key to Success," *Baseball Magazine*, November 1931, 545; "Behind the Red Sox Turnabout," *Sport*, November 1967, 24; *Sporting News*, 24 June 24 1985.

7. For a thorough overview of doping in sports history, see Rosen, *Dope*; Todd, "Anabolic Steroids," 254; Bil Gilbert, "Problems in a Turned On World," *Sports Illustrated*, 23 June 1969, 66.

8. *New York Times*, 22 August 22 1965.

9. "Should Athletes Take Pep Pills?," *Milwaukee Sentinel*, 5 January 1958, 47; "The Dandy Dominican," *Time*, 10 June 1966, 88.

10. *New York Times*, 12 July 1954; "Highlight . . . And High Life," *Sports Illustrated*, 6 May 1957, 42.

11. "*Chicago Tribune*, 23 June 1957; *Wall Street Journal*, 20 May 1957; "Out of the Bottle," *Time*, 27 May 1957, 58.

12. "Out of the Bottle," 58.

13. Perelman, *Road to Miltown*; "A New Drug Brings Relief for Tense and Anxious," *Cosmopolitan*, August 1955, 82–83.

14. "Drugs for the Mind," *Nation*, 21 July 1956, 56; "Don't Give a Damn Pills," *Time*, 27 February 1956, 98; "Happiness by Prescription," *Time*, 11 March 1957, 59; "Happiness Doesn't Come in Pills," *Readers Digest*, 1 January 1957, 60; "'Ideal' in Tranquility," *Newsweek*, 29 October 1956, 63 ; "That Wonderful Frustrated Feeling," *American Mercury*, July 1957, 20.

15. Manheimer et al., "Popular Attitudes and Beliefs," 1246.

16. "Billy Martin's Story," *Sport*, May 1954, 34; "Damndest Yankee of Them All," 34; "Love, Hate and Billy Martin," *Sports Illustrated*, 2 June 1975, 70; "Breakdown in Ball Park: Piersall's Comeback to Sanity Is Told in Heartwarming Film," *Life*, 1 April 1957, 56; "Piersall Is Still Battling," *Sport*, July 1959, 3.

17. *Wall Street Journal*, 20 May 20 1957; *Los Angeles Times*, 17 September 1958.

18. *Milwaukee Sentinel*, 5 January 1958.

19. *New York Times*, 29 May 1955; "Man With a Mission," *Time*, 14 May 1956, 44.

20. "Souped-Up Athletes?" *Time*, 17 June 1957, 39; *New York Times*, 7 June 1957.

21. Todd, "Anabolic Steroids," 254.

22. *New York Times*, 17 October 1971, 30 August 1960.

23. Rasmussen, *On Speed; Kansas City Star*, 16 May 2005.

24. Grinspoon and Hedbloom, *Speed Culture*, 13.

25. Torgoff, *Can't Find My Way Home*, 157.

26. Ryan, "Use of Amphetamines in Athletics," 562; *Chicago Tribune*, 13 August 1 1957.

27. Mandell, "Sunday Syndrome," 225–32.

28. Mandell, Stewart, and Russo, "Sunday Syndrome," 2693–98, 2697.

29. Ibid., 2697.

30. *Milwaukee Sentinel*, 5 January 1958. Branch Rickey, one of baseball's great tee-totalers, was involved in both plans to ply players with B-1 vitamins and carrots; see *New York Times*, 23 February 23 1941, 10 March 1942.

31. *Kansas City Star*, 16 May 2005; Kiner and Peary, *Baseball Forever*.

32. *Kansas City Star*, 16 May 2005.

33. Willoughby interview, quoted in Hornig, *Boys of October*, 170; Bowman and Zoss, *Diamonds in the Rough*, 326.

34. "The biggest drug dealers in the sports world are none other than the train-ers," claimed critic Paul Hoch in Hoch, *Rip Off the Big Game*, 122; Harrigan, *Detroit Tigers*, 191–192; Hornig, *Boys of October*, 171.

35. G. M. Smith and Beecher, "Amphetamine Sulfate and Athletic Performance," 542–557.

36. *Toledo Blade*, 3 November 1951.

37. "Pep Pills: How Dangerous for Major Leaguers?" *Baseball Digest*, April 1971, 47; Angell, *Summer Game*, 194; Gilbert, "Problems in a Turned On World," 66.

38. Gilbert, "Problems in a Turned On World," 66.

39. See especially Conrad, *Medicalization of Society*.

40. "Detroit's Vagabond Glover," *Baseball Digest*, January 1957, 78; discussion of use of DMSO in 1960s baseball in U.S. Congress, *Proper and Improper Use of Drugs*, 394.

41. *New York Times*, 22 August 1965.

42. "Pep Pills," 42.

43. "Don Drysdale: Anatomy of a Clutch Pitcher," *Sport*, January 1966, 20; "Don Drysdale's Pitching Litany," *Baseball Digest*, August 1965, 11.

44. *New York Times*, 22 August 1965.

45. *Chicago Tribune*, 19 November 1966; *Los Angeles Times*, 19 November 1966: "Too Many Shots, Too Many Pills," *Time*, 25 November 1966, 64.

46. *Los Angeles Times*, 3 October 1966.

47. "K is for Koufax," *Time*, 11 October 1963; *New York Times*, 4 October 1963.

48. *Los Angeles Times*, 20 August 1964.

49. *New York Times*, 22 August 22 1965.

50. "Arm and the Man," *Newsweek*, 8 August 1966, 74; Beringer quoted in Delsohn, *True Blue*, 88; Leavy, *Sandy Koufax*, 159, 189.

51. *Washington Post*, 26 July 1966; *Los Angeles Times*, 21 October 1970; "The Chosen One," *Sports Illustrated*, 9 September 2002, 66.

52. *Washington Post*, 8 May 1968; *Chicago Tribune*, 8 May 1968.

53. *Washington Post*, 3 April 1965.

54. *New York Times*, 19 July 1968, 22 August, 1965.

55. *Sporting News*, 8 October 1966; *New York Times*, 19 November 1966.

56. "Baseball: Sandy's Agony," *Time*, 9 September 1966, 50.

57. Brosnan, *Long Season*, 1.

58. R. Smith and Berkow, *Red Smith on Baseball*, 276–277.

59. Bil Gilbert, "Something Extra on the Ball," *Sports Illustrated*, 30 June 1969, 30.

60. Gilbert, "Problems in a Turned On World," 66; Gilbert, "Something Extra on the Ball," 30; Bil Gilbert, "High Time to Make Some Rules," *Sports Illustrated*, 7 July 1969, 30.

61. Gilbert, "Problems in a Turned On World," 66.

62. "Pep Pills," 47.

63. Helyar, *Lords of the Realm*, 25; M. Miller, *Whole Different Ball Game*, 19–32.

Chapter 4. Pitching around the Problem

1. Bouton, *I'm Glad*, 68–70; Kuhn, *Hardball*, 73–74; *Sporting News*, 6 June 1970.

2. Bouton, *I'm Glad*, 67, 70; Kuhn, *Hardball*, 73; *Wall Street Journal*, 11 June 1970.

3. Bouton, *Ball Four*, 81; Freehan, *Behind the Mask* is less revelatory than *Ball Four* and less literate than Brosnan's works. Freehan described it as a "story about a ballclub," but it did include some controversial allegations about star pitcher Denny McClain's destructive behavior.

4. Bouton, *I'm Glad*, 68–71; *Sporting News*, 11 April 1970.

5. Bouton suggested that pitchers who used amphetamine were taking a risk. It made them feel as if their "stuff" was far better than it probably actually was, led to grooving pitches, and ultimately resulted in them getting hammered by the opposing batter. In other words, it made pitchers feel they were better than they really were; then they would "get gay, throw it down the middle and get clobbered," in Bouton, *Ball Four*, 157, 211–212; "7 Ballplayers Answer Jim Bouton," *Sport*, October 1970, 54.

6. Holtzman, *Commissioners*, 134; *Wall Street Journal*, 22 March 1966; Kuhn, *Hardball*, 21–22; Okrent, *Nine Innings*, 240; *Sporting News*, 23 August 1969, 22 February 1969.

7. Kuhn, *Hardball*, 15; *Sporting News*, 15 March 1969, 29 March 1969, 12 April 1969.

8. M. Miller, *Whole Different Ballgame*, 293–294; *Sporting News*, 22 August 1983, 2 January 1984.

9. Helyar, *Lords of the Realm*; Korr, *End of Baseball*.

10. *Hartford (Conn.) Courant*, 2 June 1964; Sugar and Richardson, *Horse Sense*, 139; "Problems in a Turned On World," *Sports Illustrated*, 23 June 1969, 66; "Something Extra on the Ball," *Sports Illustrated*, 30 June 1969, 30; "High Time to Make Some Rules," *Sports Illustrated*, 7 July 1969, 30.

11. Meschery, *Over the Rim*; Meggyesy, *Out of Their League*; Scott, *Athletic Revolution*; Hoch, *Rip Off the Big Game*; Edwards, *Revolt of the Black Athlete*.

12. Rader, *American Sports*, 245; Patterson, *Grand Expectations*, 750–753.

13. Pipkin, *Sporting Lives*, 22–25.

14. "7 Ballplayers Answer Jim Bouton," 54; *Sporting News*, 17 October 1970; "Author Meets the Critics," *Sport*, October 1970, 30; "Pitcher in the Wry," *Newsweek*, 15 June 1970, 59.

15. U.S. Congress, *Proper and Improper Use of Drugs*, 133–134.

16. "Drugs in Sports—Congress Steps Up Drug Powers," *Newsday*, 1 May 1973, 12.

17. Ibid., 12.

18. U.S. Congress, *Proper and Improper Use of Drugs*, 37, 99.

19. Ibid., 83.

20. Ibid., 142–143.

21. Ibid., 30–39.

22. "Hearing Cites High Drug Use in All Sports," *Jet*, 7 June 1953, 51.

23. Dick Schaap, "True Grit," *New York Magazine*, 19 April 1993; Axthelm, *City Game*, 9.

24. "Players Turn on the Ease Hurt of Losing Game," *Jet*, 5 July 1973, 48. Marijuana actually had created a major controversy in the Major Leagues decades earlier when "Babe" Dahlgren, a onetime sub for the New York Yankees, was inexplicably traded several times over a seven-year period. Only in 1943 did Dahlgren learn that prominent figures such as Branch Rickey were spreading the rumor that his alleged marijuana use negatively influenced his play. See Dahlgren, *Rumor in Town*, 113–116.

25. *St. Louis Post-Dispatch*, 20 June 1973.

26. U.S. Congress, *Proper and Improper Use of Drugs*, 107, 374, 378; *Sporting News*, 21 February 21 1970; "Baseball Probes Jones' Florida Arrest with Nude Woman," *Jet*, 22 May 1975, 54.

27. *Sporting News*, 2 June 1973.

28. *St. Louis Post-Dispatch*, 20 June 1973; U.S. Congress, *Proper and Improper Use of Drugs*, 375.

29. *Sporting News*, 20 November 1971; *New York Times*, 3 March 1971.

30. *Sporting News*, 19 December 1970, 20 November 1971; *New York Times*, 3 March 1971.

31. *Sporting News*, 20 March 1971.

32. *Sporting News*, 6 March 1971.

33. *Sporting News*, 20 March 1971, 17 July 1971; U.S. Congress, *Proper and Improper Use of Drugs*, 535.

34. U.S. Congress, *Proper and Improper Use of Drugs*, 535–555, 769.

35. Vecsey, *Baseball*, 201; "Pete Rose Slams Fans, Management, Media, Plugs Self," *Playboy Magazine*, September 1979, 77–79, 102–107.

36. *Trenton Times*, 8 July 1980; *New York Daily News*, 10 July 10 1980; *Sporting News*, 26 July 1980.

37. Kashatus, *Almost a Dynasty*, 182; "The Continuing Saga of Dr. Mazza and His 'Good Friends,'" *Sports Illustrated*, 16 February 1981, 11.

38. *Sporting News*, 28 November 1981; *Boca Raton News*, 8 November 1983; *Los Angeles Times*, 15 January 15 1984.

39. *Sporting News*, 22 March 1980; Kuhn, *Hardball*, 307.

40. Kuhn, *Hardball*, 308; "Law and Disorder," *Sports Illustrated*, 22 September 1970, 11; *Sporting News*, 28 November 1981.

41. *Sporting News*, 13 October 1979.

42. *Sporting News*, 6 May 1978.

43. *Sporting News*, 16 August 1980; Stainback, *Alcohol and Sport*, 73.

44. *Sporting News*, 16 August 1980.

45. U.S. Congress, House, *Cocaine*, 1–2; *Sporting News*, 6 May 1978, 19 November 1977.

46. Committee on Problems of Drug Dependence, *Problems of Drug Dependence*; "Drugs Will Ruin Sports," *Jet*, 2 July 1981, 48.

47. *People*, 6 January 1978; "America's Crusade," *Time*, 15 September 1986, 32.

48. *New York Times Sunday Magazine*, 1 September 1974; *High Times*, June 1979, 29; National Institute on Drug Abuse, "Household Survey on Drug Abuse," 68–71; "It's the Real Thing," *Newsweek*, 27 September 1971, 124.

49. U.S. Congress, House, *Cocaine*, 1–2; *Sporting News*, 6 May 1978, 19 November 1977.

50. *Pittsburgh Press*, 16 July 1982; *Dallas Observer*, 16 June 2005.

51. *New York Times*, 11 January 1973; *Modesto (Calif.) Bee*, 19 January 1973; *Chicago Tribune*, 20 December 1976; *Los Angeles Times*, 20 December 1976. For a fictionalized treatment of real-life NFL experience with drugs, see Gent, *North Dallas Forty*; *Miami News*, 6 September 1977; "Speed Is All the Rage," *Sports Illustrated*, 28 August 1978, 30.

52. Reese, "'I'm Not Worth a Damn,'" *Sports Illustrated*, 14 June 1982, 66. Reese's admission was so profound that it served as the cover page for the magazine.

53. Reese, "'I'm Not Worth a Damn,'" 66; *St. Petersburg (Fla.) Times*, 2 July 1982; *New York Times*, 11 August 1977.

54. *Pittsburgh Post-Gazette*, 22 December 1984.

55. "Sport: Scoring off the Field," *Time*, 25 August 1986, 13; "Sports vs. Drugs," *Time*, 15 September 1986, 23.

56. "Letter to Dr. George Beecher," November 19, 1980, Marvin J. Miller Papers, Wagner 165, Box 2, Folder 36,Tamiment Library/Robert F. Wagner Labor Archives.

57. *Chicago Tribune*, 19 June 1980; *Spokesman-Review*, 23 May 1980.

58. *Evening Independent* (St. Petersburg, Fla.), 28 January 1981.

59. *Orlando (Fla.) Sentinel*, 24 January 1988; Gallagher, *You Don't Forget Homers.*

60. *New York Times*, 3 September 1980.

61. *New York Times*, 31 July 1983.

62. *Sporting News*, 28 November 1981.

63. Ibid., 13.

64. Kuhn, *Hardball*, 305–307; *Sporting News*, 11 October 1980 ; "Law and Disorder," *Sports Illustrated*, 22 September 1970, 11. The Montreal Expos were owned by the Bronfman family, themselves owners of the Seagram's empire.

65. *Sporting News*, 28 November 1981.

66. *Sporting News*, 21 November 1981; Welch and Vecsey, *Five O'Clock Comes Early.*

67. *Eugene (Ore.) Register-Guard*, 18 December 1980; Porter and Deerfield, *Snap Me Perfect!*

68. *Philadelphia Inquirer*, 14 July 1981.

69. *Sporting News*, 28 November 1981.

70. Sands and Gammons, *Coming Apart at the Seams*, 52–54; "Back to the Dark Ages," *Sports Illustrated*, 11 July 1983, 15.

71. *Los Angeles Times*, 16 June 1982; *Palm Beach Post*, 18 June 1982.

72. Kuhn, *Hardball*, 308.

73. *Sporting News*, 13 September 1982, 31; Kuhn, *Hardball*, 313.

74. *Chicago Tribune*, 23 October 1983; *Palm Beach (Fla.) Post*, 21 March 1984.

75. *New York Times*, 21 August 1985; Kuhn, *Hardball*, 311.

76. Sullivant quoted in Kuhn, *Hardball*, 311.

77. MacPhail, *My Nine Innings*, 183–189 ; Weiler, *Leveling the Playing Field*, 63–64; *Los Angeles Times*, 22 June 1984.

78. *New York Times*, 19 December 1983.

79. *Los Angeles Times*, 20 December 1983.

80. "Interim Decision of the Arbitration Panel, Decision No. 60," 1984, Marvin J. Miller Papers, Wagner 165, Box 3, Folder 1; "Gr. of Vida Blue, Decision No. 61," 1984, Marvin J. Miller Papers, Wagner 165, Box 2, Folder 36.

81. "Gr. of Vida Blue, Decision No. 61."

82. A letter from Liebl's girlfriend to Blue was featured in the hearing. In that letter the girlfriend asked Blue to make good on his considerable debts as Liebl was in serious financial trouble. She noted how Harry Gibbs, the chief of baseball security, had been in contact and implied the threat of damaging testimony if Blue didn't come through with money in "Gr. of Vida Blue, Decision No. 61," 1984, Marvin J. Miller Papers, Wagner 165, Box 2, Folder 36.

83. "Gr. of Vida Blue, Decision No. 61."

84. "MLBPA: For Immediate Release," June 30, 1983, Marvin J. Miller Papers, Wagner 165, Box 4, Folder 1.

85. *Sporting News*, 23 January 1984; "MLBPA: For Immediate Release."

86. *Ocala-Star Banner (Fla.)*, 16 December 1983; *Gainesville (Fla.) Sun*, 17 December 1983.

87. *Gainesville Sun*, 2 June 1984; *New York Times*, 2 June 1984.

88. Kuhn, *Hardball*, 319.

89. *Sporting News*, 2 July 1984, 14 May 1984; "The Long Season," *Commonweal*, 4 October 1985, 517.

Chapter 5. This Is Not Just a Test

1. *Sporting News*, 12 March 1984; "Thing Called Baseball," *Minneapolis Review of Baseball*, April 1984.

2. "Inside Baseball: Drugs, Money and Expansion (Interview with Peter Ueberroth)," *U.S. News & World Report*, 28 October 1985, 68; Herzog and Pitts, *You're Missin' a Great Game*, 187–192. Herzog explains how a key part of managing in the 1980s was recognizing which players were using cocaine, how the problem was, indeed, widespread, and how Montreal was a critical point of purchase for most National League franchises.

3. Tom Callahan, "Larger and Darker by the Day," *Time*, 7 October 1985, 64.

4. Pete Axthelm, "Baseball's Bad Trip: Some Star Players Testify to Widespread Use of Cocaine during the Trial of an Alleged Dealer in Pittsburgh," *Newsweek*, 16 September 1985, 106; "The Long Season," *Commonweal*, 4 October 1985, 517; "Drugs in Baseball," *Los Angeles Daily Journal*, 13 September 1985, 4.

5. "Critical Time in Pittsburgh," *Sporting News*, 16 July 1984, 20; "A Flood of Mighty Waters," *Pittsburgh Tribune-Review*, 12 June 2005; "The Pirate Problem: Pittsburgh's Family Falls on Tough Times," *Sporting News*, 9 September 1985, 2; "In Ruins: The State of the State," *Philadelphia Inquirer*, 9 January 1983, A01; "In the Steel City, Sports Are Going to Pot: Pittsburgh's Baseball, Hockey and Soccer Teams Threatening to Move," *Los Angeles Times*, 2 July 1985, 5.

6. Tom Callahan, "An Illusion of Constant Values," *Time*, 16 September 1985, vii. Stargell's restaurant was the All-Pro Chicken parlor; see "Homer's Cook Free Chicken," *St. Petersburg (Fla.) Times*, 11 July 1971, 37.

7. Callahan, "Larger and Darker," 64.

8. "Baseball's Drug Scandal," 26–29.

9. Ibid., 27.

10. Ed Magnuson, "Baseball's Drug Scandal," *Time*, 16 September 1985, 28–29; "The Baseball Drug Scandal," *Macleans*, 10 June 1985, 58; *Los Angeles Times*, 1 September 1985.

11. Collins, *Transforming America*, 93, 120; Silas L. Warner, "To What Are Athletes Entitled? Not to Cocaine," 29 September 1985, Marvin J. Miller Papers, Wagner 165, Box 3, Folder 1.

12. "Heroes Are Made," *Nation*, 28 September 1985, 8.

13. *Sporting News*, 14 February 1984.

14. Callahan, "Illusion of Constant Values," 55.

15. *New York Times*, 24 September 1985, 21 September 1985.

16. *Chicago Sun Times*, 2 March 1986; *Dallas Morning News*, 5 March 1986; "Citizen Ueberroth," *Esquire*, February 1987, 69; "Striking Out . . . ," *Scholastic Coach*, August 1987, 14.

17. *San Francisco Chronicle*, 26 September 1985; *New York Times*, 7 October 1985, C9; CBS-TV, *Sixty Minutes*, 6 October 1985.

18. *New York Times*, 7 October 1985; CBS-TV, *Sixty Minutes*, 6 October 1985.

19. CBS-TV, *Sixty Minutes*, 6 October 1985.

20. "The Owner's Moral Grandstanding," *Nation*, 26 April 1986, 581; *San Diego Union*, 7 November 1985.

21. Amerikaner, *Pros Say It's OK*; *Sporting News*, 21 October 1985.

22. *Sporting News*, 4 November 1985, 7 October 1984, 9 December 1985; "Owners Moral Grandstanding," 581; *ABC World News Tonight*, transcript, 24 September 1985.

23. *Sporting News*, 10 February 1985, 7 October 1985.

24. "American Notes Sports," *Time*, 10 March 1986; *Chicago Sun-Times*, 2 March 1986; "Groping for a Drug Plan That Will Work," *Sports Illustrated*, 10 March 1986, 7; "Ueberroth's Plutocracy," *National Review*, 28 March 1986, 24.

25. *Chicago Sun-Times*, 2 March 1986; "Groping for a Drug Plan," 7; *Sporting News*, 2 December 1985, 14 April 1986.

26. *Beaver Country Times*, 9 March 1986.

27. "Ueberroth's Plutocracy," 24; "Groping for a Drug Plan," 7.

28. *Toronto Star*, 9 May 1985; *Chicago Sun-Times*, 2 March 1986.

29. "Baseball's New Family Image," *Nation*, 26 April 1986, 581.

30. *Chicago Sun-Times*, 31 January 1986; "Drugs and the Disaffected Public," *Macleans*, 14 July 1986, 7; *Sporting News*, 14 July 1986.

31. "Scoring off the Field," *Time*, 25 August 1986, 26.

32. *Sporting News*, 14 April 1986, 31 March 1986, 42 ; *New York Times*, 22 August 1985.

33. *New York Times*, 22 August 1985.

34. *Minneapolis Star Tribune*, 14 January 1987; "NBA Drug Program Works," *USA Today*, 25 February 1988, 6C; *New York Post*, 9 May 1985.

35. *Los Angeles Times*, 19 May 19 1985.

36. *New York Times*, 29 July 1986.

37. *Washington Post*, 20 June 1987.

38. *Los Angeles Times*, 26 January 1988; *The Little League Drug Education Program*, Little League Home Video, 1990.

39. *New York Times*, 18 August 1986.

40. *Milwaukee Journal*, 27 March 1987.

41. Ibid.

42. Ibid.

43. *New York Times*, 4 May 1984; *Sporting News*, 9 April 1984.

44. *New York Times*, 4 May 1984.

45. *Philadelphia Daily News*, 3 April 1984; *Miami Herald*, 11 March 1984.

46. Morgan, "Problems of Mass Urine Screening," 301–317.

47. Hansen, Caudill, and Boone, "Crisis in Drug Testing."

48. Morgan, "Problems of Mass Urine Screening," 301–317.

49. Ibid.; "Drug Testing an Invasion of Basic Rights," *New York Times*, 9 February 1986.

50. *Spartanburg (S.C.) Herald-Journal*, 27 January 1985; *San Francisco Chronicle*, 26 September 1985.

51. *New York Times*, 4 May 1984; *Philadelphia Daily News*, 3 April 1984.

52. *Sporting News*, 9 April 1984.

53. *New York Times*, 4 May 1984.

54. *New York Post*, 24 October 1985.

55. Callahan, "Larger and Darker by the Day," 64.

56. "The Commissioner Gets Tough," *Sports Illustrated*, 20 May 1985, 32.

57. *Lodi (Calif.) News-Sentinel*, 6 September 1984.

58. *New York Times*, 22 August 1985.

59. *Chicago Sun-Times*, 2 March 1986.

60. *Milwaukee Journal*, 27 March 1987.

61. *Los Angeles Times*, 10 May 1985.

62. *Los Angeles Times*, 25 September 1985, 6 October 1985.

63. *New York Post*, 9 May 1985.

64. *New York Post*, 24 October 1985.

65. Ibid.

66. *Milwaukee Journal*, 23 August 1985; *Chicago Tribune*, 22 August 1985.

67. "Drug Tests Needed—For Players Too," 13 May 1985, Marvin J. Miller Papers, Wagner 165, Box 3; Folder 1.

68. *Sporting News*, 9 December 1985.

69. *Sporting News*, 10 February 1986.

70. *Boston Globe*, 25 September 1985.

71. *Milwaukee Journal*, 7 August 1985; J. E. Miller, *Baseball Business*, 317.

72. Letter from Ted Simmons to Scott McGregory, 3 February 1986. Marvin J. Miller Papers, Wagner 165, Box 3, Folder 1.

73. Memorandum from Donald Fehr, 21 July 1986, Marvin J. Miller Papers, Wagner 165, Box 2, Folder 50.

74. *Los Angeles Times*, 10 March 1986; "Groping for a Drug Plan," 7.

75. *Miami Herald*, 20 November 1985.

76. *Chicago Sun-Times*, 19 January 1986.

77. *Los Angeles Times*, 15 November 1985.

78. *Toronto Star*, 24 February 1986; *Sporting News*, 17 March 1986.

79. *Times Daily*, 18 December 1985; "Arena," *Newsday*, 18 December 1985, 155.

80. *Sporting News*, 21 July 1986.

81. *Fortune*, August 19, 1985; "Right to Privacy Is a Basic Principle," 9 February 1986, Marvin J. Miller Papers, Wagner 165, Box 3, Folder 1.

82. *Pittsburgh Post Gazette*, 20 January 1986.

83. West and Coombs, *Drug Testing*; McCloskey and Bailes, *When Winning Costs Too Much.*

84. "Baseball's New Family Image," 581.

85. Wong and Ensor, "Major League Baseball and Drugs," 779, 785.

86. *Los Angeles Times*, 2 June 1989.

87. *San Francisco Chronicle*, 5 June 1985.

88. Ibid.

89. "Memorandum from Donald Fehr."

90. "*Bryan (Ohio) Times*, 31 July 1986; *Philadelphia Inquirer*, 31 July 1986; *Los Angeles Times*, 31 July 1986.

91. *Los Angeles Times*, 31 July 1986, B1.

92. *Reading (Pa.) Eagle*, 31 July, 1986; "Baseball Special: Week in Review," 9.

93. *Philadelphia Daily News*, 31 July 1986.

94. Ibid.; *Ludington (Mich.) Daily News*, 31 July 1986; *Los Angeles Times*, 31 July 1986; Helyar, *Lords of the Realm*, 343; *Philadelphia Inquirer*, 7 August 1986. Roberts was reinstated in September following a union grievance, but his absence allowed the owners to sustain collusion longer than they might otherwise have done.

95. *Beaver Country Times*, 9 March 1986.

96. *Sporting News*, 28 March 1988.

97. *Wall Street Journal*, 20 May 1991; see also T. Roberts, "Before the Major League Baseball Arbitration Panel," Grievance No. 86–2, 21 September 1987; G. Nicolau, "Before the Major League Baseball Arbitration Panel," Grievance No. 87–3, 31 August 1985; Jennings, *Ball and Strikes*, 192–199.

98. *Chicago Tribune*, 9 July 1985.

99. *Sporting News*, 25 January 1988; "They Dared Cocaine—And Lost," *Reader's Digest*, July 1992, 55.

100. *Atlanta Journal-Constitution*, 2 January 1986; *Washington Post*, 31 May 1989; Helyar, *Lords of the Realm*, 342–343.

101. *St. Louis Post-Dispatch*, 7 October 1988; *Providence Journal*, 6 October 1988; *Atlanta-Journal Constitution*, 10 May 1989; "McKay Helps A's with Weighting Game," *USA Today*, 6 October 1989, C3; Canseco, *Juiced.*

Chapter 6. Summers of the Long Ball Frauds

1. See especially U.S. Congress, *Investigation into Rafael Palmeiro's March 17, 2005 Testimony*; *Washington Post*, 16 March 2005.

2. *Washington Post*, 18 March 2005.

3. Ibid.

4. National Public Radio, "Sports. Baseball's Steroid Hearings," 18 March 2005.

5. *Chicago Tribune*, 4 April 2005; *New York Times*, 24 March 2005.

6. "McGwire Mum on Steroids in Hearing," *CNN International*, 18 March 2005; *Los Angeles Times*, 17 March 2005; *Chicago Sun Times*, 18 March 2005.

7. Palmeiro's firm denunciation of steroids and of Canseco made headlines later in the summer when it was confirmed that he had failed a drug test. Palmeiro then insisted that he had never "intentionally" taken steroids. Like McGwire, Palmeiro then disappeared from the game and from the media eye. See especially U.S. Congress, *Investigation into Rafael Palmeiro's March 17, 2005 Testimony*; *New York Post*, 2 August 2005; *Chicago Tribune*, 18 March 2005.

8. U.S. Congress, *Investigation into Rafael Palmeiro's March 17, 2005 Testimony*, 3.

9. Ibid., 119.

10. Ibid., 253–254.

11. Ibid., 277–278.

12. Ibid., 307.

13. Wadler quoted in Bryant, *Juicing the Game*, 168.

14. *Washington Times*, 10 September 1998; *Minneapolis Star Tribune*, 9 September 1998; *Baltimore Sun*, 9 September 1998; *St. Louis Post-Dispatch*, 10 September 1998.

15. *San Francisco Chronicle*, 13 September 1998.

16. *Christian Science Monitor*, 9 September 1998.

17. *Washington Post*, 8 September 1998; "Making His Mark," *Sports Illustrated*, 14 September 1998, 28; Lupica, *Summer of '98*, 11.

18. Canseco describes how a mixture of testosterone, Deca-Derbolin, and weight-lifting added twenty-five pounds between his final season in the minor leagues and his rookie campaign with the Oakland A's in Canseco, *Juiced*, 50. See also *Kansas City Star*, 4 May 2005; *Boston Globe*, 4 May 2005. House recanted slightly the next day when he explained that he meant to say everyone else was using amphetamines, not steroids; see Associated Press, 5 May 2005; *Washington Post*, 25 May 2009.

19. "The Game Is Designed to Break Your Heart," *Record*, 15 September 1994, B1. "Baseball shot itself in the foot," said Richard Luker, executive director of the ESPN/Chilton Sports Poll in "Will Fans Walk? For Some, Strike May Be Last Straw," *Newsday*, 18 August 1994; *Boston Herald*, 25 July 1994.

20. A litany of articles from the early 1990s suggested baseball was falling behind other sports in terms of popularity. See, for example, *Baltimore Sun*, 8 January 1993; *Washington Post*, 17 June 1991; *San Diego Union-Tribune*, 9 May 1993.

21. Letter to the Editor, *Sports Illustrated*, 7 June 1995, 7; Bill Gallo, "Dead Ball Era," *Icon*, 26 January–1 February 1995, 4.

22. *Ocala (Fla.) Star-Banner*, 8 April 1995; *Atlanta Journal-Constitution*, 8 August 1995.

23. *Philadelphia Inquirer*, 27 May 2009; Reuters News Service, 28 April 1995; *Denver Rocky Mountain News*, 11 April 1996; *Washington Post*, 29 April 1995.

24. Tom Verducci, "Anybody Home?" *Sports Illustrated*, 8 May 1995, 18–23.

25. *New York Times*, 3 September 1995; *Washington Post*, 7 September 1995. Slugging shortstops such as Alex Rodriguez, Miguel Tejada, and Hanley Ramirez all owe something to Ripken.

26. "The Pride of the Orioles," *Newsweek*, 11 September 1995, 79.

27. *Baltimore Sun*, 7 September 1995; "Touching 'Em All," in *2,131: Cal Ripken Jr. Stands Alone*, Special Collector's Edition of *Sports Illustrated*, 1995, 15.

28. Williams quoted in Zirin, "Juice and the Noose."

29. *Los Angeles Times*, 1 August 1994.

30. "Making His Mark," 28; Richard Corliss, "Baseball: These Are the Good Old Days," *Time*, 14 September 1998.

31. *Sporting News*, 9 July 1984; "The Stuff of Legend," *Macleans*, 24 August 1987, 36; "Stroke of Genius," *Sports Illustrated*, 21 December 1998, 44.

32. *New York Times*, 27 August 1998; Canseco, *Juiced*, 170. Canseco describes how he and McGwire would inject each other with steroids in bathroom stalls, an allegation roundly denied by McGwire even after his 2010 admission that he had, in fact, used steroids during his baseball career.

33. Lupica, *Summer of '98*, 11.

34. Corliss, "Baseball."

35. *New York Daily News*, 30 August 1998.

36. *New York Times*, 22 August 1998, 23 August 1998.

37. *Gainesville (Fla.) Sun*, 30 August 1983.

38. *Pittsburgh Press*, 27 August 1983.

39. *Boston Globe*, 23 August 1983; *Los Angeles Times*, 26 June 1988; *Pittsburgh Press*, 27 August 1983.

40. *Toronto Star*, 28 September 1988.

41. *St. Petersburg (Fla.) Times*, 30 September 1988; *Orlando (Fla.) Sentinel*, 7 October 1988; *Spokane Spokesman Review*, 22 March 1988.

42. *Miami Herald*, 23 May 1987.

43. Fay Vincent, "Baseball's Drug Policy and Prevention Program," 16 June 1991, The Biz of Baseball, http://www.bizofbaseball.com/index.php?option=com_content&view =article&id=28:baseballs-drug-policy-and-prevention-program&catid=7:selection-of -docs&Itemid=25 (accessed 10 January 2009).

44. *New York Times*, 18 December 2007.

45. *Boston Globe*, 13 July 1997.

46. *Kansas City Star*, 23 June 1993; *Chicago Tribune*, 10 June 1993; "Ambiguities of DSHEA," 390–397.

47. Dickinson, *Before and after DSHEA*.

48. Sapienza, *Dietary Supplements*, 188; *Salt Lake Tribune*, 21 May 2001.

49. *New York Daily News*, 11 November 1998.

50. Ibid.

51. *San Diego Union-Tribune*, 11 February 2001.

52. *Hartford (Conn.) Courant*, 23 September 1998; "ESPN Drops Andro Ad," *Newsday*, 24 September 1998, A94.

53. The musical *Damn Yankees*, which tells the story of Joe Hardy, is based on Wallop, *Year the Yankees Lost the Pennant*.

54. *New York Times*, 23 August 1998.

55. *New York Times*, 27 August 1998.

56. Ibid.

57. *St. Petersburg (Fla.) Times*, 25 August 1998; *Rocky Mountain News*, 30 August 1998.

58. "Big Bash Theories: All-Stars Ponder Explanation for HR Explosion," *USA Today Baseball Weekly*, 11 July 1996," 32; *Wall Street Journal*, 4 March 1997; "Lifting the Game," *USA Today Baseball Weekly*, 7 May 1997, 32.

59. *San Jose (Calif.) Mercury News*, 8 October 1998; *New York Times*, 3 October 1961.

60. *New York Times*, 11 June 1999.

61. "USA Today Poll: 79% of Players Want Drug Testing," *USA Today*, 8 July 2002, A01.

62. *New York Times*, 27 August 1998; Hoberman, *Testosterone Dreams*, 272.

63. *New York Times*, 31 August 1998.

64. *Chicago Tribune*, 13 January 1999; *Dallas Morning News*, 22 December 1998.

65. *St. Louis Post-Dispatch*, 13 July 1999.

66. *St. Louis Post-Dispatch*, 17 September 1998.

67. See Pearlman, *Love Me, Hate Me*, 82–83. Barry Bonds resented not only the way the media treated his father, although Pearlman suggests the press gave the elder Bonds a fair shake, but also their attempts to understand what drove him to succeed.

68. "The Sledge-Hammer Kid," *Playboy*, May 1987, 174; " *National Sports Daily*, 14–15 September 1990.

69. "The Rising Stock of Bonds," *Newsweek*, 31 May 1993, 64.

70. For general media treatment of Bonds in his early years, see, for example, "Bonds Reputation Continues to Take Beating," *Baseball America*, 10 April 1991, 5; Peter King, "Bawl Players," *Sports Illustrated*, 18 March 1991, 5. Bill James writes about Bonds in James, *New Bill James Historical Baseball Abstract*, 361, 653; Bobby Bonds quoted in "Rising Stock of Bonds," 64.

71. Fainaru-Wada and Williams, *Game of Shadows*, x.

72. Ibid., 74; see also Pearlman, *Love Me, Hate Me*, 174, where the author describes similar behavior.

73. *Long Beach (Calif.) Press-Telegram*, 26 September 2001; "Barry Bonds against the World," *USA Today Baseball Weekly*, 18 July 2001, 4; Travers and Sheen, *Barry Bonds*, 253

74. "Smilin' Sammy," *Newsday*, 4 September 1998, A07.

75. *New York Times*, 1 July 1998.

76. *Chicago Tribune*, 2 September 1998, 7 September 1998.

77. *St. Louis Post-Dispatch*, 1 July 1998.

78. *Orlando Sentinel*, 28 August 2001; *New York Post*, 27 August 2001; *Chicago Tribune*, 28 August 2001.

79. Ezra, *Asterisk*, 279.

80. *Boston Herald*, 31 May 2002.

81. Verducci, "Totally Juiced," *Sports Illustrated*, 3 June 2002.

82. *New York Times*, 22 April 2003.

83. Fainaru-Wada and Williams, *Game of Shadows;* McCloskey and Bailes, *When Winning Costs Too Much; San Francisco Chronicle*, 3 September 2004; *Financial Times*, 6 December 2004.

84. *San Francisco Chronicle*, 16 September 2007.

85. *New York Times*, 12 February 2005.

86. Canseco, *Juiced*, 133.

87. "McGwire Apologizes to La Russa, Selig," ESPN, 12 January 2010; "Bud Selig's Long Goodbye," *Time*, 26 September 2013.

Epilogue. Brave New Game

1. Callahan, "The Fairest of Them All," *Sports Illustrated*, July 1996.

2. *New York Daily News*, 12 July 2004; *New York Magazine*, 12 December 2009.

3. Callahan, "Fairest of Them All."

4. See Roberts, *A-Rod; New York Times*, 2 May 2009; "Author Speaks about A-Rod," ESPN, 4 May 2009.

5. *Seattle Times*, 9 February 2009.

6. Elfrink and Garcia-Roberts, *Blood Sport; 60 Minutes*, CBS TV, 14 January 2014.

7. "Why Drug Testing Can't Catch Doping Athletes," ABC News, 8 August 2013.

8. Verducci, "The Good—and Bad—News about MLB's Attendance Figures, *Sports Illustrated*, 3 May 2011."

9. Jay, *More Than Just a Game*, 188.

10. Silver, "What Do Statistics Tell Us?"

11. "Stallone on a Mission," *Time*, January 24, 2008.

12. *New York Post*, 13 February 2005.

13. Elias and Dunning, *Quest for Excitement;* Stallone et al., *Rocky IV*.

14. Hoberman, *Testosterone Dreams*.

15. Lasch, *Culture of Narcissism*.

16. *Guardian*, 10 December 2004.

17. *Chicago Tribune*, 5 May 2007; *St. Louis Post-Dispatch*, 5 May 2007.

18. Hampton, "Researchers Address Use of Performance-Enhancing Drugs," 607–608.

19. *Los Angeles Times*, 10 January 2013.

20. Asinof, *Eight Men Out*, 197.

Bibliography

Archival Sources

Legacy Tobacco Documents Library, University of California, San Francisco.

Miller, Marvin. Papers. Robert F. Wagner Labor Archives. Tamiment Library, New York University.

Player Clippings Files. A. Bartlett Giamatti Research Center. National Baseball Hall of Fame, Cooperstown, N.Y.

Ritter, Lawrence S. Oral History Tapes. Joyce Sports Research Collection. University of Notre Dame, South Bend, Ind.

Publications and Other Sources

Abrams, Roger I. *The Dark Side of the Diamond: Gambling, Violence, Drugs and Alcoholism in the National Pastime*. Burlington, Mass.: Rounder Books, 2007.

Alexander, Charles. *Breaking the Slump: Baseball in the Depression Era*. New York: Columbia University Press, 2002.

Allen, Maury. *Bo: Pitching and Wooing*. New York: Dial Press, 1973.

———. *Damn Yankee: The Billy Martin Story*. New York: Times Books, 1980.

"Ambiguities of DSHEA." *Food and Drug Law Journal* 51 (1996): 390–397.

Amerikaner, Susan. *The Pros Say It's OK to Say No to Drugs Coloring Book*. New York: Playmore, 1986.

Angell, Roger. *Once More around the Park: A Baseball Reader*. New York: Ballantine Books, 1991.

———. *The Summer Game*. New York: Viking Press, 1972.

Anson, Robert Sam. *Gone Crazy and Back Again: The Rise and Fall of the Rolling Stone Generation*. Garden City, N.Y.: Doubleday, 1981.

Ashley, Richard. *Cocaine: Its History, Uses, and Effects*. New York: St. Martin's Press, 1975.

Asinof, Eliot. *Eight Men Out: The Black Sox and the 1919 World Series*. New York: Owl Books, 1963.

Assael, Shaun. *Steroid Nation: Juiced Home Run Totals, Anti-Aging Miracles, and a Hercules in Every High School: The Secret History of America's True Drug Addiction*. New York: ESPN Books, 2007.

Axthelm, Pete. *The City Game: Basketball from the Garden to the Playgrounds*. New York: Harper's Magazine Press, 1970.

Bacon, Lloyd, dir. *It Happens Every Spring*. Beverley Hills, Calif.: Fox Video, 1994. VHS.

Bailey, Beth L., and David R. Farber. *America in the Seventies*. Lawrence: University Press of Kansas, 2004.

Bainbridge, John. *The Wonderful World of Toots Shor*. Boston: Houghton Mifflin, 1951.

Bakalar, James, B., and Lester Grinspoon. *Drug Control in a Free Society*. Cambridge: Cambridge University Press, 1984.

Baker, Aaron, and Todd Boyd. *Out of Bounds: Sports, Media, and the Politics of Identity*. Bloomington: Indiana University Press, 1997.

Barnouw, Erik. *The Sponsor*. New Brunswick, N.J.: Transaction, 2004.

Barra, Allen. *Yogi Berra: Eternal Yankee*. New York: W. W. Norton, 2009.

Barrows, Susanna, and Robin Room. *Drinking: Behavior and Belief in Modern History*. Berkeley: University of California Press, 1991.

Barzun, Jacques. *God's Country and Mine; A Declaration of Love Spiced with a Few Harsh Words*. Boston: Little, Brown, 1954.

Bass, Amy. *In the Game: Race, Identity, and Sports in the Twentieth Century*. New York: Palgrave Macmillan, 2005.

Baum, Dan. *Smoke and Mirrors: The War on Drugs and the Politics of Failure*. Boston: Little, Brown, 1996.

Bell, Chris, dir. *Bigger, Stronger, Faster*: The Side Effects of Being American*. Los Angeles: Magnolia Home Entertainment, 2008. DVD.

Bennett, William. *The De-valuing of America: The Fight for Our Culture and Our Children*, New York: Touchstone Books, 1994.

Blanc, Mel. *The Essential Bugs Bunny*. Burbank, Calif.: Warner Home Video, 2010. DVD.

Borelli, Stephen. *How about That! The Life of Mel Allen*. Champaign, Ill.: Sports Pub., 2005.

Boswell, Thomas. *Why Time Begins on Opening Day*. Garden City, N.Y.: Doubleday, 1984.

Bouton, Jim. *I'm Glad You Didn't Take It Personally*. New York: Morrow, 1971.

Bouton, Jim, and Leonard Shecter. *Ball Four: My Life and Hard Times Throwing the Knuckleball in the Big Leagues*. New York: World, 1970.

Bowman, John Stewart, and Joel Zoss, *Diamonds in the Rough: The Untold History of Baseball*. New York: Macmillan, 1989.

Bradbury, J. C. *The Baseball Economist: The Real Game Exposed*. New York: Dutton, 2007.

Brochu, Claude. *My Turn at Bat: The Sad Saga of the Expos.* Toronto: ECW Press, 2002.

Brooks, Nathan. *Drug Testing in Sports Proposed Legislation.* Washington, D.C.: Congressional Information Service, Library of Congress, 2005.

Brosnan, Jim. *The Long Season.* Chicago: Ivan R. Dee, 2002.

Bryant, Howard. *Juicing the Game: Drugs, Power, and the Fight for the Soul of Major League Baseball.* New York: Viking, 2005.

Buck, Jack. *"That's a Winner!"* Champaign, Ill.: Sagamore, 1997.

Burk, Robert F. *Much More Than a Game: Players, Owners, and American Baseball since 1921.* Chapel Hill: University of North Carolina Press, 2001.

Canseco, Jose. *Juiced: Wild Times, Rampant 'roids, Smash Hits, and How Baseball Got Big.* New York: Regan Books, 2005.

———. *Vindicated: Big Names, Big Liars, and the Battle to Save Baseball.* New York: Simon Spotlight Entertainment, 2008.

Caray, Harry, and Bob Verdi. *Holy Cow!* New York: Villard Books, 1989.

Carroll, Will, and William L. Carroll. *The Juice: The Real Story of Baseball's Drug Problems.* Chicago: Ivan R. Dee, 2005.

Castro, Tony. *Mickey Mantle: America's Prodigal Son.* Washington, D.C.: Brassey's, 2002.

Casway, Jerrold I. *Ed Delahanty in the Emerald Age of Baseball.* Notre Dame, Ind.: University of Notre Dame Press, 2004.

Catton, Bruce. "The Great American Game." *American Heritage* 10, no. 3 (April 1959): 16–25.

Click, James, and Jonah Keri. *Baseball between the Numbers: Why Everything You Know about the Game Is Wrong.* New York: Basic Books, 2006.

Collins, Robert M. *Transforming America: Politics and Culture in the Reagan Years.* New York: Columbia University Press, 2007.

Committee on Problems of Drug Dependence. *Problems of Drug Dependence: Proceedings of the Annual Scientific Meeting, the Committee on Problems of Drug Dependence, Inc.* NIDA Research Monograph. Rockville, Md.: Dept. of Health, Education, and Welfare, Public Health Service, Alcohol, Drug Abuse, and Mental Health Administration, National Institute on Drug Abuse, Division of Research, 1979.

Conrad, Peter. *The Medicalization of Society: On the Transformation of Human Conditions into Treatable Disorders.* Baltimore: Johns Hopkins University Press, 2007.

Considine, Bob. *Toots.* New York: Meredith Press, 1969.

Cooper, Jeff, James A. Ellison, and Margaret M. Walsh. "Spit (Smokeless)–Tobacco Use by Baseball Players Entering the Professional Ranks." *Journal of Athletic Training* 38.2 (April–June 2003): 126–132.

Courson, Steve, and Lee R. Schreiber. *False Glory: Steelers and Steroids: The Steve Courson Story.* Stamford, Conn.: Longmeadow Press, 1991.

Cramer, Richard Ben. *Joe DiMaggio: The Hero's Life.* New York: Simon and Schuster, 2000.

Crawford, Gary. *Consuming Sport: Fans, Sport and Culture.* New York: Routledge, 2004.

Creamer, Robert W. *Babe: The Legend Comes to Life.* New York: Simon and Schuster, 1974.

———. *Stengel: His Life and Times.* New York: Simon and Schuster, 1984.

Dahlgren, Matt. *Rumor in Town: A Grandson's Promise to Right a Wrong.* Irvine, Calif.: Woodlyn Lane, 2007.

Davenport-Hines, R. P. T. *The Pursuit of Oblivion: A Global History of Narcotics.* New York: W. W. Norton, 2002.

DeLillo, Don. *Underworld.* New York: Scribner, 1997.

Delsohn, Steve. *True Blue: The Dramatic History of the Los Angeles Dodgers, Told by the Men Who Lived It.* New York: Perennial, 2002.

Dickinson, Annette. *Before and after DSHEA: The Regulation of Dietary Supplements before and after the Dietary Supplement Health and Education Act of 1994.* Washington, D.C.: Council for Responsible Nutrition, 1994.

Dimeo, Paul. *A History of Drug Use in Sport, 1876–1976: Beyond Good and Evil.* London: Routledge, 2007.

Dolan, Edward F. *Drugs in Sports.* New York: F. Watts, 1986.

Dreifort, John E. *Baseball History from Outside the Lines: A Reader.* Lincoln: University of Nebraska Press, 2001.

Drucker, Susan J., and Gary Gumpert. *Voices in the Street: Explorations in Gender, Media, and Public Space.* Cresskill, N.J.: Hampton Press, 1997.

Dubbert, Joe L. *A Man's Place: Masculinity in Transition.* Englewood Cliffs, N.J.: Prentice-Hall, 1979.

Duren, Ryne, and Bob Drury. *The Comeback.* Dayton, Ohio: Lorenz Press, 1978.

Duren, Ryne, and Tom Sabellico. *I Can See Clearly Now: Ryne Duren Talks from the Heart about Life, Baseball and Alcohol.* Chula Vista, Calif.: Aventine Press, 2003.

Durocher, Leo, and Edward Linn, *Nice Guys Finish Last.* New York: Simon and Schuster, 1975.

Eaves, Ted. "The Relationship between Spit Tobacco and Baseball." *Journal of Sport and Social Issues* 35.4 (November 2011): 437–442.

Edwards, Harry. *The Revolt of the Black Athlete.* New York: Free Press, 1969.

Elfrink, Tim, and Gus Garcia-Roberts. *Blood Sport: Alex Rodriguez, Biogenesis, and the Quest to End Baseball's Steroid Era.* New York: Dutton, 2014.

Elias, Norbert, and Eric Dunning. *Quest for Excitement: Sport and Leisure in the Civilizing Process.* Oxford: B. Blackwell, 1986.

Elias, Robert. *Baseball and the American Dream: Race, Class, Gender, and the National Pastime.* Armonk, N.Y.: M. E. Sharpe, 2001.

Ellis, Dock, and Donald Hall. *Dock Ellis in the Country of Baseball.* New York: Simon and Schuster, 1989.

Erickson, Hal. *Baseball in the Movies: A Comprehensive Reference, 1915–1991.* Jefferson, N.C.: McFarland, 1992.

Ewen, Stewart. *All Consuming Images: The Politics of Style in Contemporary Culture.* New York: Basic Books, 1988.

Ezra, David. *Asterisk: Home Runs, Steroids, and the Rush to Judgment*. Chicago: Triumph Books, 2008.

Fainaru-Wada, Mark, and Lance Williams. *Game of Shadows: Barry Bonds, BALCO, and the Steroids Scandal That Rocked Professional Sports*. New York: Gotham Books, 2006.

Falkner, David. *The Last Yankee: The Turbulent Life of Billy Martin*. New York: Simon and Schuster, 1992.

Ford, Whitey, and Phil Pepe, *Slick: My Life in and around Baseball*. New York: Morrow, 1987.

Ford, Whitey, Mickey Mantle, and Joseph Durso. *Whitey and Mickey: A Joint Autobiography of the Yankee Years*. New York: Viking Press, 1976.

Freehan, Bill. *Behind the Mask: An Inside Baseball Diary*. New York: World, 1970.

Frommer, Harvey. *New York City Baseball: The Last Golden Age, 1947–1957*. New York: Macmillan, 1980.

Fu, Freddie H., and David A. Stone. *Sports Injuries: Mechanisms, Prevention, Treatment*. Baltimore: Williams and Wilkins, 1994.

Gallagher, Danny. *You Don't Forget Homers Like That: Memories of Strawberry, Cosby, and the Expos*. Toronto: Scoop Press, 1997.

Gent, Peter. *North Dallas Forty*. New York: Morrow, 1973.

Giamatti, A. Bartlett. *Take Time for Paradise: Americans and Their Games*. New York: Summit Books, 1989.

Gilbert, James Burkhart. *Men in the Middle: Searching for Masculinity in the 1950s*. Chicago: University of Chicago Press, 2005.

Goldman, Bob, Patricia J. Bush, and Ronald Klatz. *Death in the Locker Room: Steroids & Sports*. South Bend, Ind: Icarus Press, 1984.

Goldman, Bob, and Ronald Klatz. *Death in the Locker Room: Drugs and Sports*. Chicago: Elite Sports Medicine, 1992.

Goldman, Steven, *Forging Genius: The Making of Casey Stengel*. Washington, D.C.: Potomac Books, 2005.

Golenbock, Peter. *Wild, High and Tight: The Life and Death of Billy Martin*. New York: St. Martin's Press, 1994.

Good, Howard. *Diamonds in the Dark: America, Baseball, and the Movies*. Lanham, Md.: Scarecrow Press, 1997.

Gooden, Dwight, and Bob Klapisch. *Heat: My Life on and off the Diamond*. New York: Morrow, 1999.

Gooden, Dwight, and Richard Woodley. *Rookie*. Garden City, N.J.: Doubleday, 1985.

Greenfield, Robert. *Timothy Leary: A Biography*. Orlando, Fla.: Harcourt, 2006.

Grinspoon, Lester, and Peter Hedbloom. *Speed Culture: Amphetamine Use and Abuse in America*. Cambridge, Mass.: Harvard University Press, 1975.

Gunn, Brian. "Championship Hangover: The 2007 St. Louis Cardinals." *The Hardball Times Baseball Annual 2008*. Skokie, Ill.: Acta, 2007.

Gutman, Dan. *Baseball Babylon: From the Black Sox to Pete Rose, the Real Stories behind the Scandals That Rocked the Game*. New York: Penguin Books, 1992.

Guttmann, Allen. *A Whole New Ball Game: An Interpretation of American Sports.* Chapel Hill: University of North Carolina Press, 1988.

Halberstam, David. *Summer of '49.* New York: Morrow, 1989.

Hamilton, Josh. *Beyond Belief: Finding the Strength to Come Back.* New York: Faith Words, 2008.

Hampton, T. "Researchers Address Use of Performance-Enhancing Drugs in Nonelite Athletes." *Journal of the American Medical Association* 295, no. 6 (2006): 607–608.

Hansen, H. J., Samuel P. Caudill, and Donald Joe Boone. "Crisis in Drug Testing: Results of CDC Blind Study." *Journal of the American Medical Association* 253, no. 16 (26 April 1985): 2382–2387.

Harrigan, Patrick J. *The Detroit Tigers: Club and Community, 1945–1995.* Toronto: University of Toronto Press, 1997.

Harris, Mark, *The Southpaw.* Indianapolis: Bobbs-Merrill, 1953.

Heiman, Lee, Dave Weiner, and Bill Gutman. *When the Cheering Stops: Ex-Major Leaguers Talk about Their Game and Their Lives.* New York: Macmillan, 1990.

Helyar, John, *Lords of the Realm: The Real History of Baseball.* New York: Villard Books, 1994.

Hernandez, Keith, and Mike Bryan. *If at First: A Season with the Mets.* New York: McGraw-Hill, 1986.

Hernon, Peter, and Terry Ganey. *Under the Influence: The Unauthorized Story of Anheuser Busch.* New York: Simon and Schuster, 1991.

Hershiser, Orel, and Hank Aaron. *The Little League Drug Education Program.* Williamsport, Penn: Little League Baseball, 1990. VHS.

Herzog, Whitey, and Jonathan Pitts. *You're Missin' a Great Game: From Casey to Ozzie, the Magic of Baseball and How to Get It Back.* New York: Berkley Books, 1999.

Hoberman, John M. *Mortal Engines: The Science of Performance and the Dehumanization of Sport.* New York: Free Press, 1992.

———. *Testosterone Dreams: Rejuvenation, Aphrodisia, Doping.* Berkeley: University of California Press, 2005.

Hoch, Paul. *Rip Off the Big Game: The Exploitation of Sports by the Power Elite.* Garden City, N.Y.: Anchor Books, 1972.

Holtzman, Jerome. *The Commissioners: Baseball's Midlife Crisis.* New York: Total Sports, 1998.

Hornig, Doug. *The Boys of October: How the 1975 Boston Red Sox Embodied Baseball's Ideals and Restored Our Spirits.* Chicago: Contemporary Books, 2003.

Howe, Steve, and Jim Greenfield. *Between the Lines: One Athlete's Struggle to Escape the Nightmare of Addiction.* Grand Rapids, Mich.: Masters Press, 1989.

Isaacs, Stephen L., and James Knickman. *To Improve Health and Health Care, 1998–1999: The Robert Wood Johnson Foundation Anthology.* San Francisco: Jossey-Bass, 1998.

Jacobson, Kristi, prod. *Toots.* New York: Catalyst Films, 2006. DVD.

Jay, Kathryn. *More Than Just a Game: Sports in American Life since 1945.* New York: Columbia University Press, 2004.

Jenkins, Philip. *Decade of Nightmares: The End of the Sixties and the Making of Eighties America.* New York: Oxford University Press, 2006.

Jennings, Kenneth M. *Balls and Strikes: The Money Game in Professional Baseball.* New York: Praeger, 1990.

Jennison, Christopher. *Wait 'Til Next Year: The Yankees, Dodgers, and Giants, 1947-1957.* New York: Norton, 1974.

Johnson, L. A. "Amphetamine Use in Professional Football." Ph.D. diss., U.S. International University, San Diego, Calif., 1972.

Jonnes, Jill. *Hep-Cats, Narcs, and Pipe Dreams: A History of America's Romance with Illegal Drugs.* New York: Scribner, 1996.

Kahn, Roger. *The Boys of Summer,* New York: Harper and Row, 1972.

———. *The Era: 1947–1957, When the Yankees, the Giants, and the Dodgers Ruled the World.* New York: Ticknor and Fields, 1993.

———. *Games We Used to Play: A Lover's Quarrel with the World of Sport.* New York: Ticknor and Fields, 1992.

———. *Memories of Summer: When Baseball Was an Art and Writing about It a Game,* New York: Hyperion, 1997.

———. *October Men: Reggie Jackson, George Steinbrenner, Billy Martin, and the Yankees' Miraculous Finish in 1978.* Orlando, Fla: Harcourt, 2003.

———. *A Season in the Sun.* New York: Harper & Row, 1977.

Kashatus, William C. *Almost a Dynasty: The Rise and Fall of the 1980 Phillies.* Philadelphia: University of Pennsylvania Press, 2008.

Katz, Lawrence S. *Baseball in 1939: The Watershed Season of the National Pastime.* Jefferson, N.C.: McFarland, 1995.

Kimmel, Michael S. *Manhood in America: A Cultural History.* New York: Free Press, 1996.

Kiner, Ralph, and Danny Peary, *Baseball Forever: Reflections on 60 Years in the Game.* Chicago: Triumph Books, 2004.

Klapisch, Bob. *High and Tight: The Rise and Fall of Dwight Gooden and Darryl Strawberry.* New York: Villard, 1996.

Koppett, Leonard. *The Rise and Fall of the Press Box.* Toronto: Sport Classic Books, 2003.

Korr, Charles P. *The End of Baseball As We Knew It: The Players Union, 1960–81.* Urbana: University of Illinois Press, 2002.

Kowet, Don. *The Rich Who Own Sports.* New York: Random House, 1977.

Kuhn, Bowie. *Hardball: The Education of a Baseball Commissioner.* New York: Times Books, 1987.

Lapchick, Richard Edward. *Fractured Focus: Sport as a Reflection of Society.* Lexington, Mass.: Lexington Books, 1986.

Larsen, Don, and Mark Shaw. *The Perfect Yankee: The Incredible Story of the Greatest Miracle in Baseball History.* Champaign, Ill.: Sagamore, 1996.

Lasch, Christopher. *The Culture of Narcissism: American Life in an Age of Diminishing Expectations.* New York: Norton, 1978.

Leavy, Jane. *Sandy Koufax: A Lefty's Legacy.* New York: HarperCollins, 2002.

Lee, Bill, and Dick Lally. *The Wrong Stuff.* New York: Viking Press, 1984.

Lender, Mark Edward, and James Kirby Martin. *Drinking in America: A History.* New York: Free Press, 1982.

Lieb, Fred. *Baseball as I Have Known It.* New York: Coward, McCann and Geoghegan, 1977.

Lipsyte, Robert. *Sportsworld: An American Dreamland.* New York: New York Times Book Co., 1975.

Lombardo, John. *A Fire to Win: The Life and Times of Woody Hayes.* New York: Thomas Dunne Books, 2005.

Lowe, Stephen R. *The Kid on the Sandlot: Congress and Professional Sports, 1910–1992.* Bowling Green, Ohio: Bowling Green State University Popular Press, 1995.

Lucas, John, and Joseph Moriarity. *Winning a Day at a Time.* Center City, Minn.: Hazelden, 1994.

Lupica, Mike. *Summer of '98: When Homers Flew, Records Fell, and Baseball Reclaimed America.* New York: G. P. Putnam's Sons, 1999.

MacPhail, Lee. *My 9 Innings: An Autobiography of 50 Years in Baseball.* Westport, Conn.: Meckler Books, 1989.

Mandell, Arnold. "The Sunday Syndrome: A Unique Pattern of Amphetamine Abuse Indigenous to American Professional Football." *Clinical Toxicology* 15, no. 2 (1979): 225–232.

Mandell, Arnold, Kim D. Stewart, and Patrick Russo. "The Sunday Syndrome: From Kinetics to Altered Consciousness." *Federation Proceedings* 40, no. 12 (1981): 2693–2698.

Manheimer, Dean I., Susan T. Davidson, Mitchell B. Balter, Glen D. Mellinger, Ira H. Cisin, and Hugh J. Parry. "Popular Attitudes and Beliefs about Tranquilizers." *American Journal of Psychiatry* 130, no. 11 (1973): 1246–1253.

Mantle, Mickey, and Ben Epstein. *The Mickey Mantle Story.* New York: Holt, 1953.

Mantle, Mickey, and Herb Gluck. *The Mick.* Garden City, N.Y.: Doubleday, 1985.

Mantle, Mickey, and Mickey Herskowitz. *All My Octobers: My Memories of Twelve World Series When the Yankees Ruled Baseball.* New York: HarperCollins, 1994.

Mantle, Mickey, and Phil Pepe. *My Favorite Summer, 1956.* New York: Doubleday, 1991.

Marcus, Norman, and David Klatell. *Sports for Sale: Television, Money and the Fans.* New York: Oxford University Press, 1988.

Marshall, William. *Baseball's Pivotal Era, 1945–1951.* Lexington: University Press of Kentucky, 1999.

Martin, Billy, and Peter Golenbock. *Number 1.* New York: Delacorte Press, 1980.

McCloskey, John, and Julian E. Bailes. *When Winning Costs Too Much: Steroids, Supplements, and Scandal in Today's Sports.* Lanham, Md.: Taylor Trade Pub., 2005.

McKay, Jim, Michael A. Messner, and Donald F. Sabo. *Masculinities, Gender Relations, and Sport.* Thousand Oaks, Calif.: Sage, 2000.

Meggyesy, Dave. *Out of Their League.* Berkeley, Calif.: Ramparts Press, 1970.

Meschery, Tom. *Over the Rim.* New York: McCall, 1970.

Miklasz, Bernie, Ron Smith, Mike Eisenbath, Dave Kindred, and Jack Buck. *Celebrating 70: Mark McGwire's Historic Season*. St. Louis: Sporting News/St. Louis Post Dispatch, 1998.

Miller, James Edward. *The Baseball Business: Pursuing Pennants and Profits in Baltimore*. Chapel Hill: University of North Carolina Press, 1990.

Miller, Marvin. *A Whole Different Ball Game: The Inside Story of the Baseball Revolution*. Chicago: Ivan R. Dee, 1991.

Miller, Patrick B., and David K. Wiggins. *The Unlevel Playing Field: A Documentary History of the African American Experience in Sport*. Urbana: University of Illinois Press, 2003.

Mitchell, George J. *Report to the Commissioner of Baseball of an Independent Investigation into the Illegal Use of Steroids and Other Performance Enhancing Substances by Players in Major League Baseball*. New York: Office of the Commissioner of Baseball, 2007.

Mohun, Janet, and Khan Aziz. *Drugs, Steroids, and Sports*. New York: F. Watts, 1988.

Montville, Leigh. *The Big Bam: The Life and Times of Babe Ruth*. New York: Doubleday, 2006.

Morgan, John P. "Problems of Mass Urine Screening for Misused Drugs." *Journal of Psychoactive Drugs* 16, no. 4 (1984): 305–317.

Most, Marshall G., and Robert Rudd, *Stars, Stripes and Diamonds: American Culture and the Baseball Film*. Jefferson, N.C.: McFarland, 2006.

Musto, David F. *Drugs in America: A Documentary History*. New York: New York University Press, 2002.

Nathan, Daniel A. *Saying It's So: A Cultural History of the Black Sox Scandal*. Urbana: University of Illinois Press, 2005.

National Institute on Drug Abuse, Division of Epidemiology and Prevention Research. *National Household Survey on Drug Abuse: Highlights 1990*. Rockville, Md.: U.S. Dept. of Health and Human Services; Alcohol, Drug Abuse, and Mental Health Administration, 1991.

Nylund, David. *Beer, Babes, and Balls: Masculinity and Sports Talk Radio*. Albany: State University of New York Press, 2007.

Office of the Commissioner of Baseball. *Baseball vs Drugs: An Education and Prevention Program*. Bayonne, N.J.: Ranno Pub. Group, 1977.

Okrent, Daniel. *Nine Innings*. New York: Ticknor and Fields, 1985.

Okrent, Daniel, and Steve Wulf. *Baseball Anecdotes*. New York: Oxford University Press, 1989.

Olson, James, and Randy Roberts. *Winning Is the Only Thing: Sports in America since 1945*. Baltimore: Johns Hopkins University Press, 1989.

Palmer, Harry Clay, J. A. Fynes, Francis C. Richter, W. I. Harris, and Henry Chadwick. *Athletic Sports in America, England and Australia: Comprising History, Characteristics, Sketches of Famous Leaders, Organization and Great Contests of Baseball, Cricket, Football, La Crosse, Tennis, Rowing and Cycling*. Philadelphia: Hubbard Bros., 1889.

Parker, Clifton Blue. *Fouled Away: The Baseball Tragedy of Hack Wilson.* Jefferson, N.C.: McFarland, 2000.

Parrott, Harold. *The Lords of Baseball,* New York: Praeger, 1976.

Patterson, James T. *Grand Expectations: The United States, 1945–1974.* New York: Oxford University Press, 1996.

Pearlman, Jeff. *The Bad Guys Won: A Season of Brawling, Boozing, Bimbo-Chasing, and Championship Baseball with Straw, Doc, Mookie, Nails, the Kid, and the Rest of the 1986 Mets, the Rowdiest Team to Put on a New York Uniform, and Maybe the Best.* New York: HarperCollins, 2004.

———. *Love Me, Hate Me: Barry Bonds and the Making of an Antihero.* New York: HarperCollins, 2006.

Peary, Danny. *We Played the Game: 65 Players Remember Baseball's Greatest Era, 1947–1964.* New York: Hyperion, 1994.

Pepe, Phil. *The Ballad of Billy and George: The Tempestuous Baseball Marriage of Billy Martin and George Steinbrenner.* Guilford, Conn: Lyons Press, 2008.

Perelman, S. J. *The Road to Miltown; or, Under the Spreading Atrophy.* New York: Simon and Schuster, 1957.

Pipkin, James W. *Sporting Lives: Metaphor and Myth in American Sports Autobiographies.* Columbia: University of Missouri Press, 2008.

Pollack, William S. *Real Boys: Rescuing Our Sons from the Myths of Boyhood.* New York: Henry Holt, 1999.

Porter, Darrell P., and William Deerfield. *Snap Me Perfect! The Darrell Porter Story.* Nashville: T. Nelson, 1984.

Pound, Richard W. *Inside Dope: How Drugs Are the Biggest Threat to Sports, Why You Should Care, and What Can Be Done about Them.* Mississauga, Ont.: J. Wiley and Sons Canada, 2006.

Prager, Joshua. *The Echoing Green: The Untold Story of Bobby Thomson, Ralph Branca, and the Shot Heard round the World.* New York: Pantheon Books, 2006.

Prince, Carl E. *Brooklyn's Dodgers: The Bums, the Borough, and the Best of Baseball, 1947–1957.* New York: Oxford University Press, 1996.

Rabin, Robert L., and Stephen D. Sugarman, eds. *Regulating Tobacco.* New York: Oxford University Press, 2001.

Rader, Benjamin G. *American Sports: From the Age of Folk Games to the Age of Spectators.* Englewood Cliffs, N.J.: Prentice-Hall, 1983.

———. *Baseball: A History of America's Game.* Urbana: University of Illinois Press, 1992.

———. *In Its Own Image: How Television Has Transformed Sports.* New York: Free Press, 1984.

Radomski, Kirk. *Bases Loaded: The Inside Story of the Steroid Era in Baseball by the Central Figure in the Mitchell Report.* New York: Hudson Street Press, 2009.

Rasmussen, Nicolas. *On Speed: The Many Lives of Amphetamine.* New York: New York University Press, 2008.

Ribowsky, Mark. *The Power and the Darkness: The Life of Josh Gibson in the Shadows of the Game.* New York: Simon and Schuster, 1996.

Roberts, Selena. *A-Rod: The Many Lives of Alex Rodriguez*. New York: Harper, 2009.

Robinson, Brooks, and Danny Peary. *We Played the Game: Memories of Baseball's Greatest Era*. New York: Black Dog and Leventhal, 2002.

Robinson, Phil Alden, dir. *Field of Dreams*. Produced by Lawrence Gordon. Universal City, Calif.: Universal, 2004. DVD.

Rosen, Daniel M. *Dope: A History of Performance Enhancement in Sports from the Nineteenth Century to Today*. Westport, Conn: Praeger, 2008.

Rosenthal, Harold. *The 10 Best Years of Baseball: An Informal History of the Fifties*. Chicago: Contemporary Books, 1979.

Rossi, John P. *A Whole New Game: Off the Field Changes in Baseball, 1946–1960*. Jefferson, N.C.: McFarland, 1999.

Rotskoff, Lori. *Love on the Rocks: Men, Women, and Alcohol in Post–World War II America*. Chapel Hill: University of North Carolina Press, 2002.

Roy, George, dir. *Mantle*. New York: Home Box Office, 2006. DVD.

Russell, Bill, and Taylor Branch. *Second Wind: The Memoirs of an Opinionated Man*. New York: Random House, 1979.

Ryan, Allan. "Guest Editorial: Use of Amphetamines in Athletics." *Journal of the American Medical Association* 170, no. 5 (1959): 562.

Sandel, Michael. *The Case against Perfection: Ethics in the Age of Genetic Engineering*. Cambridge, Mass: Belknap Press of Harvard University Press, 2007.

Sands, Jack, and Peter Gammons. *Coming Apart at the Seams: How Baseball Owners, Players, and Television Executives Have Led Our National Pastime to the Brink of Disaster*. New York: Macmillan, 1993.

Sapienza, Dorothy M. *Dietary Supplements: Regulatory & Legal Challenges*. Southborough, Mass.: International Business Communications, 1998.

Scheinin, Richard. *Field of Screams: The Dark Underside of America's National Pastime*. New York: Norton, 1994.

Schmidt, Mike, with Glen Waggoner. *Clearing the Bases: Juiced Players, Monster Salaries, Sham Records, and a Hall of Famer's Search for the Soul of Baseball*. New York: HarperCollins, 2006.

Scott, Jack. *The Athletic Revolution*. New York: Free Press, 1971.

Seiler, Lewis, dir. *The Winning Team*. Ronald Reagan: Signature Collection. Burbank, Calif.: Warner Bros., 2006. VHS.

Shapira, Will. "The Booze of Summer: Ryne Duren's Story." *Physician and Sportsmedicine* 3, no. 10 (October 1975): 81.

Shelton, Ron, dir. *Bull Durham*. Santa Monica, Calif: MGM Home Entertainment, 2002. DVD.

Shropshire, Mike. *Seasons in Hell: With Billy Martin, Whitey Herzog, and "the Worst Baseball Teams in History," the 1973–1975 Texas Rangers*. New York: D. I. Fine, 1996.

Silver, Nate. "What Do Statistics Tell Us about Steroids?" In *Baseball between the Numbers: Why Everything You Know about the Game Is Wrong*, edited by James Click and Jonah Keri, 326–342. New York: Basic Books, 2006.

Skipper, John C. *Wicked Curve: The Life and Troubled Times of Grover Cleveland Alexander*. Jefferson, N.C.: McFarland, 2006.

Smelser, Marshall. *The Life That Ruth Built: A Biography*. Lincoln: University of Nebraska Press, 1993.

Smith, Curt. *Voices of the Game: The First Full-Scale Overview of Baseball Broadcasting, 1921 to the Present*. South Bend, Ind.: Diamond Communications, 1987.

Smith, Gene M., and Henry K. Beecher. "Amphetamine Sulfate and Athletic Performance: I. Objective Effects." *Journal of the American Medical Association* 170, no. 5 (1959): 542–557.

Smith, Red, and Ira Berkow. *Red Smith on Baseball: The Game's Greatest Writer on the Game's Greatest Years*. Chicago: I. R. Dee, 2000.

Spalding, A. G. *America's National Game: Historic Facts Concerning the Beginning, Evolution, Development, and Popularity of Base Ball, with Personal Reminiscences of Its Vicissitudes, Its Victories and Its Votaries*. New York: American Sports Pub., 1911.

Spalding's Base Ball Guide and Official League Book for 1885: A Complete Hand Book of the National Game of Base Ball . . . Together with the Season's Averages of the Four Professional Associations for 1884, and Also the College Club Statistics for 1884, Added to Which Is the Complete Official League Record for 1884. St. Louis: Horton, 1987.

"Spit (Smokeless)—Tobacco Use by Baseball Players Entering the Professional Ranks." *Journal of Athletic Training* 38, no. 2 (2003): 126–132.

Stainback, Robert D. *Alcohol and Sport*. Champaign, IL: Human Kinetics, 1997.

Stallone, Sylvester, Talia Shire, Burt Young, and Carl Weathers. *Rocky IV*. Santa Monica, Calif.: MGM/UA Home Video, 1985. VHS.

Strawberry, Darryl. *Straw: Finding My Way*. New York: Ecco, 2009.

Strawberry, Darryl, and Art Rust. *Darryl*. New York: Bantam, 1992.

Streatfeild, Dominic. *Cocaine: An Unauthorized Biography*. New York: Thomas Dunne Books, 2002.

Suchon, Josh. *This Gracious Season: Barry Bonds and the Greatest Season in Baseball*. San Diego: Winter Pub., 2002.

Sugar, Bert Randolph, and Cornell Richardson. *Horse Sense: An Inside Look at the Sport of Kings*. Hoboken, N.J.: Wiley, 2003.

Sullivan, Dean A. *Final Innings: A Documentary History of Baseball, 1972–2008*. Lincoln: University of Nebraska Press, 2010.

Sullivan, Neil J. *The Diamond Revolution: The Prospects for Baseball after the Collapse of Its Ruling Class*. New York: St. Martin's Press, 1992.

Sunday, Billy, and William T. Ellis. *"Billy" Sunday, the Man and His Message, With His Own Words Which Have Won Thousands for Christ*. Philadelphia: John C. Winston, 1914.

Taylor, Lawrence, and Steve Serby. *L.T. over the Edge: Tackling Quarterbacks, Drugs, and a World beyond Football*. New York: HarperCollins, 2003.

Taylor, William N. *Macho Medicine: A History of the Anabolic Steroid Epidemic*. Jefferson, N.C.: McFarland, 1991.

Tellem, Susan M., and Gerald McKee. *Sports Medicine: Facts for the 80's.* Van Nuys, Calif.: PM, 1984.

Thompson, Fresco, and Cy Rice. *Every Diamond Doesn't Sparkle: Behind the Scenes with the Dodgers.* New York: David McKay, 1964.

Thompson, Teri. *American Icon: The Fall of Roger Clemens and the Rise of Steroids in America's Pastime.* New York: Alfred A. Knopf, 2009.

Todd, Terry. "Anabolic Steroids: The Gremlins of Sport." In *Sport in America: From Wicked Amusement to National Obsession,* edited by David Kenneth Wiggins. Champaign, Ill.: Human Kinetics, 1995.

Torgoff, Martin. *Can't Find My Way Home: America in the Great Stoned Age, 1945–2000.* New York: Simon and Schuster, 2004.

"Tributes to A. Bartlett Giamatti (1938–1989)." *Seton Hall Journal of Sport Law* 1, no. 1 (Winter 1991): xii-6.

Ungerleider, Steven. *Faust's Gold: Inside the East German Doping Machine.* New York: Thomas Dunne Books/St. Martin's Press, 2001.

U.S. Congress. *Investigation into Rafael Palmeiro's March 17, 2005 Testimony at the Committee on Government Reform's Hearing, "Restoring Faith in America's Pastime: Evaluating Major League Baseball's Efforts to Eradicate Steroid Use."* Third Report by the Committee on Government Reform. Washington, D.C.: Government Printing Office, 2005.

U.S. Congress. *Proper and Improper Use of Drugs by Athletes: Hearings, Ninety-Third Congress, First Session, Pursuant to S. Res. 56, Section 12.* Washington, D.C.: Government Printing Office, 1973.

U.S. Congress. House. *Anabolic Steroids Control Act of 1990.* Hearing before the Subcommittee on Crime of the Committee on the Judiciary. 101st Cong., 2nd sess., 17 May 1990. Washington, D.C.: Government Printing Office, 1990.

U.S. Congress. House. *Anabolic Steroid Control Act of 2004.* Hearing before the Subcommittee on Crime, Terrorism, and Homeland Security of the Committee on the Judiciary. 108th Cong., 2nd sess., 16 March 2004. Washington, D.C.: Government Printing Office, 2004.

U.S. Congress. House. *Cocaine: A Major Drug Issue of the Seventies.* Hearings before the Select Committee on Narcotics Abuse and Control. 96th Cong., 1st sess., 24, 26 July 1979; 10 October 1979. Washington, D.C.: Government Printing Office, 1979.

U.S. Congress. House. *Legislation to Amend the Controlled Substances Act (Anabolic Steroids).* Hearing before the Subcommittee on Crime of the Committee on the Judiciary. 100th Cong., 2nd sess., 27 July 1988. Washington, D.C.: Government Printing Office, 1989.

U.S. Congress. House. *Restoring Faith in America's Pastime.* Hearing before the Committee on Government Reform. 19th Cong., 1st sess., 17 March 2005. Washington, D.C.: Government Printing Office, 2005.

U.S. Congress. House. *Sports and Drug Abuse Prevention.* Hearing before the Select Committee on Narcotics Abuse and Control. 100th Cong., 1st, sess., 10 September 1987. Washington, D.C.: Government Printing Office, 1988.

U.S. Congress. House. *Steroids in Sports: Cheating the System and Gambling Your Health.* Joint hearing before the Subcommittee on Commerce, Trade, and Consumer Protection and the Subcommittee on Health of the Committee on Energy and Commerce. 109th Cong., 1st sess., 10 March 2005. Washington, D.C.: Government Printing Office, 2005.

U.S. Congress. Senate. *Proper and Improper Use of Drugs by Athletes.* Hearings, 93rd Cong., 1st sess., 18 June 1973; 12, 13 July 1973. Washington, D.C.: Government Printing Office, 1973.

U.S. Congress. Senate. *S. 1114, the Clean Sports Act of 2005, and S. 1334, the Professional Sports Integrity and Accountability Act.* Hearing before the Committee on Commerce, Science, and Transportation. 109th Cong., 1st. sess., 28 September 2005. Washington, D.C.: Government Printing Office, 2006.

U.S. Congress. Senate. *Steroid Use in Professional Baseball and Anti-Doping Issues in Amateur Sports.* Hearing before the Subcommittee on Consumer Affairs, Foreign Commerce and Tourism of the Committee on Commerce. 107th Cong., 2nd sess., 18 June 2002. Washington, D.C.: Government Printing Office, 2005.

Veblen, Thorstein, and Stuart Chase. *The Theory of the Leisure Class: An Economic Study of Institutions.* New York: Modern Library, 1934.

Vecsey, George. *Baseball: A History of America's Favorite Game.* New York: Modern Library, 2006.

Vincent, Fay. *It's What's Inside the Lines That Counts: Baseball Stars of the 1970s and 1980s Talk about the Game They Loved.* New York: Simon and Schuster, 2010.

———. *The Last Commissioner: A Baseball Valentine.* New York: Simon and Schuster, 2002.

———. *We Would Have Played for Nothing: Baseball Stars of the 1950s and 1960s Talk about the Game They Loved.* New York: Simon and Schuster, 2008.

Voigt, David Quentin. *American Baseball.* Vol. 1: *From Gentleman's Sport to the Commissioner System.* University Park: Pennsylvania State University Press, 1983.

———. *American Baseball.* Vol. 2: *From the Commissioners to Continental Expansion.* University Park: Pennsylvania State University Press, 1983.

———. *American Baseball.* Vol. 3: *From Postwar Expansion to the Electronic Age.* University Park: Pennsylvania State University Press, 1983.

Voigt, Don, and Bill Veeck. *View from the Bleachers: The Bill Veeck Show.* Video. WTTW Chicago Public Media, 30 May 1982. VHS. Available from Media Burn Independent Video Archive, http://mediaburn.org/video/view-from-the-bleachers-5/.

Von Borries, Philip. "Requiem for a Gladiator." *Baseball Research Journal: Twelfth Annual Historical and Statistical Review of the Society for American Baseball Research* 12 (1983). http://research.sabr.org/journals/requiem-for-a-gladiator.

Voy, Robert O. *Drugs, Sport and Politics.* Champaign, Ill.: Leisure Press, 1991.

Wadler, Gary I. *Drugs and the Athlete.* Philadelphia: F.A. Davis, 1989.

Wall, Dick, *The Broom Is Out: Confessions of a Budweiser Beer Drummer.* Kansas City: Leathers, 1996.

Wallop, Douglas. *The Year the Yankees Lost the Pennant*. New York: W. W. Norton, 1954.

Walton, Stuart. *Out of It: A Cultural History of Intoxication*. New York: Harmony Books, 2002.

Waterman, Guy. "Racial Pioneering on the Mound: Don Newcombe's Social and Psychological Ordeal." *Nine: A Journal of Baseball History and Social Policy Perspectives* 1, no. 2 (Spring 1993): 185.

Weiler, Paul C. *Leveling the Playing Field: How the Law Can Make Sports Better for Fans*. Cambridge, Mass.: Harvard University Press, 2000.

Welch, Bob, and George Vecsey. *Five O'clock Comes Early: A Young Man's Battle with Alcoholism*. New York: Quill, 1986.

Wells, David, and Chris Keski. *Perfect I'm Not: Boomer on Beer, Brawls, Backaches, and Baseball*. New York: Morrow, 2003

Wenner, Lawrence A. *Mediasport*. London: Routledge, 1998.

West, Louis Jolyon, and Robert Coombs, eds. *Drug Testing: Issues and Options*. New York: Oxford University Press, 1991.

Wieting, Stephen G. *Sport and Memory in North America*. London: F. Cass, 2001.

Wiggins, David Kenneth. *Sport in America: From Wicked Amusement to National Obsession*. Champaign, Ill.: Human Kinetics, 1995.

Will, George F. *The Morning After: American Successes and Excesses, 1981–1986*. New York: Free Press, 1986.

———. *The Pursuit of Virtue and Other Tory Notions*. New York: Simon and Schuster, 1982.

Wills, Maury. *My Last Chance in Life: Maury Wills Talks about Drugs*. Mendocino, Calif.: Lawren Productions, 1985. VHS.

Wilson, Thomas M. *Drinking Cultures: Alcohol and Identity*. Oxford: Berg, 2005.

Wolff, Bob. *It's Not Who Won or Lost the Game, It's How You Sold the Beer*. South Bend, Ind.: Diamond Communications, 1996.

Wong, Glenn M., and Richard J. Ensor. "Major League Baseball and Drugs: Fight the Problem or the Player?" *Nova Law Review* 11, no. 2 (1987): 779–813.

Wright, James Edward, and Virginia Cowart. *Anabolic Steroids: Altered States*. Carmel, Ind.: Benchmark Press, 1990.

Yesalis, Charles E. *Anabolic Steroids in Sport and Exercise*. Champaign, Ill.: Human Kinetics, 1993.

Yesalis, Charles E., and Virginia Cowart. *The Steroids Game*. Champaign, Ill.: Human Kinetics, 1998.

Zeiler, Thomas W. *Ambassadors in Pinstripes: The Spalding World Baseball Tour and the Birth of the American Empire*. Lanham, MD: Rowman and Littlefield, 2006.

Zimbalist, Andrew. *Baseball and Billions: A Probing Look inside the Big Business of Our National Pastime*. New York: Basic Books, 1992.

Zirin, Dave. "The Juice and the Noose." *International Socialist Review*, no. 50 (November/December 2006).

Index

NATHAN MICHAEL CORZINE is an instructor in history at Coastal Carolina Community College.

Pay for Play: A History of Big-Time College Athletic Reform
    Ronald A. Smith
Globetrotting: African American Athletes and Cold War
    Politics   *Damion L. Thomas*
Cheating the Spread: Gamblers, Point Shavers, and Game Fixers
    in College Football and Basketball   *Albert J. Figone*
The Sons of Westwood: John Wooden, UCLA, and the Dynasty
    That Changed College Basketball   *John Matthew Smith*
Qualifying Times: Points of Change in U.S. Women's Sport
    Jaime Schultz
NFL Football: A History of America's New National Pastime
    Richard C. Crepeau
Marvin Miller, Baseball Revolutionary   *Robert F. Burk*
I Wore Babe Ruth's Hat: Field Notes from a Life in Sports
    David W. Zang
Changing the Playbook: How Power, Profit, and Politics Transformed
    College Sports   *Howard P. Chudacoff*
Team Chemistry: The History of Drugs and Alcohol in Major
    League Baseball   *Nathan Michael Corzine*

REPRINT EDITIONS
The Nazi Olympics   *Richard D. Mandell*
Sports in the Western World (2d ed.)   *William J. Baker*
Jesse Owens: An American Life   *William J. Baker*

The University of Illinois Press
is a founding member of the
Association of American University Presses.

Composed in 10.5/13 Adobe Minion Pro
by Lisa Connery
at the University of Illinois Press
Manufactured by Cushing-Malloy, Inc.

University of Illinois Press
1325 South Oak Street
Champaign, IL 61820-6903
www.press.uillinois.edu